Motherhood Reconceived

Motherhood Reconceived

Feminism and the Legacies of the Sixties

Lauri Umansky

New York University Press
New York and London

NEW YORK UNIVERSITY PRESS
New York and London

Library of Congress Cataloging-in-Publication Data

Umansky, Lauri, 1959-
Motherhood reconceived : feminism and the legacies of the sixties
/ Lauri Umansky.
p.   cm.
Includes bibliographical references and index.
ISBN 0-8147-8561-1 (cloth).—ISBN 0-8147-8562-x (pbk.)
1. Feminism—United States.   2. Motherhood—United States.   3. Sex
role—United States.   I. Title.
HQ1421.U43 1996
305.42—dc20   96-8798
                    CIP

New York University Press books are printed on acid-free paper,
and their binding materials are chosen for strength and durability.

Manufactured in the United States of America

10 9 8 7 6 5 4 3 2 1

For Peter, Carenna, and Wendy

Contents

Acknowledgments

Many thoughtful and generous people made this project possible. My thanks to them run deep.

For her unflagging enthusiasm, rigor, and patience as thesis advisor, I wish to thank Mari Jo Buhle. Always exacting, always supportive, she has seen this work through many drafts. Though I have not always heeded her advice, her guidance has been invaluable. So, too, have the critiques offered at various stages by Richard Meckel and Howard Chudacoff, my dissertation readers at Brown University.

The research was aided by a Woodrow Wilson Women's Studies Research Grant for Doctoral Candidates, and by the efforts of the staff of the Schlesinger Library at Harvard University. Special thanks go to the librarians at Suffolk University, who never balked at my piles of interlibrary loan requests.

Grateful acknowledgment is made to *Critical Matrix* for publishing a version of chapter 3 of this book. The article appeared in *Critical Matrix: The Princeton Journal of Women, Gender, and Culture* 8, no. 2 (1994): 19–50.

To the following people, who read drafts, discussed with me the ideas presented here, or just helped keep me on course, I am grateful: Robert Allison, Lucy Barber, Robert Bellinger, Teresa Bill, Gwen Brown, John Cavanagh, Ruth Feldstein, Carroy Ferguson, Kevin Gaines, Jane Gerhard, Janet Gray, Ken Greenberg, Claire Griffler, Keith Griffler, Molly Ladd-Taylor, Sharon Lenzie, Karen Lindsey, Melanie MacAllister, Sally Mills, Kate Monteiro, Louise Newman, Doris Onek, Peter Onek, Elaine Phillips, Michele Plott, Miriam Reumann, Charles Rice, Jessica Shubow, Lyde Sizer, Judy Smith, Howard Umansky, and Muriel Weckstein.

It is my good fortune that Regula Noetzli and Niko Pfund, as agent and editor, have turned their sharp minds and discerning eyes toward this work. Our communications invariably invigorate me.

The years I spent researching and writing this book have been punctuated by my own experience of mothering. My daughters, Carenna and Wendy, enrich my life more than I could have imagined. Born in the first and the last years of this project, respectively, they have witnessed all its stages. Thanks to them, motherhood has been concrete and vivid for me, even as I have delved far into theory.

Time away from my children has been important to the completion of this work, too. For the loving care they have provided, I especially wish to thank Paula Blundell and Annette Buccheri. In the final weeks of writing, my mother and stepfather, Aviva and Carl Griffler, added to their years of moral and intellectual support generous hours of child care. It really does take a village to raise a child. Our village has been filled with many special people.

Finally, I wish to express my gratitude to Peter Onek, my husband, my dearest friend, my partner in all that matters. Everyone should have the depth and breadth of support he has given me. The creative ferment of everyday life with him keeps my mind alert and my spirits lifted. I attribute the best in all I do to his presence in my life.

Introduction

Motherhood: The Problem That Modern Feminists Can Face

*I*n 1986, when Sylvia Ann Hewlett wrote about the plight of mothers in the United States, many accepted unflinchingly her assertion that the women's movement had ignored the needs of mothers and children, or worse, treated those needs with an active contempt. "One might say that *motherhood is the problem that modern feminists cannot face*," Hewlett wrote in *A Lesser Life*. She claimed that "many contemporary feminists have reviled both mothers and babies. Some feminists rage at babies; others trivialize or denigrate them. Very few have attempted to integrate them into the fabric of a full and equal life." [1] In the world's wealthiest nation, she argued, heirs to the triumphs of technology and free enterprise, hundreds of thousands of women and children are destined to live in poverty. Divorce leaves women destitute. A majority of working women has no secure maternity leave. Day care remains a haphazard and expensive proposition. "The bottom line is that American women (and often their children) are in bad shape." [2] And worst of all, according to Hewlett, feminists are providing neither solutions nor empathy.

Hewlett's book addressed real problems in U.S. society. The United States lags behind all other major industrialized nations in infant mortality. Approximately half of all American children will spend part of their childhood in a female-headed household, and

57 percent of those households are below the poverty line.[3] Unlike countries such as France, Sweden, or Denmark, the United States has no viable public day care policy. However, when Hewlett named the women's movement as a leading culprit in perpetuating these problems, she began to lose her credibility.

The women's movement—or more accurately, movements— has been propelled by long-term shifts in the economy and the gender makeup of the workforce, which have had profound implications for the family and other cultural configurations. Seizing the opportunities presented by these shifts, feminists have introduced a wide array of initiatives for social and cultural change. Feminists can count among their successes the institutions and increased awareness now existing around such issues as rape, reproductive freedom, battering, and more. But while struggling to articulate diverse goals, and while fighting to translate those goals into material change in women's lives, the women's movements of the United States have faced enormous pressure, both from the organized Right and from the push of a social, cultural, and economic system that has benefited from women's subordination. However radical they might or might not have been in their various guises, the women's liberation movements of the past three decades have been *protest* movements. We have to ask ourselves whether protest movements should be blamed for the inequities of the very society they seek to alter.[4]

Critics who accuse feminists of ignoring mothers or motherhood are not only wrong. They are completely off the mark. Arguably, American feminist discourses have subjected the institution of motherhood and the practice of mothering to their most complex, nuanced, and multifocused analysis. On the one hand, feminists have focused on motherhood as a social mandate, an oppressive institution, a compromise of a woman's independence, and a surrender to the half-human destiny that biology supposedly decrees to women. This "negative" discourse has occurred in conjunction with political agitation for birth control and abortion rights, and alongside a critique of the nuclear family. On the other hand, feminists have focused on motherhood as a positive force. Motherhood minus "patriarchy," theorists have claimed, holds the truly spectacular potential to bond women to each other and to nature, to foster a liberating knowledge of self, to release the very creativity and generativity that the institution of "motherhood" in our culture denies to women. The women's peace movement attributes to mothers the potential to save the human race from nuclear destruction. Feminist psychoanalysts posit that changes in our current mothering arrangements could alter not only sex role socialization, but the mesh of inner being that defines human desire, development, and interaction; if people were different, society would be different, and mothering holds the key to changing both. In short, far from dismissing motherhood out of hand, feminist thought has concentrated on the topic from every possible angle. Motherhood has become an organizing metaphor for farflung, seemingly unrelated feminist concerns. It has at times been a safe and utterable substitute for what has been too controversial or unthinkable for feminists to confront directly. The mother has been rejected at times, almost deified at others, but she has never been ignored by feminists.

By virtue of sheer volume, feminist writing on motherhood deserves analysis. More deeply, the questions that inhere in an analysis of motherhood sit at the nexus of many feminist concerns. An argument for the primacy of motherhood in women's lives has, of course, been made by all of feminism's foes: biology is destiny, and women must fill their creche of "inner space" in order to find fulfillment; all that women do eventually circles back to this primal need. But this type of essentialism aside, the concerns that the subject of motherhood has tapped in a late twentieth-century American cultural context have influenced feminist thought in a broad and determinative way.

As women situated within a highly pronatalist, Freudian-influenced wider culture, women's liberationists of the 1960s, 1970s, and 1980s could not easily ignore the topic of motherhood. Some fashioned a conscious rejection of what they called the bourgeois wife and mother syndrome. Ironically, in the process of rejecting motherhood, they paid heavy homage to the topic. In the writing of others, the subject of motherhood acquired a privileged position less deliberately. The enemy always has a hand in setting the agenda.

Feminist thinking about motherhood draws even more directly from the women's liberation movement's commonly acknowledged progenitors: the Civil Rights movement, the New Left, and the counterculture. In their organized as well as their more inchoate forms, these groups included among their goals the rejection of technology, the search for "authentic experience," the prizing of youth and innocence, the revalorization of nature, the reclamation of the body and reinscription of sexuality, and the search for community.[5] Feminists recast these goals by submitting them to a gender-based power analysis, and the pursuit of each goal eventually led to an analysis of motherhood. Feminists have asserted that natural childbirth and breastfeeding challenge the male-dominated, technocratic medical establishment and celebrate the female body; that women, as creators of life, stand closer to nature, further from the machines of destruction that have come to define male culture; that the liberation of sexuality in a male-dominated society could be dangerous to women, while motherhood redeems sexuality by harnessing libido to a clear-cut, interpersonal, and nonsexual relationship; and that in daughterhood, and in potential or actual motherhood, all women participate in a community of shared experience. If we assess when, why, and precisely how feminists developed these theories, we are led to reconsider the common scholarly conclusion that the women's movement broke with the Left in an ideological as well as more obvious organizational sense.[6] Attention to the topic of motherhood especially highlights a continuity of influence between the Left and the women's movement.

In addition, feminist discourses of motherhood reveal the bedrock importance of race to late twentieth-century American feminism. Much has been written about racism within the women's movement. Too often, white feminists have posed the question, Why have women of color not joined "our" movement? But the question itself defines the participation of feminist women of color as derivative, as an act of joining an already existing white and largely middle-class movement. On the level of organized politics, black women often have responded to their "double jeopardy" by joining "black" and mixed-gender, as opposed to "women's," struggles.[7] On the level of theory, however, an African American feminist promother voice rings clear, early on, articulating many of the sentiments and concerns that white feminists would later endorse. If this voice could be called protofeminist, then so too must the white cultural feminists whose arguments sometimes build on the feminist theory of women of color.

Race (along with class) has been of central importance to American feminism in another way. Again, motherhood has been an important axis around which theory has revolved. Early on, white middle-class theorists of women's liberation were forced, by women of color, by working-class women, and by the integrity of their own leftist politics, to deal with the contradictions of race and class difference among women supposedly united worldwide by their gender. How could these theorists claim to be fighting for the rights of all women if few black women or poor women seemed to join the cause? Short of retreating to Leninist self-definitions of vanguard status, they were pressured to reach out to women in the community. When they did, they frequently spoke in terms of women's common needs as mothers. Similarly, when various women's liberation groups began to founder in the early 1970s on the shoal of extreme internal tension over questions of race, class, and sexual orientation, many theorists pushed motherhood to the fore as a powerful universalizing issue: As women, we have more in common than not, feminists began to proclaim. We are all daughters, and most of us will be mothers during our lifetimes. Let us unite and celebrate![8] With their attention focused on this assertion, many women's liberationists in the early 1970s began to shift from a radical to a cultural feminist perspective.

All students of recent American feminism face a dilemma, namely, how to define the "movement" itself. At once a grassroots groundswell and an academic assemblage, a collection of local initiatives and a national phenomenon, an action-based political force and a theory-based ideological fount, the "women's movement" is replete with internal contradictions. Perhaps the most compelling problem lies at the core: Whom do we speak of when we refer to feminists, or to the "women's movement"? Some of the harshest critics of feminist ideas about mothering, for example, seem to locate sources haphazardly, citing an antinatalist tract here, an unsympathetic consciousness-raising group there, and then conclude that the sum total of these incongruent parts presents a circumstantially strong indictment of the women's movement.

Historian David Hollinger, in a materialist interpretation of the concept of discourse, provides a more meaningful analytic framework: "Discourse is a social as well as an intellectual activity; it entails interaction between minds, and it revolves around something possessed in common. Participants in any given discourse are bound to share certain values, beliefs, perceptions, and concepts— 'ideas,' as these potentially distinctive mental phenomena are called for short—but the most concrete and functional elements shared, surely, are questions." [9] To extend and modify Hollinger's wording slightly: Discourse involves not just interaction between minds, but between individuals and groups situated socially. And while people engaged in discourse sometimes share "ideas," they also, because they are socially situated, often have somewhat competing interests and agendas. Thus participants in the discourses that make up feminism share a common goal, roughly stated as the desire to understand and change women's subordination. [10] They interpret that goal and the means to its achievement in many different ways as they actively define themselves within the rubric of feminism, and as they generate new questions that further their common cause.

The discourses of feminism, defined in this way, have occurred on many levels, ranging from spontaneous kitchen-table conversations to elaborately planned scholarly conferences. This project includes in its purview the works of authors—in books, periodical literature, or unpublished but publicly disseminated political writings—who define themselves as radical, cultural, or socialist feminists, and who address the range of concerns being raised by their contemporaries as "feminist." Scholars, professionals of various sorts, artists, and "ordinary" people all contributed to these discourses. Individual participants might have belonged to any of the organized women's liberation groups that began to form in the late 1960s, or they might have been involved only in a specific form of activism informed by feminist analysis, such as women's health activism or rape crisis work. On the other hand, many writers had no formal affiliation with feminist activist groups per se. Some were academics operating within their professional milieux but influenced by feminist thought to the extent that their scholarship took up the questions of "feminism." Some had been activists and in time became academics. Additionally, many women involved in forms of activism not traditionally defined as "feminist"—for example, some participants in the Black Power movement—addressed questions central to an evolving set of feminist discourses.

Feminists found a wide range of outlets for their views. Discussion took place not only in publications self-defined as feminist, but also in scholarly, political, and mainstream journals that sometimes published feminist views. While not all writers or publications emerge as equally influential, that distinction resting on the further generation of questions and responses spurred by a given work, all must be considered as part of the community of "discoursers."

Because of the decentralized structure of the early movement, many of the first feminist writings appeared in political pamphlets, flyers, and leaflets, and, as time went on, in feminist newsletters and newspapers with local distributions. The most influential of these early writings were soon reprinted in anthologies with national and international readerships. By the early 1970s, mainstream publishers began to issue significant numbers of feminist books and anthologies, so that at this point it becomes possible to speak of "American feminist" discourses.

Including at any given time both old and new participants, and old and new alliances or schools of thought, the boundaries of feminist discourse have been remarkably fluid. Only as social historians undertake the meticulous work of identifying specific groups of feminists and tracing the theoretical positions they pursued will it become possible to address the further thorny problem facing students of women's liberation: the relation of theory to praxis. Should we stress the overt acts undertaken by feminists—the sit-ins, demonstrations, legal challenges, consciousness-raising groups, political unions, and community organizing initiatives? If so, then in what light should we regard the vast body of theory that feminists have produced? To what extent are these two aspects of feminist expression separate, and to what extent do they inform one another? Most scholars have treated this question implicitly, drawing a thin line between what feminists say and what they do. At times, writers have defined the act of speaking or writing itself as a political act, in light of women's centuries-long history of enforced silence.[11] We must tackle these questions as we begin to construct a rich social, cultural, political, and intellectual history of American feminism.

This study addresses what emerged between the late 1960s and the early 1980s as a public, nationwide, written feminist discussion about the meaning of motherhood. I do not claim to test the absolute pulse of feminist sentiment on the matter at any given time. At times the categories of theory and activism do blend, as for example when the women's health movement publishes a guide to help women advocate for midwife-assisted childbirth. For the most part, however, the activism of women's liberationists has been highly localized and decentralized. Studies of feminist activism will have to focus on specific localities or organizations. Here I am trying to locate a more general discussion, analyze historically its development, and discuss its intellectual roots and implications.

Printed and published sources always carry the weight of a certain elitism and privilege. The right to free speech is one thing, while access to the means to produce and distribute one's ideas in printed form is another. Nevertheless, as a study of written discourse, this one bears more egalitarian promise than many. Most participants in the women's movements of the 1960s, 1970s, and 1980s were highly literate and articulate. They had the skills to join in the written discourse if they chose. Moreover, with the proliferation of small presses and other feminist media, they did not have to battle the mainstream publishers in New York to find themselves in print. And because of the newness and explicitly antiestablishment editorial policies of many feminist publications, at least in the early years, writers did not need to display traditional academic standing to enter the fray. All of these factors help to mitigate the still withstanding nonegalitarianism of an intellectual history approach.

Moreover, a study of the internal development of any particular discourse can fall prey to the pitfall of false isolationism. American feminists operated within a wider American context, as well as within an international feminist context. I attempt to situate feminist discourses of motherhood within these wider rhetorical and social contexts, when necessary. Feminist pronatalism, for example, parallels a similar predisposition in both the mainstream and the counterculture in America in the 1960s and 1970s. In terms of an international focus, however, the isolation of American feminist thought proves to be more than a false construct. Aside from a few works, such as the writings of British psychoanalyst Juliet Mitchell, or the ambiguously feminist contribution of Australian writer Germaine Greer, few early feminist texts by "outsiders" had wide play in the United States.[12]

Although this project broaches only one aspect of a complex inquiry into the connections between feminism and motherhood, in this case theory is of more than ordinary importance. Ideological constructs form part of the mold of any social movement. In a protest movement, in which participants cannot necessarily actualize their goals, theory represents a hefty repository of intention. Critics attack feminists with a two-pronged fork: feminists have not cared about mothers; and feminists have done nothing to help mothers. To the latter charge, scholars cannot yet fully respond. But these pages address what feminists have believed they would do vis-à-vis mothering, if they held the social and political power.

In 1968, women who had been involved in the Civil Rights movement and the New Left began in earnest to organize on their own behalf. While there had been feminist dissent within the Left earlier, not until 1968 did a significant number of feminist writings begin to appear. Nor did the groundswell of grassroots activism, primarily in the form of consciousness-raising groups, really take hold until this watershed year.

Many scholars date the onset of second-wave feminism to the publication of Betty Friedan's book *The Feminine Mystique* in 1963.[13] That periodization, however, conflates two disparate bodies of thought and activism. The feminist activism sparked by Friedan's articulation of "the problem that has no name" appealed primarily to women of her generation. It drew from the liberal tradition of individual rights and sought redress through public, legal, and legislative channels.[14] The radical branch of the women's movement that emerged in the late 1960s drew its philosophy, its members, and its modus operandi from the radical cultural and political movements of that decade. While liberal and radical feminism have merged both organizationally and ideologically at various junctures—as for example in the fight for abortion rights—they are at root distinct movements and philosophies. The intense—and primarily positive—emphasis on motherhood in feminist thought draws more from the predominantly white cultural left and the black feminist discourses of the 1960s and early 1970s than from the reformist activism of liberal feminist organizations like the National Organization for Women. The cultural left, in its many 1960s guises, was most influential in shaping the attitudes toward the body, sexuality, nature, and community that would form the basis of feminist theory about motherhood.[15]

My major purpose here is to ferret out the sources of positive feminist discourses of motherhood and to show the functions of those discourses in the transition from radical to cultural feminism in the early to mid-1970s. Cultural feminist theory about motherhood took many forms and did not reach full fruition for several years. But by the early 1980s, feminists had become fully embroiled in debate about pornography, a debate that positioned a safe but asexual mother image against the dangers of unbridled sexuality. The women's peace movement and the ecofeminist movement, laden with maternalist rhetoric, had also begun to peak by this time. The women's spirituality movement, which deified the Great Mother and cast about for models of ancient matriarchy, was well mobilized by then, too. Feminist psychoanalytic theorists, most notably Nancy Chodorow, had begun to turn their attention to mothering. In 1980, Sara Ruddick published the signal article of this period, "Maternal Thinking," which posits mothering behavior as a blueprint for human caring and communion.[16] In 1983, feminist protesters planted themselves outside the Seneca Army Depot in Seneca Falls, New York, in a concrete expression of the belief that women's nature, set against men's, can save the planet.[17]

Chapter 1 confronts the image of the feminist as baby hater, covering the period from 1968 to 1973, the only time during which relatively negative assessments of motherhood influenced a substantial portion of feminist writing on the subject. Feminists drew such views from several post-World War II critiques of the nuclear family, most specifically those developed by the New Left and counterculture of the 1960s. While the Left's demand for individual sexual liberation and its more general valorization of the body as part of nature certainly influenced feminist thought, the cultural left's communitarian legacy to feminism was a strong mitigating factor against an outright rejection of mothers, children, and families of some sort.

Chapter 2 begins to locate the sources of the increasingly positive view of motherhood endorsed by many feminists and identifies those influences even in the earliest women's liberationist writings, from the mid-1960s through 1974. The counterculture, at least as much as the New Left or the Civil Rights movement, served as a key seedbed of second-wave feminism. The early women's health movement's focus on pregnancy and natural childbirth provides strong evidence of this countercultural influence.

Chapter 3 reveals that black feminist thought about motherhood was important to all feminist theory on the topic and distinguishes between that unacknowledged debt and some white feminists' rhetorical use of motherhood as an antidote to racism within the women's movement.

Chapter 4 analyzes the decline of radical feminism and the rise of cultural feminism in the mid-1970s, noting the concurrent movement-wide burst of attention to the topic of motherhood and probing why that issue, among others, was pushed to the fulcrum of feminist concern.

Chapter 5 explores the content of the reenergized feminist endorsements of motherhood, looking particularly at psychoanalytic feminism, ecofeminism, spiritual feminism, and the antipornography movement, and examining the ways in which those movements continued to wrestle with the uneasy challenge of the cultural left to reconcile sexuality, motherhood, and the desire for community.

While the study ends in 1983, I note in conclusion the trends of the last dozen years, showing how they, too, further the earliest agendas of second-wave feminism. The conclusion gathers up some of the loose ends left by the cultural feminist supposition of a "natural" connection between mother and child, looking at the ways in which feminists are still treating motherhood as the last utopian frontier for countercultural ideals, and as the metaphorical cement for a fragmented movement.[18]

A Note on Terms

A great many individuals and groups participated in the discourses traced here. While labels do not always capture the breadth or the shading of a particular viewpoint, they do provide a rough map on which to locate complex, often overlapping, strains of thought. A brief key to the terminology of this study might be helpful.

The term *women's liberation movement* refers to both radical and socialist feminist organizations, participants, and ideas. The term *liberal feminism* refers to the separate branch of reformist feminism organized under such groups as NOW and the Women's Equity Action League.

Many radical and socialist feminists came from similar political and cultural backgrounds and shared basic values and politics. In cases where the distinction is irrelevant, the term *women's liberationists* suffices. At times, however, theoretical and organizational distinctions separate radical and socialist feminism. *Radical feminism* stresses gender oppression as the original and primary oppression of women; male dominance, above and beyond all other forms of social organization, must be eradicated. *Cultural feminism,* which emerged in the early 1970s from the radical feminist movement, also views gender oppression as the central oppression, but stresses even more strongly than most early radical feminist theories the essential, perhaps biologically based, differences between women and men and seeks to create a separate women's culture that celebrates women's distinct qualities. *Socialist feminism* treats the combined influence of gender oppression and capitalism as the source of women's oppression; thus liberation entails a socialist revolution as well as the elimination of male dominance. Unlike radical and cultural feminism, which can be quite ahistorical in their emphasis on the unchanging body, socialist feminism relies on historical analysis, insofar as it recognizes capitalism and socialism as temporal and dynamic historical phases.[19]

These definitions, descriptively accurate in a general sense, have themselves been the subject of an evolving body of feminist theory.

While for purposes of clarity and continuity I use the labels of "radical," "cultural," and "socialist" feminist, I use them advisedly, with the understanding that the categories have been in flux since their inception.

Similarly, the actual membership of the movement has always been in flux. No single, fixed group of feminists, or even clearly defined generations of feminists, ever comprised "the movement." Individuals have shifted camps, and newcomers have affiliated themselves with well-established groups or ideologies. As the site of a number of complex and intersecting discourses, the women's movement has been highly permeable. It has, in fact, eluded definition as a single movement, consisting more accurately of a multiplicity of movements. Indeed, an underlying task here is to trace and to interrogate many feminists' insistence on delineating a unitary movement, for feminist mothering theory has often been deployed toward that end.

A final word about the use of the terms *cultural left, New Left,* and *counterculture.* I discuss, broadly, the views that arose from the writing and activism of people in all segments of the 1960s "subculture." However, that subculture actually consisted of a more organized political wing, referred to as the New Left, and a more loosely defined cultural wing, referred to as the counterculture. To be even more specific, the New Left refers to particular organizations, and to a broader social movement, that appeared on college campuses and beyond in the 1960s. These groups include Students for a Democratic Society, the free speech movement, the antiwar movement, the Yippies, and others (often splinter groups or infiltrators of the above). The New Left fashioned itself not only against the Right, or the "establishment," but also against the Old Left, especially the anticommunist League for Industrial Democracy. The counterculture can be tied less easily to specific groups but in general refers to the "lifestyle" subcultures of the 1960s—the hippies, communards, and so on—and to aspects of that lifestyle: marijuana and psychedelic drugs, folk and rock'n'roll music, sexual "freedom," long hair, and other idiosyncrasies of personal style. In addition, the predominantly white Left of the 1960s had interactions with and, more important, corollaries to the black activism of the period: the youth branch of the Civil Rights movement, especially the Student Nonviolent Coordinating Committee (SNCC), and, in the latter part of the decade, the Black Power movement, which incorporated SNCC, the Black Panther Party, cultural nationalists, and others.

The New Left and the counterculture were never entirely separate, in participants or in ideas. In terms of the critique of the nuclear family, for example, the interplay between the New Left and the counterculture was so thorough that the distinctions become meaningless. However, certain ideas, values, and beliefs did receive more attention among those people who identified most heavily with the counterculture, even when highly regarded New Left intellectuals first posed the ideas. This is the case with many of the utopian and liberationist ideas concerning the body, nature, sexuality, and community. First suggested by New Left thinkers, they received widest play in the counterculture. Countercultural ideas continued to influence feminist thought even after many feminists disavowed any affiliation with the organized Left. I use the labels "countercultural" and "New Left" to specify the principal arenas in which ideas took hold. When the distinction is not particularly relevant to the discussion, I refer more generically to the "cultural left." [20]

Chapter One

Down with Motherhood?
Ambivalence in the Emerging
Feminist Movement

The stereotype that feminists disdain mothers and children appeared almost simultaneously with the emergence of radical feminism in the late 1960s. Many of the first feminist actions and publications did target traditional marriage and motherhood as oppressive institutions. The media, the New Right, and feminist revisionists have seized on that critique over the years to gain a handle on an unwieldy movement, to link sexual politics with standard Cold War right-wing politics, and to redirect American feminism toward a more mainstream "profamily" platform.[1] As a result, the negative critique of motherhood, never hegemonic within feminism, has achieved an exaggerated reputation.

What was the genuine critical stance toward motherhood in women's liberationist writing from the late 1960s through the early 1970s, the only period during which "negative" views of motherhood gained any prominence in feminist writing?[2] Clearly, some feminist writers did develop a negative stance toward motherhood, but that stance was part of a wide-ranging and complex critique of the nuclear family, drawn largely from the New Left and the counterculture of the 1960s, rather than a simple dismissal of mothers and mothering. Alongside even the most trenchant attacks on current mothering arrangements, feminists usually proposed strategies for improving the material lot of mothers and children.[3]

Indeed, both the cultural left and women's liberation activism must be understood not only in terms of what they wished to destroy, as is so common, but in terms of what they wished to create. Rejecting the traditional family as destructive of individuality, sexual expressiveness, and authentic interpersonal communication, New Leftists, counterculturalists, and then radical feminists proposed new forms of community to replace the old. Utopianist and visionary, members of the cultural left of the 1960s sought both individual liberation, as mediated through the body, and community. Feminists, too, sought such a reconciliation. But as feminists subjected the ideas and values of the Left to a gender analysis, they discovered a problem: Much of the "new" communalism of the Left rested on very old ideas about women's relationship to childbearing and child rearing. Although they were influenced by the cultural left's critique of traditional domesticity and drawn to many of the same values and visions, feminists needed to analyze the nuclear family even more critically. That analysis led at times to starkly rejectionist views of marriage and motherhood. More often, however, early radical and socialist feminists added to the utopianism of the cultural left provisions that would allow women, as well as men, to participate fully in the creation of new and liberated family arrangements.

Sources of Ambivalence

Post-War Critiques of the Family

Decades before the cultural revolution of the 1960s, a pool of disaffected thinkers in the United States and Europe had submitted the nuclear family to a sustained critique. Anthropologists theorized that the values of a culture were reflected in the individual personality structures of its members, and that family structures mediated personality. Frankfurt School intellectuals warned that if the state took over too many functions of the family, and if it assumed the authority of the father, the result could be a personality willing to commit atrocities in the name of obedience. Unlike the Frankfurt theorists, American sociologist Talcott Parsons cheered the interposition of state institutions into the family: As an affective and socializing unit, with many of its onerous tasks lifted, the family could concentrate its energies fully on its young, rearing children with the unprecedented guidance of many trained professionals.

By the 1950s, however, even some Parsonians expressed uncertainty about the institution of the family. The nuclear family, snuggled cozily on its suburban plot, concentrated *too* heavily on its young, felt Kenneth Keniston. The pressure is so unbearable, Philip Slater wrote, that the children of the stiflingly isolated suburbs learn to numb themselves to cope with their intrusively doting mothers. By the early 1960s, American sociology contained a whole body of literature about the felt discontent of the middle-class American, the dullness of suburban life, and the smothering nature of the family. This discourse commented critically on motherhood as an institution to the extent that it linked "family" to a mother-centered domesticity.[4]

As this critique entered both the popular and the psychological literature, the condemnation of mothers became more vitriolic. Philip Wylie, in the 1942 book *Generation of Vipers,* had already announced that the over-involved "Mom" who had supplanted the old-fashioned, self-effacing mother was bad for men, bad for society, and, worst of all, bad for her children.[5] In a more scholarly vein, Theodore Lidz, in his well-known clinical studies of schizophrenia, blamed mothers both for their excessive closeness to their children *and* for their "pseudo" closeness.[6] In the 1960s, numerous mainstream mother-blaming tracts, imbued with bowdlerized psychoanalytic wisdom, and markedly misogynist in tone, popularized the personage of the schizophrenogenic mother as a woman too fully involved in her children's lives, coddling, berating, intruding, and eventually destroying their human potential.[7] Philip Roth's novel *Portnoy's Complaint* labeled the Jewish mother as the exemplar of maternal transgression, portraying life with her as a series of harangues that sent fathers and sons alike in retreat to the bathroom, seeking refuge in solitude and slabs of cold calves' liver.[8] Mothers could hardly sustain harsher criticism.

The family as a whole, however, could still be subjected to criticism. Long before feminists launched their critique, a male revolt against domesticity surfaced. In the 1950s, the Beats rejected American materialism and the constraints of domestic life, seeking more "authenticity" and less responsibility in their lives.[9] A radical individualist perspective, Beat philosophy linked women and the family with the deadening of a free, male, pioneer-of-the-open-road spirit. Jack Kerouac in particular wrote of an American landscape strewn with the corpses of temporary domestic arrangements.[10]

Appearing just before the Beats, but outliving them, Hugh Hefner's *Playboy* magazine channeled a similar dissatisfaction with the burdens of twentieth-century domesticity into a less nihilistic release. By embracing bourgeois materialism, and by including the female body in the panoply of items to be purchased on the open marketplace, *Playboy* offered freedom from family responsibility in conjunction with sexual pleasure.[11]

Thus, even at the outset of the 1960s, the traditional family had already been scrutinized by a wide range of critics, and much of the criticism centered on the mother. The New Left, with the women's movement as its dissenting progeny, did not suddenly reject 1950s domesticity in an explosive fit of generational conflict.[12]

As babyboomers entered college, they nevertheless faced a culture that remained strongly pronatalist. On the level of rhetoric, the rejections of domesticity were more strident in the 1960s than in the 1950s, and they would eventually claim a broader popular base of support. On the level of cultural prescription, however,

American women in the 1960s were still expected to bear and rear children. Although the role of the mother had been riddled with post-Freudian angst, so that it was nearly impossible to be considered a *good* mother, the dictate to "go forth and mother" remained in place.[13] Children's games and literature continued to present motherhood as the eventual occupation of choice for all adult women. The venerable Dr. Spock and other pediatricians still considered employment outside the home a kind of child desertion: A woman's job was to mother, full-time, period. Women were still shunted into pink-collar ghettoes in jobs with little promise of advancement, on the rationale that a woman worked only temporarily until motherhood pulled her back into the home. Family planning literature assumed that every woman would, in time, bear children. Married couples with children received tax breaks denied to childless couples. Abortion remained illegal until 1973 in the United States. These were but some of the seemingly discrete social and economic inducements to parenthood that, taken together, constitute a pronatalist norm.[14]

The prevalence of this pronatalist norm seems at odds with changing patterns in marriage and childbearing in the United States. Beginning in 1960, Americans began to marry later or not at all. The birthrate, meanwhile, began to drop.[15] One explanation for the persistence of pronatalist attitudes, despite this newly emerging demographic pattern, is that because the baby boom persisted until 1964, most American women were ensconced in the details of childrearing well into the 1970s. They created and responded to a primary identification of women as mothers. The demands of this role created a lag between the imperatives of everyday life and any potential receptivity they might have had to the wider array of options becoming available to women during the same period.

This explanation does not suffice, however, because the ideology of domesticity that matured in the 1950s and then persisted into the 1960s was more than a direct and "natural" result of the baby boom. The domestic ideal of the 1950s made a conceptual link between the self-contained American family and the containment of a nuclear threat from the "evil empire" abroad. The American way, and the American nuclear family, contraposed the Soviet way, with its presumed lack of respect for family, domesticity, and privacy. "Mom," in other words, was a fundamental late-twentieth-century capitalist, imperialist icon.[16] And as American policy in Vietnam confirms, the Cold War persisted well through the 1960s, promoting on an ideological level the linkage of the privatized, consumerist, male-headed, mother-centered nuclear family with the glorification of the flag and the stock market.

The New Left and the Counterculture: Decoding the Nuclear Family

Establishing what would become the fundament of radical feminist theory, the cultural and political radicals of the 1960s attempted to open up all that the Cold War consensus tried to contain.[17] With varying levels of perspecuity, New Leftists and counterculturalists rejected the external symbols of 1950s security. Their cry rang with clarity: Oppose the United States government in its anticommunist, imperialist aggression! Reject the materialism and consumerism of the suburban middle class! Do away with the corporations! Run from the rat race! And, finally, Smash the nuclear family![18]

The "Port Huron Statement," the earliest cohesive presentation of New Left philosophy, linked these elements of protest implicitly, using the cry for "authenticity" as a connector. Decrying the moribund condition of the American political and social landscape, Tom Hayden, writing for Students for a Democratic Society (SDS), articulated a new set of values:

The goal of man and society should be human independence; a concern not with image of popularity but with finding meaning in life that is personally authentic; a quality of mind not compulsively driven by a sense of powerlessness, nor one which unthinkingly adopts status values, nor one which represses all threats to its habits, but one which has full, spontaneous access to present and past experiences, one which easily unites the fragmented parts of personal history, one which openly faces problems which are troubling and unresolved; one with an intuitive awareness of possibilities, an active sense of curiosity, an ability and willingness to learn.[19]

According to SDS, the consensus that had resulted in the Cold War depended on the denial of individual, personal, authentic, spontaneous, and intuitive impulses or drives. Idealism had been shunted into bureaucratic, technocratic inertia. Life-affirming impulses had been repressed and molded into status-affirming institutions. Those artificial institutions needed to be stripped away, replaced with the channels of human intercourse that would interfere least with natural, unmediated "men," beings "infinitely precious and possessed of unfulfilled capacities for reason, freedom, and love."[20]

Because the cultural left eventually spawned the women's liberation movement, with its complex views of the body and the body's reproductive capacity, it is crucial to this analysis to highlight the deeply essentialist implications of the New Left's premier document. The "Port Huron Statement" both recognized the all-powerful influence of socialization and valorized those human qualities that precede and, in exceptional cases, survive the current socialization process. In other words, society always shapes people. The nature of the social, political, economic, and cultural environment determines how we will develop as human beings. We might contribute initial, positive potential to our own lives, but that potential has no shape until set in motion by "human interdependence." And here lies the contradiction. What does it mean to get back to the core of an organism that is socially constructed? What exactly lies at the core? Only potential, housed in the flesh. While the "Port Huron Statement" does not tackle the implications of its own paradoxical stance directly, its implicit resolution of this contradiction presages the fundamental essentialism of New Left, countercultural, and eventually radical feminist thought: The physical organism appears to exist a priori, outside of civilization, governed by inexorable "natural" drives, susceptible to repression, but short of death, not fully vulnerable to social mediation. The body, perceived as a site of "authentic" human experience beyond the absolute reach of societal manipulation, would soon become the closest thing to a holy land for the New Left and the counterculture.

Jerry Rubin, the flamboyant leader of the Yippies (Youth International Party), made the same point more pungently: "The New Left sprang, a predestined, pissed-off child, from Elvis' gyrating pelvis."[21] America looked pretty, all neat, combed, and repressed, but "under the surface, silent people railed at the chains upon their souls."[22] Symbols of happy domestic containment abounded in America: "Dad looked at his house and car and manicured lawn, and he was proud. All of his material possessions justified his life."[23] He tried to fit his children into the same mold, telling them that "fucking was bad because it was immoral."[24] But it felt good, and so Jerry and his contemporaries got confused. "We went crazy. We couldn't hold it back any more. Elvis Presley ripped off Ike Eisenhower by turning our uptight young awakening bodies around. . . . Elvis told us to let go!"[25]

The budding cultural left thus used a radical essentialism to drive a wedge into the marriage of domesticity and anticommunism. The separation of sexuality from domesticity and the celebration of sexuality for its own sake allowed the new generation to step outside of the Cold War consensus. If only the body, and most particularly its sexual impulse, could be liberated—decontained, as it were—then people could escape the hateful imperatives of the Cold War. Not mere hedonism, this radical emphasis on sexual liberation attempted to decode the corporate family, that alleged bulwark against foreign domination. The "family," in this view, was best seen as a collection of individual organisms, each with its own animal drives. "Domesticity" and "containment," on the other hand, required that the family be seen as a corporate whole, a single defensive apparatus in which individuals could fulfill certain prescribed roles, but which, ultimately, took meaning in its functional wholeness. With intense dismay, a generation of college-bound youth was beginning to perceive that the ultimate purpose of that functional wholeness was to promote an international arena for hatred and warfare. They saw the body, especially the sexualized body, as a way to decode the functionalist family.

This apparently sudden wave of protest did have antecedents. Yet the radical nature of the New Left revolt, its ability to conjoin the currently reigning Freudian understanding of human relations with a socialist historical overview and program, catapulted the critique of the nuclear family into a new era. With both "high" and "low" theory, New Left and counterculturalist thinkers ventured radical interpretations of the family, sexuality, and the meaning of community.

Herbert Marcuse and Wilhelm Reich, two of the leading social theorists embraced by the New Left, criticized capitalism for its repression of human instinct. Marcuse argued that what passed for genuine pleasure in modern society was in fact a superficial, numbing replica of pleasure that repressed human instincts beyond the point necessary for civilization, even while claiming to liberate them. Lured into a pacified state of conformity, people became subject to the deep totalitarianism of advanced capitalist society. To attain liberation, people needed to reject this tricky "surplus repression" and reclaim the realm of genuine instinct. Reich similarly stressed the damage done to the instincts, especially to human sexuality, by capitalism. By siphoning our deepest drives into the tasks of its own perpetuation, capitalism creates a character structure crippled by sexual repression. Socialism, free of the tyranny that impels people toward repression in the name of private property, could bring the sexual liberation that, in Reich's view, would equate with progress.[26]

The counterculturalists of the 1960s quickly translated these ideas into the vernacular. Declaring marriage and monogamy superfluous, hippies celebrated "free love," sex, and sensuality. They believed that people should control their own bodies and minds, with "nature" as the only legitimate higher authority (the obvious exception to this belief being those artificial substances used in the service of mind expansion and spiritual quest). National boundaries divided the earth unnaturally. Advanced technology, administrated through massive bureaucracies, signaled the death knoll of nature. In hundreds of communes across the country, young people reinterpreted the meaning of "family," seeing its essence not in biological or property ties, but rather in the chosen sharing of values and living space, in the moment.[27]

Beyond indulging in a wide range of sexy new choices, the Left and the counterculture pursued an avowedly radical agenda through their cultural politics. In their conjoined critique of the nuclear family and rejection of Cold War politics, they eschewed containment in the broad cultural definition of the term. Clearly, the family reflected the imperatives of the social and economic order. The family, according to even the relatively unpoliticized segments of the counterculture, had to be understood as a key socializing institution of an entire social order bent upon breaking the human spirit.[28] Indeed, as the widely read radical psychiatrist R. D. Laing theorized, the family was something of an insanity generator, socializing people to fit into an insane world; the sanest people were schizophrenics, who refused to bend to the dictates of the nuclear family.[29]

Yet, as the rapid proliferation of communal living arrangements suggests, the counterculture and the Left were antifamily only in the prescriptive sense. Along with the call to smash the nuclear family rose the plea for community.[30] The Civil Rights movement had defined its ethos in terms of Christian humanism, aspiring to create a "beloved community" based around activism.[31] The Left grafted the traditions of anarchism, utopian socialism, and Marxist humanism onto the communitarianism of the Southern Civil Rights movement.[32] The counterculture, in addition, drew selectively from the tradition of American pastoralism, finding in nature's encomiasts an alternative to the ills of urban individualism.[33]

The cultural left faced the difficult task of reuniting sexuality to a group ethos. The traditional American family had ascribed particular gendered functions to its members, presuming that the balance of the group could be achieved by containing and directing the "natural," biologically determined proclivities of each member. The New Left and the counterculture rejected this corporate-functionalist view of the family, redefining sexuality as an individual, sensorily "authentic" experience. But if the establishment had masked the internal turmoil of the nuclear family with declarations of "togetherness," the cultural radicals faltered by declaring a false egalitarianism within their own communities, based on the assumption that sexuality functions as a leveler: If the restrictions on sex are removed, then all people can partake freely and equally of its pleasures.

Failing to problematize the family in terms of gender, the cultural left did not recognize that the corporate family "contained" men's and women's sexuality in different ways, and for different purposes. Casting individuals back onto the mandates of their "authentic" physical selves, and then seeking to create community among these freed packages of libido, the counterculture failed especially to tackle the meaning of sexual liberation for women, whose "authentic" bodies would produce children if nature ruled the day. The birth control pill succeeded only partially in muting these contradictions. With the counterculture's increasing valorization of nature, hippie women, reputedly in touch with the earth and moon, gave birth to plenty of babies. And the exceedingly traditional division of labor that ensued on many of the nation's communes testifies to the limitations of the countercultural critique of traditional domesticity.[34]

In summary, without a social constructionist understanding of gender, the cultural left presented the triumvirate of liberated sex, nature, and reproduction as a refutation of the bourgeoisie's fussy, technologically mediated counterparts. But as feminists would soon point out, counterculturalists could attempt to unite sex, community, and motherhood without fearing the encroachment of a familiar domesticity only because they ignored the specific, material realities of motherhood for women, and because they attempted to incorporate mothering into the holistic, eroticized rubric of "authentic" experience.[35] It would remain for feminists to examine the tripartite meaning of sexual freedom, community, and reproduction.

Women's Liberation and Motherhood
The Puzzling Legacies of the Cultural Left

Early radical and socialist feminist writers seized the leftist and countercultural discourse that separated sexuality from domesticity, seeing in it a particular message for women. As a starting point, they often condemned the sexual revolution as exploitive of women. According to Pat Mainardi, of the radical feminist group Redstockings,

The entire alternate lifestyle revolutionary subculture was in some ways a giant step backwards for women, despite its attractive aspects and the hopes some women had for it being an improvement over "traditional marriage." It was a classic case of "men's liberation," because the freedom these men gained—freedom from the burdens of wife and children—was gained at our expense. Free love communes were exposed as places where women not only did all the traditional women's work, cooking, housekeeping, etc., but were also pressured to be available sexually to all, without birth control which was considered "unnatural." As one woman put it, "all of the women were pregnant all of the time," until dirty diapers and crying babies began to "bring down" the men, so they "split" to a newer freer commune, leaving women to go on welfare and support their children as best they could.[36]

Despite their bitterness, most early women's liberationists understood that the basic premises of the cultural left's discourse of sexuality—the loosening of the corporate bonds of family and the separation of sexuality from traditional domesticity—held out a great promise of power and liberation for women.[37] What feminists began to add to the Left's message was that the family had oppressed men and women *differently*. Women, too, suffered the effects of truncated libido and stifled human potential. Beyond that, however, they were consigned for life to the domain of the family, known by now as the seat of personal oppression. Feminists began to pry the façade of domesticity open further, seeking to understand exactly how and why women suffered most within its strictures.

On the one hand, early radical feminists succumbed even more than their New Left and countercultural predecessors to the temptations of essentialism. They theorized that women's bodies were most easily coopted by the state and its cultural apparatus because the female body brought forth the child, the heir, the bundle of flesh that linked the control of property with the control of sexuality, that is to say, the historical culprit in the formation of family.[38]

On the other hand, and ironically, feminists used the counterculture's romanticization of nature—tied closely to the cultural left's essentialism—to broach a social constructionist view of gender. Beginning with the supposition that the body, ungendered, is part of nature and therefore not only good, but also rightfully beyond the jurisdiction of culture, possessing an a priori mandate to self-determination, feminists began to analyze the apparatuses of culture that ascribe particular meaning to the female body versus the male body. They theorized that in the beginning there is only the body, which has no particular meaning. Societies, in their development of social organization, begin to ascribe meaning to men's and women's bodies as they create kinship systems posited on the economic and symbolic exchange value of women. Thus, the body-in-relation, the gendered body, serves as the basis for culture. Significantly, the gendered body also serves as the basis for women's subordination, because the division of culture and nature results in the domination of nature by culture. Women, with their childbearing functions, are perceived as more connected to nature.[39]

This analysis differs crucially from a simple essentialist view in that it faults male-dominated culture, and not women's bodies, for women's oppression.[40] In addition, and of significance for this discussion, feminist theory here parallels the Left's critique of the nuclear family. In linking women's subordination to their consignment to the private, domestic, natural or "precultural" sphere, this theory finds fault with that sphere. Indeed, the entire feminist social constructionist understanding of gender builds upon a critique of the bond between women and the domestic sphere.

Thus, with ambivalence and with rather different goals, early participants in the women's liberation movement took on two of the major battles assumed by the cultural left: the freeing of libido and the overturning of traditional domesticity. For the Left, these battles were linked, not only to each other, but to a reconstructed vision of human community imbued with the pleasure principle. In principle, feminists eschewed no aspect of this agenda, but when they submitted the Marcusian/Reichian theory of sexual liberation to a gendered power analysis, they found that women suffered an additional layer of mediation between instinct and everyday reality. Feminists noted that men within institutions like marriage, and perhaps men in general, carried the state's usurpation of true human potential into the innermost reaches of personal life. For women, the simple freeing of libido, in a society in which women are assigned sole responsibility for child rearing, could diminish rather than increase the potential for self-determination. For women, in short, the rejoining of sexuality, procreation, and community represented both the pleasure that the Left awaited and the danger that it feared.[41]

In sum, early radical feminists endorsed the cultural legacy of the Left. Yet the additional filter of gender analysis riddled that legacy with problems. For the Left, the oppression of women, albeit unacknowledged and largely unrecognized, had absorbed many contradictions. But virtually all feminist analyses have struggled to reconcile the valorization of nature, the reclaiming of sexuality, and the search for community with women's relationship to reproduction and mothering. Such reconciliation eludes them, and feminists have often sacrificed one or the other of the Left's goals in striving to create their own visions of the good society.[42]

Utopianism and the Revisioning of Motherhood

Most of the early radical and socialist feminist groups, though comprised primarily of young, childless women, did pay close attention to the topic of motherhood, and did, in concrete terms, discuss its amelioration. Perhaps the combined influence of youth and utopianist New Left politics directed many women's liberationists to view motherhood as something that could be totally restructured. Indeed, in the earliest phases of the movement, roughly from 1968 to 1973, radical and socialist feminists began to dismantle traditional expectations about motherhood. They undertook a deep analysis of the family. Critics of the movement have focused on the "negative" points of that analysis, failing to recognize that feminists, even in the early, ostensibly "antimother" period, also often endorsed the utopian goal of a restructured community, *with* children, as their ultimate vision.[43]

Juliet Mitchell, a British psychoanalyst, provided the American feminist movement with one of its earliest and most prescient analyses of the family. In her 1966 article "Women: The Longest Revolution," and in the more fully developed work *Woman's Estate*, Mitchell named the family as a key site of women's oppression.[44] Mitchell, like the many socialist feminists to follow, advanced a historical materialist analysis of women's oppression, in the tradition of Engels. The family, as a prime organizer of the social relations requisite to a society built on the ownership of private property, directs women's biological capacity for childbearing in the interests of the capitalist state. Women, removed from the visible realm of productive labor, reproduce and maintain the workforce. Their domestic and maternal duties comprise an invisible but essential base for the workings of the capitalist profit-making enterprise. Within the family, the superstructural overlay of domestic ideology seeks to justify this exploitation of women's labor; all that capitalism in fact imposes on women for its own utilitarian purposes gets mystified as the "natural," biological proclivities of women themselves. Thus, a belief in the "maternal instinct" serves to condemn proposals for restructuring the economy along gender lines, a restructuring that would deprive capitalism of its ever-replenished, maintenance-free pool of laborers.[45]

Socialist feminists, following Mitchell, saw the need to demystify the family and reveal the true economic workings beneath the veil of domestic ideology. They argued that the false division between the private and public realms, between "productive" and "reproductive" labor, renders women's work invisible and provides infinite opportunity for the superexploitation and abuse of women, in the private and the public realms—all in the name of domestic bliss, maternal instinct, and the like. The work performed by women in the home, including childbearing and child rearing, declared socialist feminists, is real work of real value to society. Women, induced by necessity to endorse their own oppression, are alienated laborers. The false privatization of the family needs to end, so that women, like other workers, can see their common cause and rise collectively toward socialism. Socialism must not be built on the backs of women's invisible labor. "Reproductive" labor must be recognized as an integral part of the economy; its constituent tasks must be taken over by society as a whole. The community benefits from the rearing of children; the community must take responsibility for that task. Only then, socialist feminists theorized, will women be freed from the hidden, oppressive conditions of their traditional labor, and only then will the labor itself be valued.[46]

Juliet Mitchell and other socialist feminists were not the only women's liberationists during this period to attempt a materialist interpretation of childbearing and child rearing. In 1970, Shulamith Firestone, more properly labeled a radical feminist than a socialist feminist, published *The Dialectic of Sex*,[47] in which she argued that the initial inequality between men and women can be traced to the most concrete and material source of all: the body. Women are weakened physically by pregnancy. Human infants, dependent for so long after birth, limit their biological mothers' potential. The physical fact of childbearing leads to a particular division of labor, with women tied to the care of the children they produce. To achieve liberation, women must be freed from the burden of producing children in their bodies, a burden that limits, distorts, and degrades women. Firestone proposes extrauterine gestation in test tubes as a liberationist strategy. Only then, she argues, will the biological family cease to define women's lives.[48]

If Firestone's notions of extrauterine procreation seemed bizarre to her many critics on the Right, she received her share of scorn from feminists as well. Juliet Mitchell charges that Firestone's theory fails as a historical materialist explanation of women's oppression; it is hardly dialectical.[49] Other critics have noted that Firestone fails to explain the ways in which society links the biological fact of childbearing to the social act of child rearing.[50] Common to all her critics is the belief that Firestone is too extreme in her rejection of motherhood.

In two ways, Firestone's critique of motherhood does surpass that of virtually all other early feminists. First, whereas many radical feminists during this period include the institution of motherhood in the litany of patriarchal oppressions, Firestone further suggests that the physical condition of pregnancy would remain oppressive no matter what social, political, or economic alterations were made. Her singular stigmatization of pregnancy placed Firestone at the far end of the spectrum of feminist antinatalism.

Second, Firestone, later to be joined by Ti-Grace Atkinson, a radical feminist theorist and founder of the New York-based group The Feminists, differed from her contemporaries in her belief that technology could provide a solution to women's oppression. Like the New Left and the counterculture, most feminists of this period expressed a profound mistrust of technology, seeing it as the establishment's medium for the worst violations of authentic experience. Firestone, with apparent disregard for the body of theory that linked liberation to "nature," instead linked an. essentialist view of technology to an equally essentialist view of maternity. She theorized that by harnessing technology as a neutral force, the worst aspects of motherhood could be neutralized.[51]

Yet Firestone, like her contemporaries, maintains a level of ambivalence about motherhood in her writing. Her work cannot be understood out of the context of the New Left and the counterculture, even though she herself made a point of disavowing the Left.[52] Like the psychoanalytically oriented Marcusian New Left, Firestone attempts to meld Marxism and Freudianism in her analysis. Like the cultural left, Firestone considers the human body the site of self-realization. Also like the cultural left, Firestone does not reject children per se. She rejects the ways in which our current childbearing and child rearing arrangements preclude full realization of a countercultural utopia. Recognizing that women have been barred by their childbearing capacity from full participation in all the pleasures promised by the new social order, Firestone constructs a plan to make women men's equals in the pursuit of pleasure. This plan is as concerned with claiming a stake in sexual liberation as it is with rejecting motherhood.

Toward the conclusion of her book, Firestone begins to discuss children's rights in countercultural terms. Children, like adults, should be able to partake of the freedoms of "cybernetic socialism," she declares. All the forms of control and repression that characterize childhood must be lifted; they are but exaggerated versions of the limitations the establishment puts on all of us, the false trappings of civilization that keep us from our authentic selves. Children, in other words, should have the right to live like liberated adults. Most challenging, Firestone declares that children, like adults, should have the right to their own sexuality. "Relations with children would include as much genital sex as the child was capable of—probably considerably more than we now believe."[53] Clearly, in this instance, Firestone's theory draws heavily from the views of the cultural left. Children are not the problem; sexual repression is.[54]

In the end, Firestone's vision does not represent undistilled antinatalism. She sees pregnancy as ultraoppressive, but like the socialist feminists she offers a radical, utopian plan for the remaking of America that includes children. While to her contemporaries, who at least superficially disavowed the positive potential of technology, her plan seemed frighteningly dystopian, her gaze points forward, toward an ideal world in which children abound, but in which the physical and social relations of motherhood have been radically altered.

The Politics of Everyday Life

As radical and socialist feminists formulated their utopian theories, they faced a pressing question: What about the women who are already mothers? What about the married women living in apparent compliance with the dictates of the "patriarchy"? This was actually a new version of the question faced by the Left: How could the Left relate to the society it sought to change? Did the radicals constitute a vanguard group? Were the masses deluded, or dangerous, or were they making conscious choices for their own survival? In the Civil Rights movement, many activists had felt that they should take "the people's" lead, rather than impose more "advanced" theory from the outside. But by the late 1960s, at least some branches of the Left, such as the Weathermen, deemed an extreme version of vanguardism the only viable strategy. Women's liberationists, with their ideological and organizational ties to the Left, debated these questions with equal vigor.[55]

Radical and socialist feminists were forced quickly to consider the question of motherhood from a practical perspective. The sheer intensity of the early women's movement, its demand that members attend frequent long meetings, made mothers' participation logistically difficult. Early on, feminists realized that they would have to make some provisions for the mothers in their midst.

Genuine concern for mothers surfaced at many radical feminist meetings, with groups discussing everything from how to draw mothers into the movement to how to provide childcare during meetings and conferences. At the National Women's Liberation Conference, held in Lake Villa, Illinois, in 1968, for example, "the women ranged in age from about seventeen to sixty, and there were three or four small children running around. . . . We volunteered to take shifts with the children." [56] In cases like this, the radical belief that children were the responsibility of the entire community, and not solely the charge of the women who bore them, began to take form.

At times, however, feminist groups paid mere lip service to mothers' needs. The group Women's Liberation of Berkeley, California, wrote in its *Let's Liberate Women!* newsletter about the need for childcare during its upcoming conference in 1969: "Mothers should be looking for a house with fenced yard and men to baby-sit during the conference. If no one does anything about this, then nothing will be done. Amen." [57] Clearly, this group thought of mothers as a species apart, responsible for their own problems.

Other radical feminist groups demonstrated a more blatant disregard for mothers and children. The testimony of various women involved in the early phases of feminist activism reveals, at times, a perception of actual hostility toward mothers in the movement. In an angry letter to the Bay Area journal *It Ain't Me, Babe,* a pregnant woman excoriated the women's movement for its treatment of mothers:

> The women's movement isn't only for bright, young middle-class women who have decided never to marry or never to have children. . . . A movement which vomits at the sight of a pregnant woman or a child leaves out quite a few sisters. . . . I somehow can't believe that children are inherently bad, or that having a child is necessarily a sinful thing to do. It is because this society refuses to accept any responsibility for those children that things are fucked up. Who can I turn to now sisters? . . . I have been so much as told that sisters will not dig my "bringing the kid around to bother them" and will have no part of that child or my life with that child.[58]

Numerous other women recounted similar experiences, and some spoke of a serious divide between mothers and nonmothers in the movement.

Some radical feminist insensitivity to mothers can be attributed to youth and to the general ignorance of the childless about the daily needs of mothers. Many young feminists had no understanding of the daily responsibilities of caring for a child. Some of them, believing that one should organize around one's own experiences of oppression, simply considered mothers and mothering to be irrelevant. Moreover, the undercurrent of hostility to mothers evident at times among feminists relates to the fact that the early women's movement, like the New Left and the counterculture, was a generational protest movement. When feminists pilloried the traditional housewife, they were referring only too clearly to their own mothers. To some extent, their "political" condemnations of traditional motherhood reveal a direct and personal desire to escape the drudgery their mothers suffered.[59]

Separatism and the Rejection of Motherhood

To some individuals and groups within the early women's liberation movement, mothers and motherhood seemed too hopelessly enmeshed with the problems created by capitalism and patriarchy to warrant a significant share of feminist attention. Some early radical feminist activists tended to reject mothers as women suffering from false consciousness, at best, and not women with whom to get entangled. According to these writers, separation from men and their institutions might not be a drastic enough step; the enemy could include not only men and male supremacism, but anyone who bought into male supremacism or engaged voluntarily in intimate relationships with men. The enemy, in other words, could easily include the kind of woman who made men, and not other women, her priority.

The earliest, most ephemeral strand of this rejectionist impulse drew its political style directly from the increasingly splintered American Left. Clearly influenced by the Yippies, whose theatrical "actions" burlesqued America's politics and populace, many of the earliest feminist activists showed little regard for the average woman's perception of their activism.[60] Having invaded the New

York Stock Exchange and attempted what Abbie Hoffman called the "rising of the Pentagon" in 1967, the Yippies went on the next year to nominate a pig for president at the Democratic National Convention in Chicago.[61] Similarly, when members of New York Radical Women, the first organized radical feminist group in New York City, staged a protest at the Miss America Pageant in Atlantic City in 1968, they named a sheep as Miss America.[62] In a less derivative action, the leftist feminist group WITCH protested a bridal fair held at Madison Square Garden in 1969, chanting, "Here come the slaves, off to their graves."[63] Also in 1969, Ti-Grace Atkinson's group, The Feminists, publicly accused the New York City Marriage License Bureau of trying to trick women into a status not unlike slavery.[64] Clearly, although these actions were intended to alert the media and the public to feminism, they were not designed as recruitment devices for the movement.[65]

Media attention was more than forthcoming. By 1970, many of the major national magazines had run articles on the women's liberation movement. Although purporting to take the movement seriously, the articles tended to focus on the most controversial and theatrical examples of feminist activism: bra-burning, freedom trash cans (intended as receptacles for bras, girdles, and other restrictive accoutrements of femininity), young women denouncing sex and motherhood. An article in *Newsweek* characterizes the women's movement as a movement for the liberation of breasts: "It all began last fall when some 150 uprighteous members of the Women's Liberation Movement gathered in front of Convention Hall in Atlantic City and burned their brassieres. . . . With that, a solid grassroots rebellion was under way to threaten the foundations (possibly moral, certainly garment) of this country."[66]

The Miss America protest in particular raised many questions within the feminist movement. Replete with posters declaring that "Miss America Sells It" and that "Miss America is a Big Falsie," the action seemed to blame nonfeminist women for their own plight.[67] Although the organizers of the event later claimed that they had not intended to blame or alienate other women, they recognized how easily their behavior could have been misinterpreted: "Women chained to a replica, red, white and blue bathing suited Miss America could have been interpreted as against beautiful women. Also, crowning a live sheep Miss America sort of said that beautiful women *are* sheep."[68]

Yet New York Radical Women was not alone in its tactics. With equal flair and boldness, the Cleveland branch of WITCH printed a flyer imploring women to "Bury Mother's Day." The top half of the flyer detailed the horrors of motherhood:

Today, one day of the year, America is celebrating Motherhood, in home . . . church . . . restaurant . . . candy shop . . . flower store . . . The other 364 days she preserves the apple pie of family life and togetherness, and protects the sanctity of male ego and profit. She lives through her husband and children . . . she is sacrificed on the altar of reproduction . . . She is damned to the world of dreary domesticity by day, and legal rape by night . . . She is convinced that happiness and her lost identity can be recovered by buying—more and more and more and more.[69]

In contrast, the bottom half of the flyer showed a leaping, joyful, bare-breasted woman under the caption "Resurrect Woman." The resurrected woman would be called a WITCH—of the new feminist variety: "A witch lives and laughs in every woman. She is the free part of each of us, beneath the shy smiles, the acquiescence to absurd male domination, the make-up or flesh-suffocating clothing our sick society demands. If you are a woman and dare to look within yourself, you are a witch. You make your own rules. You are free and beautiful."[70] So antimotherhood was this message that it actually made an explicit and mutually exclusive comparison between mothers and women.

As Carol Hanisch, an early member of New York Radical Women, wrote ruefully in *Notes from the Second Year,* all of these types of actions were marred by "antiwomanism" and could hardly be expected to draw apolitical women into the movement. To the small group of women involved in the actions, the protests felt worthwhile. "When the Miss America Protest was proposed there was no question but that we wanted to do it. I think it was because we all saw how it related to *our* lives. We *felt* it was a good action." In essence, says Hanisch, the group was engaging in a "personal solutionary" approach to politics.[71] As self-expression for a select group of young women, Yippie-style feminism had its purpose. Although the alienation of nonmovement women was often not the *intended* result of these early, poorly conceived actions, the language and style of the movement's participants clearly needed to be thought through more carefully. In order to build a mass movement, said Hanisch, "we must give up all the 'in-talk' of the New Left/Hippie movements—at least when we're talking in public."[72] For the purposes of building a movement, all women would have to be taken seriously—even Miss America; even wives and mothers.

For Ti-Grace Atkinson and The Feminists, probably the best known of the separatist groups of this period, the condemnation of marriage and traditional domestic arrangements was not inadvertent, although it seems to have had as much to do with building a feminist movement as with constructing a thoroughgoing analysis of marriage and motherhood as institutions, current or historical. The Feminists became known in the movement for their prescriptions for members' private lives. Only one-third of the group's members was allowed to be married, formally or informally.[73] Presumably, a primary commitment to a male partner would preclude a primary commitment to The Feminists, in terms of time if nothing else. For The Feminists, the rejection of marriage was largely an initiation rite into feminism, a symbolic statement of serious intent. This symbolism was not without practical roots, because married women tended to have commitments that made life-as-endless-feminist-meeting untenable.

This is not to minimize the critique to which Atkinson submitted the institutions of marriage and motherhood. In her early writings, men and women constitute the oppressor and the oppressed, in absolute terms.[74] If the marriage contract codifies women's oppression, childbearing cements it. Because sexual intercourse constitutes the "bridge" between marriage and family, for Atkinson that deceptively benign institution needed to be jettisoned.[75] No longer linked by shaky ties to sensuality and pleasure, the institution of motherhood could then shed the sugar-coating called "maternal instinct" to reveal its true, brutal nature:

> Does anyone wish to try to hold that the blood-curdling screams that can be heard from delivery rooms are really cries of joy? . . . How are you going to account for the fact that as much as two-thirds of the women bearing children suffer post-partum blues, and that these depressions are expressed in large numbers by these women killing their infants, or deserting them, or internalizing their hostility to such an extent that the woman must be confined in mental hospitals for "severe depression" (often a euphemism for attempted murder). Either it's necessary to fall back on some physiological explanation which will irrevocably damage the claim that child-bearing is good for a woman's health, or it's necessary to admit that an overwhelming number of women do not *like* to bear children regardless of whether or not there is some theory that it is a woman's natural function to bear children. . . . As for women wishing to possess children, it will be necessary to account for the fact that parents (and we all know who that is) are the second highest cause of children's deaths ("accidents" rank first). If the theory is still maintained that women by their nature like to have, or take care of, children, and that this constitutes at least a necessary part of what is called "maternal instinct," it would seem that it is the duty of men, i.e. society, to protect children from women's care just because of this instinct.[76]

Like Firestone, Atkinson considered the physicality of maternity to be oppressive to women. She too proposed that fetuses be gestated in test tubes rather than in uteri. The human race had to be reproduced, but it was unjust, even unnatural, to consign women's bodies to that task. Maternity, properly understood, was merely a political tool operated by men to bind women irrevocably to the oppressive institution of marriage.

Although Atkinson's rejection of sexuality distances her from the cultural left, her writing reveals her struggle with the same problem confronting Firestone and other radical feminists: They were steeped in the liberationist and communitarian yearnings of the Left but refused to sacrifice women's liberation to the Left's vision of community. In Atkinson's view, because sexuality and motherhood both stem from women's biology, and because biological definitions of womanhood have historically been used to steer women toward men, toward the oppressive nuclear family, and away from other women, the only route to the desired community of women lies in the eradication of both sex and motherhood. Had Atkinson, in these early writings, been able to integrate the idea of lesbian sex into her theory, she might have stopped short of condemning sex as integral to women's subordination. But even with its radical rejection of sexuality, Atkinson's solution to women's oppression retains a great deal of the Left's critique of the family, along with the overriding imperative to create a new and better community.[77]

By 1970, a clearly articulated theory of lesbian vanguardism had arisen in the women's movement. In this view, lesbians stood as the only "true" feminists, because only they could eschew contact with the enemy in the arena of intimacy, where one is most likely to forsake one's sisters. Lesbians *had* to be revolutionaries; they faced contempt in all areas of their lives because they refused all the small comforts that male-dominated society offered in exchange for real freedom. Some groups, such as Radicalesbians, defined heterosexuality as an unmitigated form of slavery. Women internalize a definition of themselves as men's slaves, they said, and thereby suffer horrible psychic consequences, for "that definition consigns us to sexual and family functions, and excludes us from defining and shaping the terms of our lives."[78] To marry and have children, in this view, would be to volunteer to go into the belly of the beast.

The Radicalesbians' condemnation of traditional societal roles is not altogether different from that of The Feminists or other separatist groups, except that it emphasizes the radical impact of a chosen lifestyle far more than other groups did. Whereas The Feminists declared that women who arranged their personal commitments in particular ways would be freer to devote themselves to political activism, the Radicalesbians, as clear descendants of the counterculture, began to assert that everyday life was in itself political. This emphasis on the everyday process of living high-lighted the importance of *values* and helped to lay the groundwork for the cultural feminist belief that women possess inherent and acquired traits that differ from those possessed by men. The ability to nurture, a most "motherly" quality, would be one of the princi-pal traits ascribed to women by cultural feminists. And lesbian feminists, by the mid-1970s, would be among the chief architects of cultural feminist theory.[79]

Prior to the mid-1970s, lesbian feminist writings on motherhood were usually aimed at the child custody rights of lesbians who had previously been involved in heterosexual relationships.[80] Locally and nationally, groups in support of lesbian mothers' legal right to the custody of their children began to form, as did emotional support groups for lesbian mothers.[81] Even NOW passed a resolu-tion in 1971 in support of lesbian mothers' custody rights.[82] All of these groups treated the existence of children in lesbians' lives as a vestige, usually welcome, of a formerly heterosexual life. An affirmative notion of deliberate lesbian motherhood would not enter the discourse fully until the mid to late 1970s.[83] This was seen as so distant a choice that Martha Shelley, a member of Radicalesbians writing in 1969, listed the forfeiture of motherhood as one of the lamentable losses of life as a lesbian.[84]

Nonseparatist Reassessments of Motherhood

While separatist groups gained the most notoriety inside and outside the movement, theirs was in fact a minority position among feminists before the rise of cultural feminism in the early to mid-1970s. Much of the debate within feminism lay not over whether to reject the "typical" woman outright, but in how to understand her oppression.[85] Feminists agreed that traditional marriage harmed women and limited their potential. Why, then, did women marry? One answer was that women were deluded, suffering from false consciousness. Perhaps they had internalized the negative messages about themselves and were in fact contributing to their own oppression. Some organizations recognized this and advised women to separate themselves from the influences that inspired self-sabotage. Other groups recognized that it was not just the "other" woman—the heterosexual married one with four children—who had a problem. All women were defined through a sex caste system and limited materially and psychically by an encompassing grid of male dominance. The first step toward liberation would be to raise one's consciousness to a level of individual and collective awareness of the assumptions that a male-dominated culture needed to present as "natural." The critical wedge opened by consciousness raising was that of perceived commonality with other women. Whereas some groups veered toward real woman-blaming, most of the influential feminist groups critiqued the institutions of motherhood and marriage for the limits they placed on a woman's life choices, but they were careful to avoid reviling wives or mothers as people.

The divergent positions taken on the marriage and motherhood question by the New York Radical Feminists and Redstockings reveal these groups' fundamentally differing analyses of oppression. Venturing essentially psychological and materialist analyses, respectively, the two groups arrived through separate channels at a position critical of motherhood as situated within a male-dominated culture, yet supportive of mothers and true to the lingering values of the cultural left.

In its earliest manifesto, "Politics of the Ego," New York Radical Feminists describes the oppression of women in terms of sex role socialization.[86] Through socialization, the little girl learns to be feminine. "Her life is already determined. She is not given the choice of exploring activity toys. Her brothers play astronaut, doctor, scientist, race-car driver. She plays little homemaker, future mother (dolls), and nurse (doctor's helper). . . . Already she is learning that her future will be the maintenance of others. Her ego is repressed at all times to conform with this future submissiveness."[87] While the "institutions of marriage, motherhood, love, and sexual intercourse" reinforce this limiting set of messages in both practical and psychological terms, the linchpin of oppression lies in the psychological process of "internalization." Sounding much like Frantz Fanon and Herbert Marcuse, New York Radical Feminists writes that "it is politically necessary for any oppressive group to convince the oppressed that they are in fact inferior, and therefore deserve their situation. For it is precisely through the destruction of women's egos that they are robbed of the ability to resist."[88]

Political change requires first and foremost a change of consciousness. Women must realize exactly what they are being tricked into believing: "Biology is destiny, she is told. . . . Because she has childbearing capacity she is told that it is her function to marry and have the man economically maintain her and make the decisions."[89] Ti-Grace Atkinson and The Feminists also referred to this "brainwashing" of women, but unlike New York Radical Feminists, they insisted that a conscious woman must reject all that is "male." New York Radical Feminists, sounding quite like Betty Friedan on this point, argued that consciousness raising frees women to make their own choices, and that one viable choice was to remain in the heterosexual sphere and fight. Surpassing Friedan, however, and echoing the cultural left, the group made it clear that the private realm was prime territory for radical change, that women's full acquisition of public equality with men would be a partial solution at best. "The personal is political," the group declared.

Redstockings also refused to condemn women for their participation in marriage and motherhood. Like the other feminist groups of the late 1960s and early 1970s, Redstockings theorists recognized the problems of marriage and motherhood as currently structured. Unlike almost all other radical feminists, who said that women were mistaken, for various reasons, to participate in these harmful institutions, Redstockings developed what it called the "prowoman line." Women, in all circumstances, must be recognized as having done the best they could with what they had to work with. Women made rational choices based on the material circumstances they confronted. The responsibility of feminists was not to condemn any woman for trying to survive, but to work to make the material conditions under which women lived better. "We . . . reject the idea that women consent to or are to blame for their own oppression. Women's submission is not the result of brainwashing, stupidity, or mental illness but of continual, daily pressure from men. We do not need to change ourselves, but to change men." [90]

In a strongly anti-Left and antilesbian article, Pat Mainardi of Redstockings chided other feminists for their outright condemnation of marriage and motherhood. She portrayed "advocates of free love" and lesbians as virtual terrorists, denying other women within the movement the right to make their own decisions about domestic arrangements. [91] The only acceptable feminist position, according to Redstockings, was to "identify with all women," to "define our best interest as that of the poorest, most brutally exploited woman." [92] Housewives and mothers might be among the most brutally exploited people in our society, but they were sisters.

As anti-Left as Mainardi appeared to be, she and other Redstockings theorists remained well within the purview of leftist thought in several significant ways. In a feminist version of "let the people decide," Redstockings maintained that the most oppressed women—that is, those most securely ensconced in the privacy of the marital relationship—were the key constituency of the feminist revolution; *their* material condition must guide the movement's analysis. This view rejected elitist politics, vowing instead a commitment "to achieving internal democracy." [93] Like the New Left, Redstockings believed strongly in the political content of personal experience; also like the Left, it decried the isolation and alienation wrought by the nuclear family. [94] But Redstockings theorists recognized that most women could not simply abandon their domestic situations. They could use consciousness raising, however, to create a community of felt commonality among women; eventually, with the development of class consciousness among women, the problems stemming from male supremacy could be "solved collectively." [95] Redstockings refused to problematize sex and motherhood systematically, believing that such analysis called into question the life choices of the masses. But in an ironic twist, given their overt rejection of the Left, Redstockings' allegiance to the Left's belief in grassroots organizing allowed the group to avert the separatism of other radical feminist groups in favor of an absolute female rapprochement, mothers not excluded.

The Practical Legacy of the Cultural Left: Day Care As a Collectivist Priority

In keeping with the collectivist vision of the cultural left, most early participants in the women's liberation movement recognized women's need for viable day care options and viewed the provision of day care as a communal responsibility. While the political orientations of the various groups produced a wide array of solutions to the dearth of high quality, affordable day care in the United States, the near unanimous attention paid by feminists to the issue demonstrates the communitarian imperative that accompanied even the earliest and most bitter feminist critiques of the traditional family.

Liberal groups such as NOW demanded that "childcare facilities be established by law on the same basis as parks, libraries, and public schools, adequate to the needs of children from the preschool years through adolescence, as a community resource to be used by citizens from all income levels." [96] Additionally, NOW called for the "immediate revision of tax laws to permit the deduction of home and child care expenses for working parents." [97]

Radical and socialist feminist groups ventured more daring proposals. The Boston radical feminist group Cell 16, which often advocated separatism, tackled the question of childcare, at least in the abstract. Tying the provision of childcare to the larger goal of eliminating the nuclear family, one of the group's prominent theorists, Roxanne Dunbar, perhaps unwittingly ascribed to the "traditional" woman a pivotal role in the feminist revolution:

How will the family unit be destroyed? After all, women must take care of the children, and there will continue to be children. Our demand for full-time childcare in the public schools will be met to some degree all over, and perhaps fully in places. The alleviation of the duty of full-time childcare in private situations will free many women to make decisions they could not before. But more than that, the demand alone will throw the whole ideology of the family into question, so that women can begin establishing a community of work with each other and we can fight collectively. Women will feel freer to leave their husbands and become economically independent either through a job or welfare.[98]

The Feminists, no less committed to vanguard politics, similarly acknowledged the restructuring of daycare as a crucial feminist demand. Going beyond the liberal demand that mothers and fathers, within the confines of the nuclear family, share equally all aspects of childcare, The Feminists wrote that "child-rearing to the extent to which it is necessary is the responsibility of all; children are part of society but they should not be possessed by anyone. . . . Marriage and the family must be eliminated."[99]

Socialist feminists made more concrete demands. Bread and Roses, a Boston-based group founded in 1969, ventured in its declaration, entitled "The Rights of Women," that "central to the liberation of women is the provision of alternatives to the present patterns of child-rearing and housekeeping, which results in each mother's bearing virtually the entire responsibility for her children and her home. Such alternatives would go far towards eliminating the untenable choice most women must make between bearing children and developing independent work."[100] Prerequisite to the long-range goal of socialist and feminist revolution, women must be empowered as individuals and as workers. That empowerment requires that the full burdens of childcare be lifted. Aware that the responsibility for childcare could simply be shifted from one relatively empowered group of women to another more exploited group, namely from white women to black women, Bread and Roses specifies that childcare should be a valued, community-controlled concern; it should not be viewed simply as a service available on the capitalist marketplace.[101]

Berkeley Women's Liberation, also avowedly socialist or "politico" in its perspective, discussed the relative merits of cooperative nurseries versus "daycare facilities provided by an institution . . . (e.g. universities, corporations, businesses, city governments, etc.)." [102] The group decided that the latter bore greater revolutionary potential, because it would "make demands upon the system," while a coop nursery would be "essentially reformist." [103] Starting a cooperative amounts to "setting up as a counter-institution—a noncooperation with the establishment. It does your own thing, by dropping out and encouraging other people to do the same. Fighting for a coop ignores the question of privelege [*sic*] and class— not all women can participate in it (i.e. for those who work, it has no value at all. Furthermore it involves no struggle with the establishment, with the capitalist class, it puts no demands upon it. The coop is essentially a personal liberation for those who are lucky enough to be able to afford it." [104] A truly progressive day care platform, like a truly progressive women's liberation movement, would recognize the crisscrossing of oppressions and attempt to address questions of class privilege, even as it focused on the common plight of mothers.

Various groups discussed the need for national legislation concerning day care. NOW successfully lobbied the White House Conference on Children, held in December 1970, to endorse a federally financed child care program. Calling for sliding scale fees and substantial community control, the program met some of the women's movement's more progressive demands. Nixon finally vetoed the bill in 1971, claiming that it endangered the family.[105]

The Congress to Unite Women, which met in New York in November 1969 and drew over five hundred women from many different groups across the Eastern United States, listed "childhood education and care" as its first concern: "We demand nationwide free twenty-four-hour-a-day child care centers for all children from infancy to early adolescence regardless of their parents' income or marital status, with child care practices decided by those using the centers. . . . Until these free child care centers are established, we demand immediate national and state legislation for deduction of child care expenses from income before taxes." [106]

Local groups began to act on this mandate. As an outgrowth of a subsequent congress held in 1971, a Cambridge, Massachusetts coalition, the Cambridge Childcare Referendum Committee, formed to demand that a proposal for free, twenty-four-hour, community-controlled childcare be put on the November ballot. The referendum question made it onto the ballot and passed by a vote of almost two to one. That the city did not fulfill its mandate to provide the daycare does not diminish the genuinely activist, promother, and prochild stance of the feminist coalition. [107]

Across the nation, diverse groups of feminists began to set up childcare centers. Many such enterprises differed from traditional childcare centers primarily in their attention to curriculum, namely their caution about the sex-role stereotyping of children. These centers paid careful attention to the toys and books chosen for the children, and to the ways in which girls and boys were encouraged to interact with the materials. The successful preschool at Princeton University, cosponsored by the university and NOW in 1970, was the first of many feminist forays into the licensed childcare realm. [108]

More commonly, grassroots groups of mothers (and sometimes fathers) formed cooperative nurseries in which parents shared the cost and labor of childcare. Rosalyn Baxandall, writing in 1970 about the Liberation Nursery in which she and her child participated, described the cooperative nursery as an early attempt to create an alternative institution according to feminist and radical precepts. Baxandall reports, "Some of us in the new nursery were in Women's Liberation and wanted to fuse the operation of the nursery with Women's Liberation: we have avoided segregating girl's games from boy's; both girls and boys play with trucks and dolls, all dressed in pants, and we invested $22 in a petit frere boy doll with genitals because we didn't want to give the impression that all dolls were female." [109] The nursery collective also opened a storefront mothers' coop exchange, where "mothers bring in their old clothes and toys and get others in exchange." [110] Encouraged by the positive response of the community, Baxandall concluded that "mothers in the nursery have also grown more interested in Women's Liberation and radical politics as a result of participating in our cooperative effort." [111]

Many cooperatives suffered from lack of funds, poor facilities, and harassment by the authorities, and as a result many were shortlived. Nevertheless, childcare centers were among the first alternative institutions created by feminists. Even in the period of its harshest criticism of traditional motherhood, the often-divided feminist movement rallied enough gender solidarity to attempt collectivist solutions, consistent with the values of the Left, to address the material needs of mothers and children. [112]

Conclusion

Most feminist activists, even in the earliest years of second-wave feminism, did not ignore mothers and children, nor did they take a wholly negative view of motherhood. An unmitigated rejection of motherhood emerged from only a few of the early women's liberationists. Most feminists, even in the late 1960s and early 1970s, critiqued motherhood as embedded in "patriarchal" culture, and then proceeded to devise ways to improve the material conditions of mothering in contemporary society.

Significantly, radical and socialist feminism drew from the New Left and from the counterculture of the 1960s a set of priorities that are hard to reconcile with one another. The cultural left's essentialism, its critique of the nuclear family, its belief in the liberatory power of sexuality, and its search for community collide when subjected to a gender analysis. In a few instances, and only early on in the movement, feminist writers have suggested that a simple unity of these concerns could be achieved if motherhood, along with the nuclear family, could be jettisoned. However, the great bulk of feminist writing suggests that feminists have turned their attention toward motherhood as they have confronted and reconfronted the contradictory implications of the Left's legacy. Contrary to their stereotyped reputation as baby haters, feminist writers attributed tremendous power and positive potential to mothering.

Chapter Two

*The Body As a Holy Land:
Feminism, Childbirth, and the
Imprint of the Counterculture*

Alongside negative views of motherhood, many feminists in the late 1960s and early 1970s promoted a distinctly promotherhood position. Seldom as rejecting of motherhood as many critics have claimed, early women's liberationists did voice strong objection to "mandatory motherhood." However, those objections never constituted the entire feminist analysis of motherhood. From the start, many feminists expressed not only a begrudging acknowledgment of already existing mothers as "sisters" in need of day care and other material aid, but also an affirmative and liberationist view of pregnancy, childbirth, and breastfeeding, as important aspects of the wider issue of motherhood. By the early 1970s, with the formation of the feminist women's health movement, and in response to the stirrings of dissension among feminists over issues of race, class, and sexual orientation, this hopeful feminist discourse of motherhood began to eclipse earlier negative views. The roots of that positive discourse trace meaningfully, though not exclusively, to the radical counterculture of the 1960s.

The Counterculture

While the roots of positive feminist mothering theory can be found in the views of the organized Left, as in organizations like Students for a Democratic Society (SDS), of the 1960s, an equally profound debt tracks to the counterculture of that era. More difficult to define, the general constellation of ideas that surrounded the New Left, the core beliefs that fueled the wider social rebellion of the 1960s, and the rather amorphous set of values and ideas that constituted the "counterculture" are crucial to the feminist reendorsement of motherhood.[1] Indeed, the joyfully, erotically essentialized views of mothering that feminists began to advance by the early 1970s become fully intelligible only in the context of countercultural thought.[2]

Extroverted and hyperbolic in style, the counterculture is vulnerable to trivialization and easy dismissal. Yet the counterculture—not entirely separate from the organized Left but sometimes divergent in its emphases—infused the entire cultural left (and perhaps the wider society, as well) with deeply restructured views of the body, nature, and human community. Enlisting the social theory of Herbert Marcuse, Wilhelm Reich, and others to fashion an ideological retort to the anticommunist conformism of the Cold War era, the New Left and, to an even greater extent, the counterculture drew from leftist intellectuals and from an array of less conventional thinkers a profound optimism and a true utopianism.[3] This strand of thought undergirded the most tenacious feminist analyses of motherhood, analyses filled with countercultural exuberance and yearning.[4]

At the deepest level, participants in the counterculture decried the "alienation" and "atomization" wrought by advanced Western industrial capitalism in all its cultural, political, and economic manifestations. In contrast, they preached the "holism" of human experience.[5] The more organized New Left voiced similar criticism in an expansive discourse of holism that drew from a disparate group of thinkers, ranging from Jacques Ellul, with his indictment of "technological society," to Herbert Marcuse, with his theory of "surplus repression."[6] But while the New Left incorporated "prefigurative" politics—that is, the actualized demonstration of political ideals through the restructuring of everyday life—into its more strategic opposition to the Vietnam War and its other programmatic goals, the counterculture offered the politics of everyday life as its only program.[7]

The means were the end. Daily living constituted the "revolution." In a society that valued products for the surplus in their exchange value, counterculturalists sought to collapse process and product, leaving no room for expropriation and resultant alienation. Whereas the culture of the assembly line, the corporation, and the suburbs accented divisions—between tasks, between dwellings, between people, between aspects of the self and the whole self—the youth culture sought to forge connections.[8] In highly romantic terms, counterculturalists posited a better time and place for human interaction. In open rebellion they acted out the contrast between their ideal and the havoc of the "plastic society." The ideal time was preindustrial; the place, rural. The hippie pastorale, though often enacted in an urban setting, celebrated the supposed uninterrupted rhythms of daily life in times and places past, as reflected most strikingly in the inexorable cycles of nature and the seemingly changeless processes of the body.[9]

Thus the symbols of the counterculture began to emerge. For every "plastic" item produced in "Amerika," the counterculture offered hand-woven rugs, home-baked bread, bodies awash in their own oils and aromas, freed from chemical tonics and polyester tunics.[10] In contrast to the killing fields of Vietnam and Watts, the counterculture offered the peacefulness of life lived simply, attuned to the dictates of nature. Advanced technology, in the hands of the few, produced napalm at worst, unhealthy consumerism at best. Minimal technology, distributed among the many, led to self-determination and the happy coexistence of human life with nature. Whereas the separation of humans from nature had produced a repressed, violent, and decadent human species, the reunion of life forms allowed the primal goodness of humanness to emerge. Naked like other animals, the unrepressed human was spontaneous, intuitive, nurturant, and healthy. Most important, the natural human was "whole," freed from the terrible dictates of a society that demanded the separation of the mind from the body, the body from the spirit, and so on. An ecosystem in miniature, each individual personified holistic purity; together, nature's people would necessarily create harmonious community. There would be no false hierarchies in such community, no rule of the "expert," for each person, in his or her intuitive completeness and connectedness to nature, was a sage. The ideal was to eliminate all false boundaries, to create "a society of free goods, freely produced, freely distributed. You take what you need, you give what you can. The world is yours to love and work for. No state, no police, no money, no borders, no property. Time and disposition to seek good, seek one another, to take trips deep into the mind, and to feel, to find out what it is to have a body, and to begin to use and make joy with it." [11]

Most of the intentional communities of counterculturalists in pursuit of these ideals reached a quick crisis of disillusionment, as human excrement and poverty complicated the pastoral simplicity of life on the land, but aspects of the dream endured. [12] The notion that the body, in all its functions, was "holy," as Allen Ginsberg had written, remained at the center of the cultural revolution. [13] In sickness, in health, in birth, in death, and especially in the joyful communion of sex, the body linked humanity to the sacred holism of nature. No government, no self-proclaimed expert, no one had the right to sever that link. Similarly, the search for connectedness, for unbesieged community among people, continued unabated in the counterculture, in spite of the establishment's raids on hippie enclaves, and in spite of the constant practical difficulties inherent to a utopian experiment without an economic base. [14]

While counterculturalists often invoked the image of children as a symbol of innocent spontaneity, they also constructed an ideal and practice of community that included children. Children were, of course, a de facto product of sexual liberation combined with haphazard birth control practices. But beyond that, to many counterculturalists children embodied the hope for a fresh start at a perfected society. Unspoiled by a corrupt culture, children's pristine little bodies were seen as evidence of human connectedness to nature. Similarly, counterculturalists valorized motherhood as a natural function. Countercultural exultations of nature frequently include the "earth mother," or, as Tom Wolfe put it, "the eternal beatific pioneer wife, in the house, at the stove, at the sewing machine, at the washing machine, with the children . . . gathered around her skirts." [15] Unashamed of her body, with milk flowing from her breasts and long hair flowing down her back, both nurturant and sexual, the hippie mother represented the quintessence of the counterculture. [16]

During childbirth, hippie women, like most other American women in the 1960s, found themselves in the care of obstetricians whose view of birth was anything but holistic or natural. These women found that the very pregnancy they celebrated for its connectedness to nature became a medical emergency in a hospital birth. With the pelvis cordoned off from the rest of the body, drapes covering the body, and the woman herself rendered passive as "experts" first drugged her and then paced the birth to meet some medically defined criteria, the traditional hospital birth defied many countercultural values. Many countercultural women responded by choosing other locations and attendants for their births. They rejected the complex technology employed by obstetricians and questioned the notion that pregnancy constituted a pathology. Instead, they cheered the example of "primitive" women who gave birth at home, attended by midwives. Particularly in rural areas, hippie women began to court local midwives, and began also to train women in their own communities to assist in childbirth. Many counterculturalists also became avid breastfeeders and advocates of a "natural" approach to childrearing. [17]

With a burgeoning birth rate and a profound mistrust of the medical establishment, counterculturalists found themselves in league with nontraditional, but hardly "revolutionary," natural childbirth and breastfeeding advocates. These movements, which had been growing slowly in the United States since the 1940s, began to gain momentum in the late 1950s and early 1960s. British physician Grantly Dick-Read published his book *Childbirth without Fear: The Principles and Practices of Natural Childbirth* in the United States in 1944. Dick-Read's method of natural childbirth stressed the connections between body and mind: If a woman approached labor with fear and dread, she would become tense and experience pain. If she could learn to relax, and if she were offered comfort and support rather than medication and isolation, she could give birth painlessly, with life-affirming joy.[18] Although Dick-Read's ideas attracted considerable attention in the United States, his method transferred poorly to the American hospital setting, where birth was not treated as a natural phenomenon, and where the artificial alleviation of pain continued to be a primary obstetrical goal.[19]

The "prepared childbirth" techniques of French obstetrician Ferdinand Lamaze, introduced popularly in the United States in 1959, proved more compatible with American obstetrical practices. In the Lamaze method, husbands usually act as coaches as their laboring wives use specific breathing and relaxation techniques to try to reduce the pain of childbirth. Discouraging the use of anesthesia, primarily out of concern for the baby's health, the Lamaze method otherwise melds quite easily with traditional, doctor-centered hospital birth. The method gained wide popularity in the 1960s, largely through the efforts of the American Society for Psychoprophylaxis in Obstetrics, founded in 1960.[20] More critical of the medical establishment, the International Childbirth Education Association compared American birthing practices unfavorably with those of many other countries, and advocated for nonmedicalized, even midwife-attended, births.[21] La Leche League, founded in 1956 by a group of Christian women seeking mutual support for breastfeeding, by the late 1960s represented a strong network of women committed not only to the nursing of infants, but to an antimedical, lay philosophy of mothering.[22] Counterculturalists sought common ground with all of these groups, and most particularly with La Leche League and homebirth advocates, with their emphasis on "nature" and "intuition."[23]

Although they agreed on natural childbirth and breastfeeding, women of the 1960s counterculture and more traditional natural childbirth and breastfeeding advocates differed in several crucial ways. Although difficult to define, personal style, sartorial and other, marked the two groups of women as different. Similarly, the philosophical underpinnings of each group's support for natural birth and nursing pushed in opposite directions. The traditionalists, especially those who supported home birth over the less controversial, hospital-based Lamaze method, saw noninterventionist birth practices as a way to promote "family togetherness" and keep the state and its medical missionaries out of the family; a birth was a deeply private happening, meant to bond wife, husband, newborn, and siblings.[24]

Counterculturalists, of course, disavowed the legitimacy of the state-sanctioned nuclear family. For them, birth promised a different kind of bonding: between woman and man, between woman and infant, but most piquantly between woman and her body. Hippies viewed childbirth and breastfeeding as highly sensual, even erotic experiences. Rena Morning Star, partner of Lou Gottlieb, the founder of one of the most famous hippie communes, Morning Star Ranch in Sonoma County, California, said, "You want to know about having a baby on the land? It's all right? Having Vishnu [her son] at Morning Star—and it's important that it's open land, because I believe the policy is 'open land, open cervix'— made childbirth much easier. We started out with a good fuck during labor. I highly recommend it! A good fuck sets the stage for a beautiful sexual orgasm. And that's what his birth was."[25] Needless to say, the heavily Christian-based natural childbirth and breastfeeding traditionalists did not laud the eroticism of birth and nursing.[26]

Counterculturalists found a different set of allies in the free clinic movement inspired by the New Left and the Black Power movement. In many U.S. cities in the late 1960s and early 1970s, "peoples' clinics" offered services in neighborhoods in which medical services were inadequate or scarce. The Black Panther Party of Boston, for example, sponsored a clinic in Roxbury, a predominantly African-American community served by only seventeen practicing physicians in the early 1970s.[27] Free clinics also served the hippie populations of many major countercultural enclaves. Operating on the principle that "health care is a human right," and decrying the profit motives of the medical establishment, these alternative clinics tried to bring the New Left ideal of participatory democracy into the medical arena.[28] Often run as collectives, some clinics attempted consensus decision-making. They encouraged patients to take an active stance toward their own health care, declaring each person the best expert on his or her own body. Critical of corporate drug manufacturers and traditional medical training and practices, they tended toward minimalist, noninterventionist, and natural treatment plans.[29] Nonjudgmental about birth control and venereal disease, the free clinic became a vital institution for the many counterculturalists whose sexually active lives benefited from the Pill and penicillin.[30] Thus the clinics, themselves inspired by many of the values incubated in the less politicized segments of the cultural left, became part of the fabric of American countercultural life.

The Women's Health Movement

As women within the New Left began to protest and exit male-dominated leftist organizations in the late 1960s, women within the free clinic movement similarly began to oppose the sexism of the alternative medical movement. In particular, they noted the insensitivity of male doctors to women's gynecological and obstetrical concerns. By the early 1970s, some of these activists began to form their own clinics. Although dissenting from the male-dominated free clinic movement, early women's health activists championed many of the same causes: "self-help," "self-determination," and minimally interventionist health care.[31] And like the "peoples' clinic" movement, the women's health movement drew its philosophy, its workers, and its clientele in large part from the counterculture. Focused on the holism of body and mind, on the benefits of sensual and sexual liberation, and on natural approaches to healing, the budding women's health movement was antiestablishment in the fashion of hippies and communards, however sexist, throughout the United States and beyond. Even the language and style of early women's health care publications and clinics bore the ambiance of the cultural left: clinics coveted a "homey," nonclinical atmosphere, replete with hanging plants and comfortable furniture; early writings featured folk and herbal remedies for common maladies, favoring the natural over the manufactured.[32]

In 1971, feminists opened clinics in Berkeley, Seattle, and Baltimore. In the next few years, they followed suit in many other cities.[33] Notably, these clinics concentrated on women's reproductive health. The Vermont Women's Health Center in Burlington, Vermont, for instance, was typical in its list of services: general gynecological treatment; counseling about menstruation, menopause, abortion, and pregnancy; training in self-examination; pregnancy testing and termination; and prenatal and postnatal care.[34] Although women's health activists spoke of the importance of treating the "whole" woman, of parting with the medical tradition that viewed all of women's complaints as stemming from disorders of the uterus, they nevertheless focused on what they saw as the arena of the most egregious medical abuses.[35] If the radical health movement as a whole critiqued the monetary motives and dehumanizing power-mongering of the medical establishment, feminists showed how sexism exacerbated those tendencies. They asserted that as the female reproductive system most clearly signaled women's biological difference from men and served, historically, as the basis for women's subordination, it was also the site of women's particular oppression in the medical arena.[36] Thus, to feminist health activists the imperative to provide "liberated" gynecological and obstetric care ranked high.

At the same time, feminists fought for abortion rights. This concerted campaign, embraced by virtually all segments of the women's movement, became popularly synonymous with feminism early on, as activists held speak-outs, lobbied legislators, and even performed illegal abortions prior to the Supreme Court's *Roe v. Wade* decision of 1973.[37] As historian Linda Gordon has pointed out, the demand for abortion did not arise suddenly in the 1960s; operating within the technological constraints of their particular era, women had long sought and obtained abortions, legal or illegal.[38] The increased abortion rights activism of the 1960s does not reduce to an increase in unwanted pregnancies created by the sexual revolution. Of equal importance for radical and socialist feminists, the Left's critique of traditional domesticity, based heavily on a regard for individuality centered in the bodily self, inspired a far-reaching discourse of bodily self-determination. For the Left, the family—or the university, acting in loco parentis—had no business regulating human desire, nor did the medical establishment or the state have the right to control what people did with their own bodies. Indeed, the cultural left posited the "liberated" body as a weapon against a decadent capitalism, with the self-determined libido spearheading the assault on conventional mores.[39] Feminists, similarly, saw sexual self-determination as crucial to women's liberation.[40] They realized clearly the importance of women's right to choose the outcome of pregnancy, a physiological state bound up intimately with women's overall social condition.

To critics on the Right, feminists' commitment to abortion rights characterized the entire feminist analysis of reproduction and health. In fact, however, early feminist writing plumbed every topic from the "mythical" vaginal orgasm, to abortion and birth control rights, to the history of gynecological and obstetrical abuses, to the liberatory potential of natural birthing practices.[41] This superficially contradictory, sweeping focus on the body gains coherence only when viewed in terms of the powerfully unifying theme of self-determination derived from the cultural left.[42]

In complex and nonlinear fashion, the feminist health movement developed as an outgrowth of the cultural left, which in turn intersected with the more traditional natural childbirth and breastfeeding movements. The women's health movement was not exclusively an organizational outgrowth of abortion activism, or the feminist corollary of the New Left "people's clinic" movement, or the latest development in a trajectory of birth reform movements. A dynamic interplay of people and ideas occurred at the intersections of these movements, and individuals often held more than one allegiance. Some women gravitated toward the women's health movement as their counterculturally influenced interest in midwifery led them to seek political allies. The feminist movement's endorsement of sexual self-determination certainly seemed more congenial to countercultural women than the sexually conservative natural childbirth movement. At the same time, abortion rights activism drew many women into the feminist movement in a way that channeled their attention to the wider array of women's health issues. Many abortion rights activists concerned themselves with sterilization abuse and the range of obstetrical malpractices. Natural childbirth, as part of the panoply of women's health concerns, also began to draw a great deal of feminist attention. Women's liberationists then allied themselves with the extant natural childbirth movement, all the while subjecting that movement to a feminist analysis and restructuring. As Nancy Mills, a lay midwife from Sonoma County, California, recalls, "Midwifery, the women's movement, the hip movement, the natural foods movement, the antiwar movement, all came to me at about the same time." [43]

For women's liberationists, involvement with this matrix of movements resulted in a heightened recognition of pregnancy, childbirth, and breastfeeding as feminist issues. From the early 1970s, the women's health movement increasingly became a principal advocate of natural childbirth and midwifery (especially lay midwifery). While feminists tended to express themselves in highly countercultural terms, both in ideology and personal style, they cast their net wide as they moved to the fulcrum of the birth reform movement. When a group of feminists in the Boston area put together a "women's health course," later to be published as *Our Bodies, Ourselves,* they focused a substantial portion of the course on the birthing conditions confronting the average American woman. While acknowledging the advantages of home birth, the Boston Women's Health Course Collective also referred women to the literature and organizations of more mainstream natural childbirth organizations.[44] In June 1973, feminists sponsored the First International Childbirth Conference, held in Stamford, Connecticut. Attended not only by feminist women's health activists, but also by a highly diverse group of counterculturalists, lay and nurse midwives, and Lamaze, home birth, and breastfeeding advocates, the conference focused on the "natural human right of a woman to determine the manner of her child's birth."[45] By hosting this event, the feminist organizers positioned the women's movement at the center of the discourse of natural childbirth, stressing the common interests of the disparate participants and casting an overlay of feminist rhetoric over the entire proceedings.[46] Similarly, in 1974, when police raided the Santa Cruz birth clinic founded by hippie midwife Raven Lang, the feminist movement rallied to the midwives' support. By the time the midwives went to court, their case was known as a feminist concern.[47] All of these examples illustrate both the prominence of positive attitudes toward childbirth among feminists and the ways in which those attitudes allowed unlikely "fellow travelers" into the fold of feminist health activism.

Reclaiming Birth

If the women's health movement proved unusually commodious in its ability to work with disparate groups toward its goal of "women-centered" birth practices, feminist theorizing of pregnancy, birth, and breastfeeding deviated little from countercultural thought. Feminist thought, as it developed, problematized the cultural left's analysis of these issues, just as it incorporated yet complicated the Left's negative critique of the nuclear family. But the deep imprint of the counterculture's utopianism and holism remains at the center of early positive feminist mothering theory. Equating the body with a vision of nature approaching the divine, championing the liberatory potential of sex, searching for authentic but selective community, and decrying the artificiality of a society that keeps self-fulfillment at bay, feminist mothering theory of the early 1970s weakens the scholarly adage that feminists during this period discarded the Left.[48]

The earliest radical and socialist feminist writings on pregnancy, birth, and related health matters subjected current and historical obstetrical practices to a scathing critique. One prong of the condemnation focused on the male domination of obstetrics and gynecology. Feminist writers traced a process, spanning several centuries, during which the newly emerging, elite, all-male medical profession in Europe, and then the United States, took over the role of "healer" from local women lay healers and midwives. That usurpation resulted in the discrediting of women healers as "witches" or primitive incompetents. With the maturation of medical science and the development of medicine as a full-fledged profession, male doctors by the nineteenth century occupied a powerful niche in the social order. To feminists, the suppression of the female midwife and concurrent rise of the male physician bespoke but one more abuse of male power, in keeping with the economic, legal, and political dominance of men. While an individual male obstetrician might treat his patients well, on a societal level the demise of female birth attendants rendered birthing women—and all women, by extension—dependent upon men at a crucial moment in the life-cycle. In the overall fight for self-determination, the loss of female control over birth was a grave one.[49]

Feminists went on to argue that the loss of female control over birth represented more than the erosion of a *symbolically* potent realm of power. In terms of women's health and well-being, the shift from female midwives to male obstetricians wrought nefarious results. In their arrogance and ignorance, male doctors exposed women to disease and to unwarranted technological intervention. From the spread of puerperal fever in the supposedly superior hospital settings preferred by doctors, to the overuse of techniques like episiotomy and tools like forceps, modern male doctors, in their rush to secure their own profession, in their love affair with technology, and in their push for the greater profits reaped by aggressive interventionism, turned birth into a more dangerous endeavor than it had been in the hands of midwives, however "untrained." [50]

To feminists, influenced by the thinkers of the cultural left, the entire model of medicine that male obstetricians had developed over the past several centuries reflected the values not only of a male-dominated society, but also a capitalist and a technocratic one. In keeping with the rationalization of the labor process that capitalism required for its advancement, obstetricians over the years had imposed a rationalized view of the body on laboring women. Whereas the preindustrial artisan had maintained control over the entire production process and had realized the value of his own labor, the industrialist separated the stages of production, and separated the worker from the product, in the push toward in-creased efficiency and maximum profits. Hence the advent of the alienated worker, stripped of the ability to determine the conditions of his labor. Likewise, feminists claimed, obstetricians trained in the ideology of the "machine age" thought of the body as a ma-chine, comprised of many parts, each to be treated separately but routinely. The physician needed to be in control of the birth process in order to regularize treatment plans and increase overall effi-ciency. With modern faith in technology, obstetricians could treat irregularities in the birth process with ever-escalating intervention-ist solutions: forceps, drugs, fetal heart monitors, and so on. This process rendered the laboring woman, as a person with agency, as obsolete as the artisan of old; the doctor worked hard, delivered the baby, and received a handsome fee for his services. [51]

According to feminist theorists, the rationalization and medicalization of birth netted the same results that capitalism and patriarchy effected in society at large, here writ indelibly on the bodies and minds of women. Childbirth, as currently practiced, was dehumanizing. It put power in the hands of "experts." The patient had no agency; the woman in childbirth became a super-alienated laborer, shut off from all the experiences the cultural left and its feminist heirs valued. Modern childbirth defied the quest for self-determination. It denied women a sense of their bodies as natural, sexual, and creative, replacing the holistic view with a model of utilitarianism, pathology, and shame. Far removed from nature, in the grips of society's most artificial products and processes, modern childbirth also separated women from one another; worst of all his depredations, the male obstetrician had disrupted a powerful, organic community of women, bound together historically and personally by the common experience of childbirth.[52]

In comparison, female midwives offered a woman-centered model of childbirth that could right all of these wrongs. The key difference between male obstetrics and female midwifery lay in the holistic philosophy of the latter. The lay midwife, usually a local woman emerging organically into prominence through the practical experience of attending many births, viewed birth as a natural process connected seamlessly to the rest of a woman's life, and not as an isolated medical emergency requiring swift treatment. As one California midwife put it, "Women birth the way they live."[53] This holistic view resonated throughout the feminist discourse of birth in the early 1970s.

If traditional obstetrics treated the body of the laboring woman as so many separate and pathologized parts, midwifery, according to its feminist advocates, operated on the premise that the body, in labor as in everyday life, was both healthy and whole. Whereas the paraphernalia of traditional hospital birth placed women in a kind of purdah, hidden behind drapes and curtains as if the female body performing its natural functions were somehow dirty or shameful, home birth advocates stressed the health, strength, and beauty of the laboring woman. Midwives described the swollen perineum of the final stage of labor, which typically sent doctors scurrying for their episiotomy tools, as a marvel of human elasticity. While doctors responded by slashing and then stitching the straining flesh, midwives massaged the area with emollients, helping it to stretch.[54] In hospitals, women were laid out on their backs, in a position that gave the obstetrician visual and manual access to the "pelvic area." Midwives, attuned to more than the cervical os and the fetus, encouraged women to find comfortable positions for laboring, believing that the efforts and relaxation of the woman's entire body contributed to the labor process. Many midwives called for the revival of "vertical delivery," made possible through the use of the obstetrical chair, a device reputedly invented hundreds of years earlier by midwives.[55] In all of these ways, midwives redefined women's bodies in general, and women's bodies giving birth, as normal and capable. In contrast to the historical obstetrical view, which claimed, in the words of historian Deirdre English, that "a woman is no more than her reproductive organs; these organs are sickly, therefore *she* is," feminists declared that childbirth was not a disease, and that women in labor were not afflicted.[56]

Equally crucial to the feminist redefinition of childbirth, natural childbirth advocates' reverence for the "whole" woman embraced more than the physical. As the author of the section on natural childbirth wrote in the earliest version of *Our Bodies, Ourselves,* "My larger aim is to unite women's minds and bodies."[57] Whereas traditional obstetricians employed every technique imaginable to distance a woman from the contractions of her uterus, midwives urged women in labor to stay in touch with their bodies, their emotions, even their deepest spirituality. Indeed, many feminists and their natural childbirth allies viewed childbirth as a unique opportunity to heal the wounds of self-alienation inflicted upon all people by a mechanistic, technocratic society. Women in particular, who suffered and internalized an extra level of objectification both in everyday life and in traditional obstetrical settings, benefited from the inner connectedness that natural childbirth could foster.[58]

According to many feminist writers and health activists, this brush with nonalienated existence gave women a feeling of empowerment and a modicum of actual control over their bodies and their lives. When the state authorities arrested the unlicensed lay midwives at the Birth Center in Santa Cruz in 1974, an article in the feminist journal *The Second Wave* declared that "the real issue, of course, is *POWER*."[59] Referring to the cumulative monetary "power" accruing to physicians from hundreds of thousand-dollar hospital deliveries, the article also stated that "we must regain our power and control over our own bodies by providing ourselves with viable alternative institutions that meet our true needs."[60] As with the cooperatives and free clinics of the Left, alternative birthing centers were viewed as a haven from the profit-oriented medical outlets, which, as feminist self-help leader Carol Downer said, treated "health care as a product instead of a process, putting human beings on an assembly line."[61] In contrast, the self-help, home-based model of midwifery placed the laboring woman in control of the pace, position, and conditions of childbirth. Whereas obstetricians spoke of "delivering" babies, in effect placing themselves in an active role and rendering the woman a passive vessel, midwives spoke of "catching" babies, crediting the laboring woman with the active, difficult work of "giving birth."[62] If women giving birth in traditional settings lost the power to determine their own bodily fate at a crucial juncture, women in natural birth settings regained that power. Ideally, women emerged from midwife-assisted births with a new sense of their own strength, their ability to endure pain, and their ability to make important decisions. The birth served as an object lesson in self-determination. Important for its own sake, a positive birthing experience could also raise a woman's consciousness about power and control. For feminists the conditions of childbirth became, like abortion and other reproductive choices, a highly charged arena for "women to control their own bodies as a step toward controlling their lives."[63]

The self-determination feminists thought could be achieved through positive birthing experiences resembled strongly the self-determination counterculturalists pursued in their daily challenge to the modern way of life. Both groups valorized nature as the crucial antidote to an overly rational, technological, and thus alienated existence. They believed that a society, or a birth practice, that relied on machines and distanced itself from the intuitive, preindustrial, even primitive, natural processes of life could not escape an ultimate inner emptiness; but a life lived close to nature, or a labor guided by the dictates of nature, offered an enticing glimpse of fulfillment and harmony. References to nature suffused feminist writings about childbirth, and ranged from a practical defense of noninterventionist birthing techniques to a fully romanticized evocation of naked bodies, gardens, and soil as spiritually redemptive.[64]

Midwives and their advocates spoke of the medical advantages of following nature's timetable during labor. As one woman, professing to be "fanatical" about home birth, said, "You know, babies just come. They come out by themselves and you catch 'em."[65] The primary function of the midwife, according to lay practitioners, is to wait, to sit in attendance, offering physical and emotional comfort to the laboring woman. "When we go to a birth we don't *do* anything to the woman except give her something to drink, suggest a position, rub her back, see that she's rested and the environment's nice, and that she's cleaned up right before delivery."[66] To make decisions at crucial moments, indeed to sense when a crucial moment has arrived, midwives claimed to use their natural intuition and faith in nature's processes, just when the obstetrician would use "his toolchest of forceps and needles to yank the baby out of the mother's body."[67] According to Kate, one of the Santa Cruz midwives, "In a hospital the only way they can tell if a woman is in second stage of labor is by doing a vaginal examination, by sticking their fingers in to see where the baby is.

We've learned to do all this by watching and listening to the woman—what she does with her body, with her baby, how she sounds."[68] Clearly, in terms of an anti-technological, "nature knows best" credo, the midwives offered sounder, and more sensitive, care.

For its enthusiasts, the implications of naturalism in childbirth extended far beyond the safety and dignity of mother and child. As with counterculturalists who invested transcendent meaning in such everyday events as baking fresh bread or weeding an organic garden, home birth advocates believed that the communion with the natural afforded by midwife-assisted birth could offset the ills of modern life. As Jackie Christeve, a feminist defender of midwifery, mused in conversation with a group of lay midwives, "As people begin to get more in touch with . . . their bodies and the natural cycles and functions of their bodies . . . the whole concept of life and death will change as a result. We will have people dying in peace, experiencing *dying as an experience,* as well as experiencing birth, and not feeling fear of that."[69] Jade, one of the midwives, concurred that "technology has taken us out of the realm of nature. Being born and dying are your two most profound experiences of life. Life is not just what happens between these experiences."[70] By attending to the process of birth, rather than trying artificially to rush its product, midwives and their clients sought to evade the emptiness of an overly rationalized culture and gain access instead to the alleged precultural holism for which counterculturalists yearned.

At times, feminist writers also invoked the precultural or primitive as they sought to redefine childbirth as natural. Many spoke euphorically of the birthing practices of nonindustrialized societies, past and present, in which childbirth was part of the rhythm of life.[71] Others urged the adoption of practices they knew or imagined to have occurred in more natural times and places. One lay midwife at the First International Childbirth Conference reported that she had "witnessed a birth where none of the participants had any clothes . . . and the act of birth was as natural as breathing is today for any of us." [72] Raven Lang, in the *Birth Book,* claimed that the preconscious, intuitive knowledge of her own birth guided her through the birth of her son:

Birth is not totally an unknown or mysterious experience. A woman while giving birth has her own birth as a frame of reference, even though there is no conscious memory of it. The memory is communicated through the rhythm that the organism has already experienced, the same rhythm deeply rooted in the pre-consciousness of her own birth. I myself felt when actually in labor and delivery that I knew exactly the process, that I had always known it all along my pregnancy and even before. [73]

Similarly, in an unrestrained expression of the primitivist, holistic, and intuitionist position, Suzanne Arms wrote that "woman gives birth, and she is one with the process. At the time that she is unable to separate herself from her body and watch herself giving birth, she is unable to understand it. The strong, sometimes violent contractions of labor throw woman back to her most instinctual and primitive state." [74] And lest anyone miss the naturalist imperative repeated dozens of times throughout the text, Arms concludes her book *Immaculate Deception* with the image of a woman, several weeks postpartum, her twins nearby, "weeding and pulling leaves of lettuce for salad." [75]

Just as counterculturalists, and now many feminists, believed that culture had alienated people from the healing holism of nature, they also believed that culture had dimmed people's capacity for sexual pleasure. Feminists began to claim that natural childbirth and breastfeeding could rekindle the sexual, in both an immediate and an ongoing sense. Arguably, the hedonistic relish with which many women's liberationists discussed the sexual and sensual benefits of birth and nursing resembles countercultural discourse more distinctly than any other aspect of the early feminist revalorization of motherhood.

Perhaps the clearest bridge between counterculturalist and feminist sensualist views of childbirth can be found in Ina May Gaskin's *Spiritual Midwifery,* first published in 1975. The wife of self-styled spiritual leader Stephen Gaskin, Ina May Gaskin practiced mid-wifery at The Farm in Tennessee, a "spiritual community of eleven hundred long-haired vegetarians."[76] Although clearly a counter-culturalist first and foremost, Gaskin also espouses a feminist view of childbirth: "We feel that returning the major responsibility for normal childbirth to well-trained midwives rather than have it rest with a predominantly male and profit-oriented medical establishment is a major advance in self-determination for women."[77] On the sexuality question, Gaskin writes that "over and over again, I've seen that the best way to get a baby out is by cuddling and smooching with your husband. That loving, sexy vibe is what puts the baby in there, and it's what gets it out, too."[78] A woman named Mary confirms the generalization: "I laid down on the bed and began to rush and everything got psychedelic. I began having beautiful, rushing contractions that started low, built up to a peak, and then left me floating about two feet off the bed. Michael was lying beside me and going through the rushes too. . . . It felt wonderful and we were having a beautiful time. As the contractions got stronger, it felt like I was making love to the rushes and I could wiggle my body and push into them and it was really fine."[79]

Going far beyond Gaskin and other counterculturalists, most early women's liberationists rejected many aspects of the "sexual revolution" as exploitive of women. Most nevertheless maintained faith in the potentially liberatory power of unrepressed sexuality. One aspect of that power related directly to the fight against male domination: Just as contemporary society objectified women's bodies for men's pleasure, feminists said, women had learned to turn that objectification inward, losing touch with their own sensations and desires in the process. Healthy sexuality for a woman would thus consist of desire *felt* from within, and incorporated holistically into the overall sense of self; sex, at its best, would be part of everyday life. In the words of the Boston Women's Health Course Collective, "It's all part of the same body that we live in every day, that defines our feelings for us, that moves us around. It can't be mysterious or alien because it's our own familiar house. A good stretch, running fast, breathing deeply—these are all orgasms of a sort." [80]

Regarded commonly as painful and traumatic, childbirth for feminists represented an experience that could be redefined as sexually pleasurable, using inward, experiential criteria that only women themselves could perceive. By naming childbirth as a sexual experience, feminists protested the male prerogative to define the sexual for women, just as they protested other aspects of male control over childbirth. "That men should be disbelieving of the capacity of the female body to carry out with ecstatic pleasure this basic biological function is understandable," said one advocate of erotic childbirth. "Like nursing a baby it is an erotic pleasure for which only the female body is equipped. Men can not share or experience it themselves. Are we therefore to deny it also?" [81] Similarly, a California midwife noted the absurdity of sexually pleasurable birth in a male-dominated hospital environment, saying, "There are women who have orgasms during delivery. I can't imagine a woman feeling comfortable about having an orgasm on a delivery table in the hospital, or possibly even *having* one." [82]

Other feminists, in true Reichian form, spoke of the perils of bodily inhibition, the sheer joy of unrepressed eroticism, and the personal and societal healing powers of sexual liberation. According to Lucille Ritvo, a participant at the Childbirth Conference held in Stamford, Connecticut in 1973, people reared in a culture that casts various orificial erogenous zones as shameful learn to sublimate all pleasure associated with the functions of those zones. In the case of childbirth, sublimation reaches the level of deformity, as pleasure is transliterated as pain. Ritvo explains,

We who are so uninhibited about the pleasures of sex and the joys of eating hide from ourselves the erotic pleasures associated with that equally important physiological function, elimination of our waste products. Perhaps, because we are all born (with the exception of those delivered by Cesarean), because we are all born between "piss and shit" we have repressed along with the normal erotic satisfaction of the eliminatory processes, the eroticism of childbirth. Whole industries have grown up to eliminate "offensive" smells which we all delighted in as children before our parents civilized us. Similarly childbirth has been surrounded with pain, perhaps to deny the pleasure—a "self-fulfilling prophecy" as the psychologists would say. Fear of pain breeds fear and pain. . . . Let us start exploring our potential for sensual pleasure.[83]

Clearly, in Ritvo's view, a society advanced enough to recognize the erotic in childbirth could rechannel the energy absorbed in fighting pain into "positive physical pleasure."[84] Similarly, numerous writers asserted that without the shame surrounding breastfeeding, nursing could provide sexual pleasure for women; that "marvelously erotic feeling," one woman suggested, could even serve as "a great antidote to the common post-partum depression."[85]

Finally, in keeping with the values of the cultural left, feminists asserted repeatedly that natural childbirth practices, especially home births attended by lay midwives, would contribute to the creation of a strong and loving community of women: As women reclaimed birth from male obstetricians, they would learn to trust and depend on one another. In a province of female concerns, they would share valuable knowledge long hoarded and mystified by doctors. With each woman considered an expert by virtue of her physicality and life experience, women would rise in each other's esteem. Women would help each other to heal from the painful isolation they had experienced during prior traditional births, as well as provide support and companionship for each other as they reared their children. With the sisterly midwife role as a model, women in the wider society would learn what women in the feminist self-help movement knew well: Self-determination is best achieved through collectivist effort.[86] As one feminist stated the case for community, "Many women coming together at the same time in life could lead to the creation of positive solutions of shared problems. Consciousness-raising could help each woman realize that society, not personal shortcomings, leads to her ambivalence."[87]

In the language of countercultural utopianism, some feminists endowed the natural childbirth experience with the power to forge something beyond the ordinary community of people of like interest. With joy and exuberance, they made broad claims for the community-building potential of liberated childbirth. They cheered the "connectedness" natural birth seemed to foster between women and nature, between women past and women present, between body, mind, and spirit, and between isolated individuals.[88] Suzanne Arms wrote that the woman in labor, "like her ancestral sister . . . is more likely to turn to someone nearby for assistance and comfort than at any other time in her life."[89] Having thus turned, received, and bonded, women would be as close to the dream of holistic community as they could hope to be. Arms's idyllic final chapter, "Your Sister Has Twins!" concludes with a springtime garden scene:

A week after her births the young woman is back out in her garden in the morning light. The friend she invited to the birth comes over daily to help with the girls, bringing her own daughter in a backpack. . . . Soon it will be summer and the carrots will be ready to pull. The women notice that another garden has been planted beside a house across the way. Perhaps next year they will have neighbors enough for a large co-operative garden, if there is interest. There is certainly time.[90]

In this vision, natural childbirth has brought forth new life of many kinds. In renewed communion with the soil and the seasons, and in a spirit of loving cooperation, women root themselves in an organic web of friendship and family.

Conclusion

Throughout the early years of the women's movement, feminists regarded the topic of motherhood as a complex one. While influenced by the cultural left to view the traditional nuclear family as constricting, feminists did not by any means adopt a narrowly rejectionist stance toward motherhood. From the start, a positive discourse of motherhood paralleled the negative. By the mid-1970s, in regard to childbirth and breastfeeding in particular, the positive overshadowed the negative.

The counterculture of the 1960s provided an ideological source for much of the feminist movement's endorsement of natural childbirth, lay midwifery, and breastfeeding. Although the women's health movement, which served as the epicenter of the earliest favorable feminist analyses of childbirth, intersected in membership, ideology, and organization with more traditional natural childbirth advocacy groups and with the "peoples' clinic" movement of the Left, its closest links, ideological and other, were with the counterculture of the 1960s and early 1970s. In the discourse of childbirth, feminists' positive valuation of bodily self-determination, sexual liberation, naturalism, holism, and community formation strongly reflects countercultural views.

These countercultural roots help elucidate the progression of feminist thought through the 1980s. The counterculture, even more than the organized Left, valorized the body and nature, sought sexual liberation and "authentic" community, and gave voice to a vivid utopianism. Many feminists maintained similar values, and sought similar goals, even after avowedly breaking with the Left by the early 1970s. The tenacity of these views among feminists makes little sense when the Left is defined in narrow organizational terms. The influence of countercultural views helps explain some of the continuities in feminist thought, which, in the case of feminist attitudes toward childbirth and motherhood, are at least as significant as the changes.

Chapter Three

Black Nationalist Pronatalism,
Black Feminism, and the Quest
for a Multiracial Women's
Movement

If the counterculture of the 1960s provided women's liberationists with one set of values that could be shaped into a positive discourse of motherhood, the radical black activist movements of the late 1960s proved an equally vital source. By the late 1960s, debates within and beyond the African American community about an alleged black "matriarchy" led many black women activists to articulate a multilayered feminist position that refuted the notion of an actual matriarchy yet viewed motherhood as a source of female strength and solidarity.

As white radical and socialist feminists sought to broaden the base of their own movement in the late 1960s and early 1970s by "reaching out" to black women, many began to heed the centrality of motherhood to black feminism and to incorporate strongly promother platforms into their own writing.[1] The shift occurred with varying degrees of deliberation on the part of white feminist writers, with many moving quite unwittingly toward the maternalist philosophy expressed by black feminists. At times, white feminists substituted promotherhood rhetoric for fuller efforts to forge a multiracial women's movement. At other times, their more genuine efforts foundered on the inadequacy of maternalist rhetoric to link people and ideas with very different material bases. Ultimately, however, the discourse of motherhood within black nationalism, the redefinition of this discourse by black feminists, and the movement toward a parallel analysis by many white feminists mark a significant shift within American feminism as a whole toward a more positive valuation of motherhood.

Black Power, Pronatalism, and the Debate about "Matriarchy"

In the mid-1960s, black activists and intellectuals focused considerable energy on defending the black family. This defense was not new—for more than a century, an array of black nationalists, social reformers, and intellectuals had championed the value of a strengthened black family, for racial self-protection, for economic advancement, indeed, for any form of social advancement. Critics, black and white, had long pointed to family structure as the source of African Americans' woes, as well. But the publication of the Moynihan Report in 1965 helped to reinspire a concerted defense. Writing under the auspices of the United States Department of Labor, Daniel Patrick Moynihan drew heavily from the 1939 book *The Negro Family in the United States* by black sociologist E. Franklin Frazier. Frazier had labeled what he believed to be an overabundance of black female-headed households as a "matriarchate," and as a source of blacks' poverty and family "disorganization."[2] Moynihan similarly referred to African American family life as a "tangle of pathology," a cross-generational morass of welfare dependency, criminality, and illegitimacy. To explain this pattern, Moynihan, like Frazier, indicted the black family itself. Lacking male heads of household, too many black families were "matriarchal," Moynihan wrote. According to the report, a matriarchal upbringing left boys enervated, without a strong work ethic, without the values that would allow them to succeed in American society. Black boys needed strong male role models. Lacking such role models in the home, black boys ought to be required to serve in the military, where they would encounter powerful male authority figures and learn to lead disciplined lives.[3]

The Moynihan Report sparked rage among American blacks. Numerous writers and activists declared that the report represented one more example of the U.S. government's covert policy of genocide against the African American people. As the nation's military involvement in Vietnam intensified, and as black soldiers fought and died there in disproportionate numbers, Moynihan's suggestion that the military serve as a surrogate role model struck many black activists as deceitful.[4] At the same time, the public was increasingly aware of the abusive sterilization of women in Puerto Rico, rural Mississippi, and the inner cities of the United States, which helped convince many black activists that the government, along with the monied forces of the white establishment, had evolved a concerted plan to annihilate the black population.[5] Finally, in light of the violence used to squelch the revolts in Watts, Newark, Detroit, and elsewhere during the late 1960s, the genocide theory seemed salient to many black commentators in America.[6]

Contemporaneously with the publication of Moynihan's incendiary report, many black activists were shifting toward a nationalist perspective, defined broadly as the recognition of African American people as a distinct group with interests—political, economic, and cultural—separate from those of white Americans or the United States as a nation. Black nationalism had emerged across a wide spectrum of organizations and ideologies by the late 1960s and early 1970s. From the eclectically Muslim and black separatist Nation of Islam, to the militant and socialist Black Panthers, to the cultural nationalist US Organization headed by Ron Karenga, nationalism dominated the growing radical sector of African American politics of this period. Culturally, it inspired a celebration of black physical beauty, the claiming of a living African heritage, and a renaissance among black artists.[7]

Soured on the dynamics of an integrationist approach to racial justice, many of the younger black participants in the Civil Rights movement had begun, by the mid-1960s, to endorse a philosophy of self-determination. Drawing on the anti-imperialist struggle of the Vietnamese people, and energized by the directive of the recently slain Malcolm X to attain liberation "by any means necessary," the Black Power movement began to gain momentum in 1966. Marching in Mississippi, Stokely Carmichael, a leader in the Student Nonviolent Coordinating Committee (SNCC), made a public cry for Black Power, declaring, "It's time to stand up and take over. Take over. Move on over or we'll move on over you." [8] The National Conference on Black Power held in Newark, New Jersey, in 1967 issued a "Black Power Manifesto," which read in part, "It is incumbent upon us to get our own house in order, if we are to fully utilize the potentialities of the revolution, or to resist our own execution." [9] Only by recognizing themselves as a colonized people, and by struggling to reconstitute as a nation, fully self-sufficient economically, politically, and otherwise, could American blacks save themselves from "ruthless extermination." [10]

This focus on potential racial genocide urged the Black Power movement from the outset toward a nationalist and pronatalist perspective. If blacks were to constitute a nation, they would need first to secure their ranks. However, as a few black women within the movement pointed out by the late 1960s, black nationalist pronatalism contained within it a starkly sexist and traditionalist message about black family and sexual politics. [11]

Ironically, many male Black Power advocates used the findings of the widely criticized Moynihan Report to underscore their own belief that a successful black revolution required, first and foremost, the reconstruction of the black *man,* as a patriarch and a warrior. Allegedly, the proposed Moynihan solution to blacks' troubles sought not only to reduce the black population overall, but also, in the short run, to kill off the men in the community. Thus, black men were thought to represent a particularly endangered population whose vulnerability needed to be recognized. Part of the problem, several leading male Black Power advocates concurred, was that black women had more opportunity for education and employment than black men in American society. That opportunity allegedly translated to more power in the family. Black men found themselves "castrated" at home by "matriarchs" and in public by white racists. According to Eldridge Cleaver, in an essay entitled "The Allegory of the Black Eunuchs," white men and black women were working together, albeit with black women unaware of the complicity, to oppress the black man: "There is a war going on between the black man and the black woman, which makes her the silent ally, indirectly but effectively, of the white man. The black woman is an unconsenting ally and she may not even realize it—but the white man sure does. That's why, all down through history, he has propped her up economically above you and me, to strengthen her hand against us."[12]

Many black nationalists asserted that the black nation needed to fortify itself with numbers. On the most basic level this meant that blacks must have more babies. The birth control pill and coercive sterilization threatened to decimate the black population, according to some leading Black Power advocates. A flyer distributed by the Black Unity Party in 1968 urged black women, in the name of revolution, to stop taking birth control pills:

It is the system's method of exterminating Black people here and abroad. To take the pill means that we are contributing to our own GENOCIDE. . . . When we produce children, we are aiding the REVOLUTION in the form of NATION building. . . . Under the cover of an alleged campaign to "alleviate poverty," white supremacist Americans and their dupes are pushing an all-out drive to put rigid birth control measures into every black home. No such drive exists within the White American world. In some cities, Peekskill, Harlem, Mississippi and Alabama, welfare boards are doing their best to force black women receiving aid to submit to *Sterilization.*[13]

Blacks were enjoined to resist by drawing themselves into father-dominated families and having many babies, for "procreation is beautiful, especially if we are devoted to the Revolution."[14] Similarly, in January 1969, the Black Panther newspaper urged black men to "deal with the situation. Educate your woman to stop taking those pills. You and your woman—replenish the earth with healthy Black warriors. You and your woman can build the black Liberation Army to end the god-fearing, god loving racist white dog monster who is piously praying to his scurvy god to WIPE YOU OUT!!"[15] Amiri Baraka, one of the most influential voices of the Black Power movement, stated his nationalism in romanticized pronatalist terms in the essay "Black Woman," writing that "it must be black consciousness that is given to our babies with their milk, and with the warmth of the black woman's loving body."[16]

Black Feminist Responses

The pronatalism of black nationalism and the discussion of "matriarchy" revived by the Moynihan Report thrust motherhood to the very center of the Black Power ideology by the late 1960s. Unlike the largely white counterculture, which incorporated but never fully articulated a revaluation of motherhood, the radical black movements of the late 1960s and early 1970s brought motherhood into positive public discourse. Those women active in Black Power movements who expressed an increasingly forceful feminist perspective, unlike their white counterparts in the New Left and the counterculture, did not need to declare to the men in their movements that mothering constituted a political issue. That was a given. Virtually all of the black women writers who contributed to a feminist analysis in the late 1960s grappled with the issues of black pronatalism and the "matriarchy" question. While they responded in a variety of ways, with many remaining in the organizations within which they were struggling for gender equality, they all helped to build an enduring feminist reassessment of motherhood.[17]

On the surface, African American activist women seemed to state their protest against male supremacy in terms similar to those of the white women who began in the late 1960s to object to sexism within the New Left. Those terms included a critique of traditional gender roles as embedded in the nuclear family. Biological motherhood, as a mandate for all women, did not escape condemnation. Yet because the pronatalist imperative for black women issued not from the wider, more definitively oppressive society, but rather from black "movement" men who were their allies in many meaningful ways, they questioned that imperative carefully.

In critiquing the edict to go forth and mother, black women activists often took pains to declare their own devotion to black liberation. Frances Beale of SNCC wrote that black men "who are exerting their 'manhood' by telling black women to step back into a domestic, submissive role are assuming a counter-revolutionary position." [18] Black women, like black men, needed to be in public, fighting "the enemy." To keep women in the home weakened the entire Black Power enterprise, in numbers of adult warriors, if nothing else. [19]

Activist and writer Toni Cade pursued a similar point, but shifted her perspective slightly to consider the damage done by blind pronatalism to *women* in the movement:

It is a noble thing, the rearing of warriors for the revolution. I can find no fault with the idea. I do, however, find fault with the notion that dumping the pill is the way to do it. You don't prepare yourself for the raising of super-people by making yourself vulnerable—chance fertilization, chance support, chance tomorrow—nor by being celibate until you stumble across the right stock to breed with. You prepare yourself by being healthy and confident, by having options that give you confidence, by getting yourself together, by being together enough to attract a together cat whose notions of fatherhood rise above the Disney caliber of man-in-the-world-and-woman-in-the-home, by being committed to the new consciousness, by being intellectually and spiritually and financially self-sufficient to do the right thing. You prepare yourself by being in control of yourself. The pill gives the woman, as well as the man, some control. Simple as that. [20]

This gendered analysis of the movement's pronatalism represented an important strain within modern black feminism. Notably, as for many white radical feminists, the base of power and individuality for many black feminist writers lay in bodily self-determination. Women, like the men and the nations of the world, needed to be able to control their own destinies. For women, that meant, first, being able to control their own bodies and procreative capacities. And Cade, like the liberationists of the New Left and the counterculture, did not want to sacrifice the pursuit of sexual pleasure to any larger social cause.[21]

Although black activist women attempted to present an analysis that was at once problack and prowoman, they often reached an impasse because the defense of "manhood" seemed to be a central and intractable aspect of Black Power ideology. With increasing frequency and increasing anger, black women began to write about the ways in which the call for traditional domesticity limited women's life options.

For some, the primary culprit in black women's oppression seemed to be white society. In Beale's assessment, those women who concurred with the domesticity edict suffered from false consciousness:

There are also some Black women who feel that there is no more productive role in life than having and raising children. This attitude often reflects the conditioning of the society in which we live and is adopted from a bourgeois white model. Some young sisters who have never had to maintain a household and accept the confining role which this entails tend to romanticize (along with the help of a few brothers) this role of housewife and mother. Black women who have had to endure this kind of function are less apt to have these utopian visions.[22]

In other cases, tensions between black men and women came to the fore, and a more militant feminist position about childbearing and child rearing emerged. A group of "poor Black women" penned a furious rebuttal to the Black Unity Party's call to abandon the birth control pill. Titled "The Sisters Reply," this rebuttal acknowledged that whites probably did want to effect the genocide of black and other poor people worldwide. The authors nevertheless declared their refusal to produce babies for a revolution run by black men who "won't support their families, won't stick by their women."[23] Birth control gave black women what little power they had to direct their own lives, to improve the lives of the children they had already borne, and to resist further exploitation by either whites *or* oppressive black men. "Having too many babies stops us from supporting our children, teaching them the truth or stopping the brainwashing as you say, and fighting black men who still want to use and exploit us."[24]

A number of black women activists wrote about the difficulties of rearing too many children under current social and economic circumstances. They pilloried the black men who were willing to sacrifice black women's lives to some larger goal of "revolution." As strategy, they wrote, that kind of nation-building would not work. Beyond that, these writers began to question the entire edifice of evidence that fueled the male-dominated Black Power movement.[25]

Black feminist writers traced the genesis of the "revolutionary" mandate to bolster the black man's masculinity to the nefarious effects of the Moynihan Report, which had itself tapped into long-standing resentments between black men and women over black men's alleged inability or unwillingness to support their families financially. A few writers simply dismissed black men as weak, lazy, and incompetent, concerned only about "the street, dope and liquor, women, a piece of ass, and their cars."[26] More commonly, black women writers began to disassemble the notion of a black "matriarchy," which they felt the Black Power movement had appropriated far too uncritically from the white establishment.

Moynihan had argued that black women held the jobs, and therefore the power, in their families. Pursuing this line of analysis, some black male activists argued that black men had been "emasculated," put in the unnatural position of subservience to their own women.[27] As black women developed an ongoing feminist analysis, they tried to disprove the notion that black women hold more power than black men in their households or communities.

Beale wrote, "Let me state here and now that the Black woman in America can justly be described as a 'slave of a slave.' "[28] While black men throughout American history had been "emasculated, lynched and brutalized," black women had been subject to that same violence and economic exploitation, coupled with sexual violence at the hands of white men, unbridled blame and resentment from white women, and rejection and violence from black men who had internalized their own oppression.[29]

Matriarchy, several writers pointed out, entailed a system of social organization in which women were vested with actual, material power. The domineering character trait attributed to black women, even if descriptively accurate, did not equate with authority to govern a family or a society. Arguing against the claim that the black male had been "castrated" by black women, Jean Carey Bond and Patricia Peery wrote, "A matriarchal system is one in which power rests firmly in the hands of women. We suggest that whatever economic power may accrue to Black women by way of the few employment escape valves permitted them by the oppressing group for their own insidious reasons, this power is really illusory and should not be taken at face value."[30] Black women were in a terribly weak and vulnerable position, Bond and Peery asserted.

In Defense of Matriarchy

In the same essays in which black feminist writers decried the misleading use of the term "matriarch," they began to redefine and reconstruct the term as a symbol of maternal fortitude. Why, they asked, did blacks need to follow suit, simply because Moynihan, a white man, criticized black women's strength as overweening and "castrating"? Black Power encompassed a reclaiming of African and African American cultural values, rather than a simple parroting of white American values. Reversing Moynihan's logic, but retaining his emphasis on family arrangements as the key to liberation, several writers suggested that families modeled after African, "egalitarian" gender relations would be able to harness rather than squelch women's strength. While chairperson of the National Black Student Association, Gwen Patton wrote that "Black people must go to the roots of African culture, and they will find that the African family acted as a unit with each member contributing productively: while the warrior went hunting for food, the mother and the children would fight off invaders and enemies; and, while the mother tilled the earth, the father would tend the children."[31]

African American feminist writers pointed out that the recognition of women's strength had benefited entire African societies, where strong women did not equate with "castrated" men:

There is nothing to indicate that the African woman, who ran the marketplace, who built dams, who engaged in international commerce and diplomacy, who sat on thrones, who donned armor to wage battle against the European invaders and the corrupt chieftains who engaged in the slave trade, who were consulted as equals in the affairs of the state—nothing to indicate that they were turning their men into faggots, were victims of penis envy, or any such nonsense.[32]

While this strand of thought might have romanticized the distant African past in much the same way that cultural nationalism reified various aspects of African culture as symbols of African American cultural pride, it nevertheless contrasted sharply with the frequent mother-blaming of the black male movement. Here, the strong African mother defied Moynihan's claim that maternal strength created paternal weakness.

In more direct defiance, black feminists asserted that the very same mothers accused by Moynihan of undermining their children and husbands, and not just their ancient African counterparts, should be praised for their fortitude. The strong black mother, in this view, was in fact an asset to the black community. In the essay "Dear Black Man," Fran Sanders wrote, "Now let's face it, it was she who caused the race to survive. And if we are now all finally finding our voices to assert ourselves as a race, let it not be at her expense." [33] If anything, mothers were the unsung heroes of black America.

In language that would later be echoed by white feminists, black feminists in the late 1960s praised their own mothers and situated themselves in a continuum of intergenerational maternal strength. The white feminist movement, so clearly an intergenerational protest movement at its inception, would not produce positive personal testimonials about the mother-daughter bond until the mid-1970s—and even then, mythical matriarchs would receive more adulation than actual mothers. For many black women writers, the reclaimed mother served as a strong basis for an affirmative feminist theory.

As many African American writers have indicated, there is at least a verbal tradition of reverence for the mother in American black culture, predating this particular debate over black "matriarchy" by a century or more. [34] As black singer Abbey Lincoln wrote in 1966, "My mother is one of the most courageous people I have ever known, with an uncanny will to survive. When she was a young woman, the white folks were much further in the lead than they are now, and their racist rules gave her every disadvantage; yet, she proved herself a queen among women, any women, and as a result will always be one of the great legends for me." [35] Lincoln's mother had instilled in her this will to survive. In their strength, Lincoln asserted, all black women were linked, across the generations. For black men to turn around and call any black woman a "black, ugly, evil you-know-what" was to betray their own mothers. [36]

The discourse of motherhood developed by women in the Black Power movement was not unique to the 1960s or 1970s. African American women activists had employed maternalist rhetoric and reasoning throughout the nineteenth and early twentieth centuries. Black club women, not unlike their white counterparts, had organized as mothers and for mothers, and in the name of the moral virtues supposedly inherent to motherhood, in their pursuit of "race betterment."[37] The reemergence of this discourse in the 1960s and 1970s, however, helped transform what was then a broad cultural praise for mothers into an explicitly feminist one.

Perhaps the most influential example of this shift came from Angela Davis, who was at the very epicenter of the Black Power movement. Davis, a professor of philosophy at the University of California, was fired because of her outspoken views as a member of the Communist Party and her support for the Black Power movement. In 1971 she published "The Black Woman's Role in the Community of Slaves" while held in the Marin County Jail on charges of murder, kidnapping, and conspiracy stemming from her alleged involvement in the attempted escape of several black prisoners from the Marin County Courthouse in 1970.[38] A symbol of black radicalism and defiance, Davis dedicated the article to George Jackson, a militant black prisoner accused of the murder of a white guard at Soledad Prison in California. Davis wrote that Jackson's life had been "precipitously and savagely extinguished" by the prison authorities; had he not been killed by a prison guard, she wrote, his grapplings with political theory and his commitment to revolution and black liberation would have led him inexorably to an enlightened understanding of the subjugation of black women.[39] By invoking the authority of Jackson, who was seen as a martyr by black militants nationwide, Davis commandeered the moral high ground of the movement for her refutation and redefinition of "matriarchy." To suggest that Jackson had been on the brink of a feminist reconsideration of black womanhood was to insist that "a systematic critique of . . . past misconceptions about black women" was central to black liberationist thought.[40]

In her article, Davis reiterated the arguments of other black activist women that a black "matriarchy" could not exist under slavery, a system that denied women not only codified power, but any assurance of an ongoing family structure. With few sources available to her in jail, Davis nevertheless penned a detailed historical analysis of the ways in which the slaveholders' refusal to accord slave women any special status as women created, ironically, a rough equality between slave women and slave men, an equality that ruling class propagandists later misinterpreted as black female dominance. But in the slave quarters, where the slaves themselves defined the division of labor, women performed the highly gender-segregated tasks relating to domesticity and motherhood. As mothers, as nurturers, as caretakers in the widest sense of the word, black women in the community of slaves performed "the *only* labor of the slave community which could not be directly and immediately claimed by the oppressor."[41] That labor of maintenance and survival, invisible to the slaveholder, enabled slaves to endure, materially and spiritually. In their domestic role, then, slave women performed a bold form of resistance to slavery. The slave woman, and by implication, the generations of black women succeeding her, was not only without fault in her reputed "strength," but was a revolutionary, a bulwark against the depredations on all black people. The positive role of the nurturing, but roughly "equal," black mother could not be overstated.

In two essays anthologized early in the women's movement, Patricia Robinson, a black psychiatric social worker and activist, also offered a historical overview of the depredations against black women.[42] Using a much looser historical method than Davis, Robinson also honored the black mother for her strength and her centrality to black survival, while simultaneously reclaiming a historical "matriarchy" and venerating the maternal body as positive and "natural." Robinson, still attempting to be historical in a sweeping sense, diverged from Davis and other writers in her conflation of materialism and essentialism. In doing so she pushed the black feminist discourse of motherhood closer to the views that would come to characterize "cultural" feminism by the mid-1970s.

In "A Historical and Critical Essay for Black Women of the Cities," Robinson identifies what she sees as the deadly dualism of Western civilization. "The American Dream is the end of a long, circuitous route away from the *animal-body, the land, woman* and *black* to condensed wealth (money, machines and property), cities, man and white. It is time now to break out of these deadly myths and this culture built on the oppression of women and blacks." [43] Robinson describes a holistic distant past in which black women, the mothers of civilization, were revered *as* mothers, with an essential, bodily bond to the nonindustrialized earth. Violent centuries of appropriation of women, blacks, and nature by white men in pursuit of urbanization, industrialization, and capitalism established the current social order. Village life, dominated by women, was communal, tied to nature, and endowed with a simple equilibrium. Cities, meanwhile, "fed by an economic surplus," were built on individualism and alienation from nature's equilibrating forces, prey to the lowest drives of power-mongering men.[44] And modern Western civilization thrives on urban alienation: "The American Dream is a bold, heady, ruthless dream—away from the black woman, the very image of the Great Earth Mother and the Black Madonna. For us black women, 'motherfucker' is now a definitive, historical term symbolizing the first murder, the murder of the Great Earth Mother repeated endlessly to this day." [45]

Robinson's abstract, essentialized understanding of motherhood radicalized matriarchy within the politics of race. In her view, the first mother, the earth mother, the earth itself, even the Madonna, had been black. Therefore, to distance oneself from mothers, nature, or communalism was to align oneself with the forces of sexism and racism. Robinson's analysis went beyond that of Davis. Where Davis redefined black women's maternal and domestic labor as a crucial revolutionary force, Robinson named black women's bodies, venerated for their procreative function, as the link to humane, communal forms of civilization.

In 1974 Alice Walker, who came into her own politically and artistically in the lap of the Civil Rights and Black Power movements, spelled out the logical conclusions of the promother stance that Davis, Robinson, and numerous other black feminist writers had intimated. Less dramatic than Robinson's, her argument was also less historical and more overtly mythologizing. Walker wrote that the mother, as a model of strength and creativity, and the mother-daughter relationship, as a symbol of the biological and spiritual bond between all women, represented a force of almost mythic power for black women. Through reverence for and identification with the mother, black women could gain insight into themselves, form alliances with each other, and place themselves in an uninterrupted historical continuum of womanly, maternal strength. In the essay "In Search of Our Mothers' Gardens," Walker writes that although black women have been called " 'Matriarchs,' 'Superwomen,' and 'Mean and Evil Bitches,' " their true strength is not malignant, but rather lies in the simple ability to maintain an inner core of creativity in the face of unbelievable oppression.[46] While the essay celebrates her own mother's artistic passion for gardening, Walker's larger point is that strong African American mothers pass an invaluable legacy to their daughters: "Guided by my heritage of a love of beauty and a respect for strength—in search of my mother's garden, I found my own."[47]

Walker's essay represents the apotheosis of the black mother, reconstructed in the aftermath of the Moynihan Report. Idealized and invested with transcendent power, the "good" mother directly refutes the negative "matriarch" stereotype and also removes the discourse from the male-centered paradigm argued by many Black Power advocates to a realm populated by women: mothers and daughters. While Walker, with her "womanist," even female separatist, perspective, had by 1974 clearly been influenced by the wider feminist movement, it is important to note that the intensely positive view of the mother that her writing epitomized, in concert with the works of numerous other black feminist writers in the late 1960s and early 1970s, helped to set a standard for subsequent feminist theory, both black and white.[48]

After a brief period of criticism in the late 1960s, motherhood rarely suffered a sustained critique in black feminist writing. Such writing since the early 1970s has focused strongly and positively on individual mothers and has used mothering as a model for everything from ecological concern to revolution. The wider feminist movement drew its positive formulation of motherhood in part from this African American model.[49]

A White Feminist Lament: How to Draw Black Women into the Movement

In the late 1960s and increasingly in the early 1970s, many white feminist groups bemoaned the absence of black women from their ranks.[50] While scholars have pointed out the shallowness and hypocrisy of much of this lament, discourses of feminism nevertheless included much discussion about how to draw black women into "the movement."[51] Repeatedly, as white feminists thought about how to attract women of color to women's liberation, they focused on motherhood as a unifying feature of women's lives.

Many white radical and socialist feminists in the late 1960s and early 1970s could not accept the idea of a women's movement geared toward white, middle-class young women. With political roots in the New Left and the Civil Rights movement, they eschewed elitism, placed a high value on mass organizing, and had a keen awareness of the particular oppression of black people in the United States. As these activists shifted their focus to women's oppression, they brought with them the skills and the strengthened sense of self acquired through successful political work.[52] The attention paid by many white feminists to the question of "outreach" to black and working-class women indicates that they also maintained their interest in the content of their earlier political activity. Most early radical and socialist feminist groups sought to expand their base to reach "ordinary" women, sometimes even adopting New Left rhetoric to argue that blacks, as the most oppressed group, must be the leaders of any viable liberation movement in this country.

As early as 1968, at a women's liberation conference held in Sandy Springs, Maryland, white feminists conducted a wide-ranging discussion of the importance of "including" black women in the feminist movement. While some participants expressed discomfort with the prominence given to blacks at many radical meetings, others insisted that a feminist movement that did not make genuine efforts toward racial inclusiveness would be ineffective by definition. Although the Sandy Springs group reached no consensus about the matter, participants introduced the idea that the integrity of the feminist movement depended at least in part on an antiracist and racially inclusive stance.[53]

Although the Sandy Springs participants expressed great ambivalence about how—or indeed whether—to include black women in the formative stages of a feminist movement, they stated clearly their perception that black women and white women had different concerns. Other groups of white feminists, with less ambivalence about the need to reach out to black women, noted this same discrepancy of concerns. What they noted, in effect, was that most black women faced more material hardship than most white women. Black women faced the "double jeopardy" of being both black and female, which often meant fighting police violence, other racial harassment, and more extreme poverty, along with the everyday problems of dealing with sexist men. If, as Redstockings and several "politico" feminist groups insisted, feminism meant fighting for the freedom of the most oppressed women, then the needs of black women would have to assume top priority. The competing argument, that feminism represented a chance for each woman to recognize her own pain, and that each woman's pain carried equal weight, seemed weak in comparison.[54]

These competing arguments set up a tension between the desire for an identity group politics for the white middle-class women who dissented from the New Left and the Civil Rights movement, and a concomitant desire on the part of many of these same women to combat racism. Many failed to see how their own consciousness raising could coexist with mass organizing around racial issues. The tension came out all too clearly at the Sandy Springs Conference, when a woman said, "We're going to get so involved with them [*sic*] that we are not going to talk about female liberation."[55]

To some very large degree the dilemma was academic, because black women did not flock to white feminist meetings. The question of how to reach black women remained largely hypothetical. When most of the predominantly white feminist groups arrived at the decision that their politics did mandate the inclusion of black women, they faced a crisis in recruitment. Several black feminist activists had made it clear that they considered current white feminist agendas irrelevant to black women's lives. Frances Beale wrote that many groups within white women's liberation had

come to the incorrect conclusion that their oppression is due simply to male chauvinism. They therefore have an extremely anti-male tone to their dissertations. Black people are engaged in a life-and-death struggle and the main emphasis of Black women must be to combat the capitalist, racist exploitation of Black people. . . . Very few of these [white] women suffer the extreme economic exploitation that most Black women are subjected to day by day. This is the factor that is most crucial for us. It is not an intellectual persecution alone; it is not an intellectual outburst for us; it is quite real.[56]

White feminists responded in manifold ways to charges such as these. On the one hand, some white feminists simply appropriated the rhetoric of black suffering by referring to the "woman as nigger."[57] All women were to all men as blacks were to whites. This claim did not usually involve an actual exegesis of the material similarities between the daily oppression of blacks and the daily oppression of women, but rather served as emotionally laden rhetoric for activists who had long privileged the oppression of blacks, fueled by no small dose of white guilt. As a strategy for drawing black women into a mass women's movement, this device had little effect, except perhaps to further alienate some black women who suspected opportunism in the expropriation.[58]

Other white feminist activists genuinely sought to reach black women by expressing solidarity with the causes for which black women activists were fighting. For example, a predominantly white coalition of feminists joined the Black Panthers and other groups in New Haven, Connecticut, in November 1969 in a demonstration to free fourteen Panthers being held on charges of conspiracy, murder, and kidnapping. Five of the imprisoned Panthers were women, two of whom were pregnant; a third had recently given birth, under allegedly wretched conditions, while in prison. In a leaflet distributed at the demonstration, entitled "Free Our Sisters, Free Ourselves," women's liberationists concentrated on the Panther women's status as mothers or expectant mothers, and declared pregnancy, prenatal care, and childbirth to be central feminist concerns. They declared that in the name of common concern over these issues, a multiracial movement for the liberation of women could be shaped. "We will no longer have to stand up alone—*now when we rise up—we rise up together. We will show the prisons, the courts, and the state that we will not tolerate the oppression of our sisters anywhere, in any way, shape or form.*"[59]

The group WITCH, better known for its condemnations of Mother's Day than for its support for mothers' rights, made similar declarations in support of the Panther women. In trying to make common cause with black activist women, WITCH distributed the flyer "Pass the Word, Sister," which used the word "confinement" to refer to the universal oppression of women. In free verse form, WITCH named the common condition of all women:

> We women are:
> in jail at Niantic
> in the mud of Vietnam
> in the slums of the cities
> in the ghetto-sinks of suburbia
> at the typewriters
> of the corporations
> at the mimeograph machines
> of the Left
> in the water at Chappaquidick
> in the brutalizing beds of Babylon
>
> We are going to stop
> all confinement of women.[60]

In the analysis framed by WITCH, confinement for the Panther women meant literal imprisonment, obviously, but more powerfully it meant loss of control over their choices as mothers or expectant mothers. This, according to WITCH, was the worst indignity visited upon the imprisoned Panther "sisters":

> How does Niantic State
> Women's Farm prepare women
> for their confinement?
> They are:
> denied their choice of doctors;
> denied information about childbirth;
> denied their choice of method
> of childbirth; deprived of proper diet,
> exercise, medication & clothing.
>
> Rose Smith weighed 132 pounds
> at the start of her pregnancy.
> Now-7 months pregnant—
> after Niantic's prenatal care,
> Rose Smith weighs 133 pounds.
>
> Guards will be there
> when the babies are born.
> Guards will be there
> to take them away.
> The state will decide
> who's "fit" and who's "not fit"
> to guard and be guardian
> of mother and child.[61]

While there is no reason to doubt the sincerity of the white feminists' concern for the physical conditions of the imprisoned Panther women, and while the New Haven demonstration must be understood in the complex context of coalition politics between the white Left and the Black Panthers, several features of the white feminist analysis emerging from the event stand out. First, the sympathetic focus on the Panther women who were pregnant or had recently given birth casts the treatment of these women as a morally, not simply legally, compelling issue. Ironically, this argument was penned by white feminists who in other contexts were decrying motherhood as a patriarchal ruse.[62] While perhaps following the pronatalist lead of the black movement itself, in its effort to align itself with black women, a group as militant as WITCH evolved a rough theory of motherhood as a universalizing issue for women.

Of course, actions such as these alone could not create an enduring multiracial feminist movement or coalition. Nor did the more vague gesture of printing black feminist writing in various feminist anthologies necessarily represent a vital, mutual recognition of common, cross-race feminist purpose. The presence of several essays by black feminists in the leading feminist anthologies of the early 1970s gave the false, if well-intended, impression of a cohesive and racially diverse women's movement.[63]

In actuality, the dilemma of outreach to black women proved difficult and ongoing for many predominantly white feminist groups in the late 1960s and early 1970s. Whereas single gestures toward solidarity, like the Panther demonstration, carried symbolic power, many feminist groups sought agonizingly to develop a gender politics that would recognize the specific, material needs of black women rather than simply appropriate and render symbolic the pathos of those needs. With the belief that a mass movement must be built "from the ground up," these groups altered their own priorities in search of a more genuine dialogue with black women.

As predominantly white feminist groups sought to reach black women "where they were," they often focused on motherhood as a point of connection. In part, this focus resulted from the fact that some of the white feminists who sought to build a mass-based women's liberation movement were veterans of the mass organizing efforts of the 1960s. They recalled that the welfare rights organizations of the 1960s, primarily comprised of welfare mothers, had been among the few successful projects of the Civil Rights movement in the North. Some activists attributed this success to the idea that "mothers will fight for their children, to supply their needs, and they will struggle for as long as it takes for their children to grow up. They possess both the will and the sustained determination to demand long and loud that the political structure allow their children enough to live on decently, and in doing so change the political structure."[64]

Beyond a general principle of maternal determination as impetus for political action, white feminists in search of black allies noted clearly the strong and positive emphasis that black feminists themselves placed on motherhood. That emphasis suffused black feminist writing, often focusing on the specific worries facing black women as they sought not only birth control and abortion rights, but also freedom from coerced sterilization. Beale challenged white feminists directly in her 1969 essay "Double Jeopardy: To Be Black and Female," anthologized widely in the women's movement: She urged white women to broaden their understanding of so-called feminist issues if they wished to ally themselves with black women. In terms of "motherhood" and reproductive rights, Beale wrote,

Black women have the right and the responsibility to determine when it is in the interest of the struggle to have children or not to have them and this right must not be relinquished to anyone. It is also her right and responsibility to determine when it is in her own best interests to have children, how many she will have, and how far apart. The lack of the availability of safe birth-control methods, the forced sterilization practices, and the inability to obtain legal abortions are all symptoms of a sick society that jeopardizes the health of black women.[65]

A number of other black feminists were making similar points by the late 1960s and early 1970s.[66]

Numerous primarily white feminist groups heeded the words of Beale and others. They recognized that if a feminist organization dealing with reproductive rights were to have any meaning to black women, it would have to recognize the fight *to* have children as well as the right to obtain an abortion. The Southern Female Rights Union of New Orleans, for example, wrote that poor and black women have "*no* access to safe abortions, and they fear forced birth control and sterilization at the hands of the white medical establishment." To create "broader alliances," women's groups had to insist upon "the right of every woman to *total* control over her body, to bear or not to bear children." [67] Similarly, the left-wing Chicago Women's Liberation Union, founded in 1969, included among its top goals, along with the support of abortion rights and the rights of pregnant teachers, the support of the Chicago Maternity Center, a much embattled clinic whose clientele, historically, had consisted heavily of inner-city black women. [68]

In Berkeley, the socialist or "politico" feminist group Women's Liberation developed strategies for outreach to various groups of women. The group's discussion of black women stressed their roles as mothers and grappled with the range of issues being raised by black feminist activists. After debating whether various ameliorative measures would constitute liberal reform rather than radical revolution, the group arrived at the conclusion that the only way to build a real revolution would be through mass organizing, which meant identifying and trying to address the disparate needs of diverse groups of women. Black women even more than other women suffered the stresses of motherhood compounded by poverty, so to reach "Third World Women" the group needed to address the material conditions of motherhood. In addition, they needed to attack the myth of the black matriarchy, which served to uphold the "white imperialist system." Following the lead of black feminists who were beginning to expose the conjoined racism and sexism of the black matriarch stereotype, Berkeley Women's Liberation vowed to join the fight against a "racist myth which is at the same time anti-woman, and which dangerously distorts reality." [69]

Conclusion

White feminist laments over the failure of outreach to African American women continued through the 1970s, and the goal of establishing *one* fully diverse women's liberation movement remained elusive. To be sure, black women worked on feminist issues and articulated feminist views in a multiplicity of settings: in

popular and scholarly writing, within mixed-gender black liberationist groups, within primarily white women's or leftist liberationist groups, and within black feminist groups such as the Brooklyn-
based Sisterhood of Black Single Mothers, the National Black
Feminist Organization, founded in 1973 in New York City, and
the Combahee River Collective, which began meeting in Boston in
1974.[70]

On the level of theory, however, black feminist thought from the
late 1960s and early 1970s influenced the focus and tenor of
women's liberationist thought as a whole. The cultural left's preoccupation with the dismantling of traditional forms of family and
the creation of new communities, coupled with its valorization of
nature and the body, pointed many white feminists toward a positive view of motherhood as a central, albeit essentialized, aspect of
women's lives. Debates about matriarchy and male dominance
within black liberation movements led some black women activists
to articulate feminist views in terms of a positive reclaiming of
motherhood. Thus, black and white feminists moved simultaneously along the same trajectory as they positioned motherhood at
the foreground of their theory and began to recast mothering in a
positive, even romanticized, light. However, in the early to mid-
1970s, some white feminists began to freight that parallel trajectory with their own desire to forge a multiracial women's movement. Noting the importance of mothering in black feminist theory,
as well as in African American culture, they sought to foster links
between black and white women based on their common capacity
to bear children. These feminists theorized that the way to reach
black women was to focus on matters that black women themselves stressed.

But ultimately the experience of motherhood, across lines of
race, class, and sexual orientation—across all lines of difference,
in other words—could remain a "universal" experience only in the
most unexamined sense. The tenuousness of this false universal, in
materialist terms, pushed many white radical feminists further and
further into essentialist and symbolic renderings of motherhood.

As the material differences between women continued to belie claims to gender-based solidarity, radical feminists in search of a single, unified movement and theory of women's liberation turned to the *most* essentialist and the *most* symbolic renderings of motherhood, garnered selectively from the radical movements of the 1960s, as they attempted to salvage their own dream of a community of women. In doing so, these "cultural" feminists were forced to confront an unsolved, implicit mandate of 1960s radicalism: to reunite sexuality, procreation, and community in a way that does not exploit women. Whereas the counterculture had prized sexuality at the expense of women's liberation, cultural feminists grew increasingly more willing to sacrifice women's sexual liberation to the dream of a community of women as "mothers."[71]

Chapter Four

Toward "Mother Right": A Universalizing Theory

*I*n the mid-1970s, many white radical feminist writers and predominantly white feminist organizations edged away from their earlier pledge to "eliminate sex roles" to the more amorphous goal of setting up a separate "female culture." This period marks a shift in much feminist theory and organization from radical to cultural feminism. In part, that shift was initiated, and continued to be developed, by writing that focused on motherhood as a unifying experience for women. Yet as feminists venerated motherhood during this period, they also mystified it. By 1976, the "mother" honored by feminists was less often one who gave birth and searched for day care, and more often an ancient matriarch or a metaphorical maternal figure. Why did so much cultural feminist theory revolve around the topic of motherhood, and why was the topic subject to such mystification?

Much of the impetus for a unifying issue stemmed from the internal turmoil that plagued women's liberation groups by 1973, as unresolved tensions inherent in the countercultural legacy of the 1960s became untenable. The counterculture's valorization of nature, which feminists in the early years of the women's health movement recast as a celebration of pregnancy, childbirth, and nursing as "natural" phenomena, coexisted uneasily with the cultural left's equally strong desire for sexual freedom and meaningful community. Deeply riven over questions of race, class, and sexual orientation by the early 1970s, feminists could not claim a simple community based on gender sameness. In material terms, all women were not the same. Bodily self-determination meant different things for poor women and middle-class women, for black women and white women. The movement toward sexual liberation brought up conflicts not only between men and women, but also between black and white women. Community among people with such different material circumstances was not easily attainable. And when open hostility compounded simple acknowledgment of "difference," romantic notions of community became absurd.

The biologically based "female culture" lauded by cultural feminists in the mid-1970s offered to palliate some of these tensions among feminists. But while carrying forward the notion advanced earlier by both the women's health movement and by black feminists—that motherhood had the transcendent power to bring women closer to each other—cultural feminists also sensed the persistence of the sexual problematic in feminist theory. By purging motherhood of its sexual content, and by seeking to substitute motherhood for sexuality, cultural feminists were able to propose a solution to the tensions, centered largely around questions of sexuality, between black and white women and between heterosexual women and lesbians in the movement.[1]

Tension within the Movement

Soured on the internal politics of the women's movement, Ti-Grace Atkinson declared sarcastically in 1970 that "sisterhood is powerful. It kills sisters."[2] From the earliest years of women's liberation, feminists had fought over questions of leadership style and identification with the Left. By the early 1970s, these disagreements extended to bitter debate about alleged classism and racism within the "sisterhood," and to deep divisions between heterosexuals and lesbians in the movement.[3] By 1973, as raucous battles even within the lesbian feminist community ensued, many feminists felt both discouraged and angry.[4] Factionalism and antipathy, rather than unity and "sisterhood," seemed to characterize the movement.

Early women's liberation conferences suffered from internal controversy, and groups splintered with regularity. Much of the early tension derived from the divergent political backgrounds of the movement's initial participants. Not surprisingly, women who had spent years in the Left, and who identified as socialists or Marxists in some way, analyzed their own oppression and their political commitments differently from women for whom feminism represented a first political identification. Early feminists challenged one another immediately about the relationship of feminism to the larger "anti-imperialist" Left. This initial "feminist" versus "politico" split haunted the movement, as women who cast gender as the primary (or sole) oppression of women opposed those who sought closer alliances with other leftist organizations, including male-dominated groups like SDS, the Weathermen, and the Black Panther Party.[5] Ideological opposition often took the brutal form of personal attack. Women accused of usurping too much power within the movement, of interacting too forcefully, or of not conforming to an antielitist, egalitarian ethos were "trashed," or purged from the very organizations they had helped to form.[6]

While some activists blamed men or outside "agents" for fomenting the divisions, others tried to salvage a sense of unity. Alice Rossi, then an associate professor of sociology at Goucher College, wrote in 1971 that "diversity within a movement can be a strength, for there is no one problem or one solution."[7] Other groups, such as Cell 16, cited the divisions between women as further evidence that women's conditioning under patriarchy led them to internalize false identifications with various oppressors; liberation could only come if women identified *as women,* and formed their strategy accordingly.[8]

But simplified gender analyses became increasingly difficult to promote as feminists began to explore the significance of class and classism in the women's movement. Working-class women began to challenge the middle-class assumptions of other women within the movement, accusing the middle class of prioritizing issues that bore little relation to working-class life. An angry opinion piece in the journal *It Ain't Me, Babe* in August 1970, for instance, proclaimed:

Everyone keeps talking about a mass women's movement. But the "women's movement" clearly doesn't want anything to do with masses, or even a few women like us; we're too needy for them. It's an elite movement exuding slimy contempt as it slips along in cahoots with various ruling class men. . . . Seems things are falling along old class lines. Seems some of us aren't nice enough, aren't polite enough, aren't smart enough, aren't slick enough, aren't revolutionary enough, aren't cool enough for the classy women's movement.[9]

Among heterosexual radical and socialist feminists, and perhaps most strongly within lesbian feminist groups, controversy over class raged in the movement by the early 1970s.[10]

Similarly, as more and more women began to identify privately and publicly as lesbians, they began to point out the heterosexist assumptions that undergirded much of the women's movement. Heterosexual women sometimes responded with hostility, rejecting the lesbian vanguardist position that "feminism is the theory, lesbianism is the practice."[11] The controversy over lesbianism had exploded early on in the liberal wing of the women's movement with Betty Friedan eschewing a feminist focus on sexuality and dubbing lesbians a "lavender menace."[12] While the radical wing of the movement treated lesbianism more seriously, fierce controversies erupted nevertheless over whether lesbians represented "truer" feminists than heterosexual women, over homophobia within the women's movement, and over a host of other, subtler issues. As the distressed editors of the Boston-based journal *Second Wave* wrote in 1973,

Tensions have recently re-emerged in Female Liberation around questions of sexuality: Lesbians and straight women each feeling oppressed by the other; women confused about their own sexuality and shy of labeling; women concerned about a lack of support for Lesbian issues. Conflicts about sexuality in general have been responsible for cross-intimidation of straight women and Lesbians; women who have not defined their sexuality have been lost in the shuffle.[13]

Finally, the ever-rankling question of racism and racial inclusiveness suffused all of the protests about class, sexuality, and other differences within the women's movement. This controversy often sounded one-sided, with black activist women chiding the primarily white women's movement for its failure to address itself to their specific concerns, and with white feminists abjuring their own ineffectiveness in "reaching" black women.[14] Among politicos and socialist feminists, the mandate to respond to the material situations of black women had always been emphasized, at least in writing. The socialist-feminist Bread and Roses collective, for example, wrote in 1970 that particular attention must be paid by feminists to the "kind of population control, on the national and international levels, which concentrates on controlling the population of non-whites," to the ways in which the "educational system and media in our country perpetuate undemocratic myths about the nature of women, working people, and black, brown, red and yellow people," and to the establishment of admissions policies at trade schools and universities "with preferential treatment of women from races and classes that have been discriminated against."[15] But many radical feminist groups, in expounding a theory of gender oppression, had defined racial oppression as secondary to, or part of, the primary subjugation of women as a sex-class. Dana Densmore of Cell 16, for instance, wrote in 1970, "Sexism is the most fundamental oppression faced by *any* woman. It is an attempt to avoid consciousness of women's oppression *as women* to concentrate on women worker's oppression as workers, welfare women's oppression as welfare recipients, black women's oppression as black, or to insist on that as being prior to women's oppression as women."[16] The tension between white feminists who sought to incorporate their analysis of racism into their understanding of sexism, and those who recognized racism as a distinct form of oppression confronting women of color, intensified in the early 1970s, especially as more black women began to challenge white feminists about their commitment to an inclusive "sisterhood."[17]

By 1973, participants in the West Coast Lesbian Feminist conference found themselves, as one woman wrote to the *Lesbian Tide,* "discouraged by the polarization and angry dialog, particularly that stemming from the issue of racism in our movement."[18] A black caucus formed at the conference, demanding that racism within the lesbian community be treated as a priority.[19] Black feminists throughout the movement issued similar demands. By the end of the year, black women had founded the National Black Feminist Organization, declaring the need to organize on their own behalf rather than struggle constantly against the racism within predominantly white women's groups.[20]

As feminists struggled with self-criticism and internal strife, they also met with growing opposition from without, as the New Right began to batten and mobilize in the wake of the Supreme Court's decision to legalize abortion. Antifeminism in mainstream politics and the press became the new weapon of an Old Right intent on reinvigorating its anticommunist, racist, and classist platforms.[21] This new assault only burdened an already freighted movement.

Attacked from every corner, battle-weary feminists listened with attentive hopefulness when some of their own began to rephrase the call for female unity in ways that promised to incorporate some of the antiracist, anticlassist, and antihomophobic analyses that had emerged in recent years.

"Mother Right": Salve for a Factionalized Sisterhood

In August 1973, *Ms.* magazine received an unexpected communiqué from Jane Alpert, a leftist militant who had become a fugitive in 1970 after failing to appear in court on charges of conspiracy to bomb federal offices.[22] Alpert was one of many militants who had

"gone underground" in the early 1970s, as factions of the American Left turned to acts of sabotage and violence to protest what
they saw as the intractability of the American "military-industrial"
establishment.[23] Alpert's former lover, Sam Melville, had been imprisoned for the attempted bombing of the National Guard armory
in New York City, in addition to various actual bombings of
government property. He died in the riots at Attica prison in 1971.
For the Left, from whose ranks so many radical feminists had
come, Alpert's name carried a certain authority and cachet. At
Alpert's request, *Ms.* published her article, which was styled in part
as an open letter to the women of the militant leftist vanguard
group, the Weather Underground.[24]

"Mother Right" opened with an account of Alpert's personal
course of disenchantment with the male-dominated Left. In contrast to the eulogistic prose she had written for the introduction to
Melville's published prison letters a year earlier, here Alpert cen-
sured his sexism so sharply that she declared herself emotionally
immune to his or his prison comrades' deaths: "I will mourn the
loss of 42 male supremacists no longer."[25] Instead, Alpert wrote,
through her fugitive peregrinations of the United States, she had
discovered a sense of commonality with the many and diverse
women she had met. She had witnessed, in organized consciousness-raising groups, but also in the unformed rumblings of ordinary women, the beginnings of feminist awareness: "I could see
women everywhere—white, black, brown, Indian—responding in
their daily lives to the fact that some women somewhere had said,
'Men oppress us.' "[26] So different in material circumstances, so
different even in the language they possessed to analyze their oppression, the women Alpert encountered, and most particularly the
women she met through her San Diego consciousness-raising
group, "discovered in each other . . . the pulse of a culture and a
consciousness which was common to us as women."[27] Feminists
had debated the source of women's apparent commonality, most
blaming men's oppressive treatment of women as a sex-class defined first and foremost biologically. In response, most feminists

had disavowed the primacy of women's biology and minimized the meaning of physical differences between men and women.[28] That feminist goal was misguided, Alpert concluded; it was counterintuitive, for *"it contradicts our felt experience of the biological difference between the sexes as one of immense significance."*[29]

Alpert called for a new feminist theory that embraces the uniqueness of female biology, because *"female biology is the basis of women's powers."*[30] The creative core of female biology, according to Alpert, is the procreative potential possessed by all women. All women, whether mothers or not, are designed to bear and to suckle children. In the service of that capacity, women, historically and currently, develop a particular set of psychological and behavioral traits. In ancient times, she said, those traits had enabled women to rule spectacular matriarchal societies, and in contemporary society they were the wellspring of the nascent feminist consciousness she applauded. Not an inevitable source of women's subjugation, as Shulamith Firestone claimed, but rather the primary source of female power, the body alone contained the seeds of liberation:

It is conceivable that the intrinsic *biological* connection between mother and embryo or mother and infant gives rise to those *psychological* qualities which have always been linked with women, both in ancient lore and modern behavioral science. . . . Feminist culture is based on what is best and strongest in women, and as we begin to define ourselves as women, the qualities coming to the fore are the same ones a mother projects in the best kind of nurturing relationship to a child: empathy, intuitiveness, adaptability, awareness of growth as a process rather than as goal-ended, inventiveness, protective feelings toward others, and a capacity to respond emotionally as well as rationally.[31]

On a basis of biological commonality, Alpert envisioned absolute female rapprochement in her theory of "Mother Right":

Because motherhood cuts across economic class, race, and sexual preference, a society in which women were powerful by virtue of being mothers would not be divided along any of these lines. Nor would any new division between women, such as between mothers and childless women, arise, because the root of motherhood and the root of female consciousness are, I believe, one and the same.[32]

Alpert proposed a strongly universalizing theory of womanhood. Unlike many radical feminists before her who had claimed that women, by virtue of their gender, and perhaps by virtue of their biology, shared certain common experiences, which were then refracted by the vagaries of culture, class, race, and sexual orientation, Alpert claimed that all women were essentially the same.

Well-versed in Marxist theory, Alpert could not make this claim on materialist grounds. She reverted, therefore, to mysticism. She subverted a historical materialist analysis by claiming a mythologized matriarchal past for all women. Admitting that research claiming to prove the existence of ancient matriarchies was tentative, Alpert minimized the importance of "scientific" historical proof. More important, she declared, was the feeling of power that belief in such theories fostered in women. In her eyes, the feminist project needed to shift from an externalized search for vestiges of female power to an internalized, spiritual quest for a feeling of connectedness to one's own body, which would in turn put one in touch with the true, essential source of female power:

It seems to me that the power of the new feminist culture, the powers which were attributed to the ancient matriarchies (considered either as historical fact or as mythic archetypes), and the inner power with which many women are beginning to feel in touch and which is the soul of feminist art, may all arise from the same source. That source is none other than the female biology: the *capacity* to bear and nurture children.[33]

In a stroke of equalizing pluralism, Alpert declared that in the deep hidden history of all societies lay a trampled matriarchal past in which women not only wielded economic and political power, but were also regarded as transcendently powerful spiritual beings. This theory allowed for unique ethnic and racial histories, while claiming a common gender history: Each woman had her own foremothers, valuable to her, while all women shared a hypothetical historical era of unity in matriarchy and mother worship. Because the seeds of this power now lay dormant in the female body, some feeling of community could once again be claimed or created, even in the presence of actual difference.

Alpert also mystified the relevance of women's current material circumstances by defining motherhood not as something relational, involving actual mothers and children, but as something immanent that was about to emerge. She wrote that "motherhood itself is only the concrete expression of that potential which defines *all* women."[34] Women, bound by a common procreative potential, shared a mythical past and a probable future. On the basis of that motherly potential and all that it implied, Alpert theorized, women ought to be able to find common cause in the present. But as Alpert herself noted, feelings of solidarity, or even actual movements for change, based on inward perceptions, were more conducive to spiritual than political revolutions. In the spirit of immanentism, Alpert believed that feminism would draw out into daily existence the abstract spirit or quality (motherliness) that was covered over by patriarchy, but that, if actualized, would bring the feminist millennium. Drawing heavily from the utopianism and essentialism of the cultural left, Alpert further mystified those tendencies and shifted her interpretation of motherhood into the terrain of religion, where felt immanence sustains belief in a perfected future. As Alpert concluded the article:

Feminism concerns more than political power, essential as *that* is. It is closely tied to theories of awakening consciousness, of creation and rebirth, and of the essential oneness of the universe—teachings which lie at the heart of all Goddess-worshipping religions. . . . Could it not be that just at the moment masculinity has brought us to the brink of nuclear destruction or ecological suicide, women are beginning to rise in response to the Mother's call to save Her planet and create instead the next stage of evolution? Can our revolution mean anything else than the reversion of social and economic control to Her representatives among Womankind, and the resumption of Her worship on the face of the Earth? *Do we dare demand less?*[35]

In retrospect, Alpert's piece appears to have ushered in an unprecedented era of feminist attention to a mystified, spiritualized vision of motherhood. From its publication on, the ideas she discussed have dominated many segments of the women's movement. Even upon its publication, some feminists declared the "Mother Right" theory revolutionary, new, and powerful.[36] But in fact, Alpert's work had been foreshadowed by numerous other feminist writings.[37] It is best read as a well-publicized, all-inclusive, and perhaps more stark version of many ideas that were beginning to be discussed in feminist circles in the early 1970s.

Both the women's health movement and black feminist activists had already begun to place motherhood at the center of feminist concern and to invest it with supposed powers beyond actual procreativity. Like many in the women's health movement, Alpert came to feminism by way of her involvement in the culture and politics of the Left. While "Mother Right" claimed to reject the Left, it nevertheless bore that movement's cultural mark: its essentialism, its belief in the elysian promise of the flesh, its prizing of "process" over "product," its search for authentic communication, and its recognition of human interconnectedness. In the late 1960s and early 1970s, many feminists had already invested motherhood with the power to bring women closer to some of those countercultural ideals; mothers, they claimed, were closer to nature, more likely to endorse peace and ecology, and inclined toward acts of protective love for their own, or the human, race. Although isolated personally, Alpert was not cut off from the vast body of feminist writing being produced during her years as a fugitive, and she drew her theory in part from the corpus of Left-influenced feminist thought that presented motherhood in a positive light.[38]

Similarly, "Mother Right" echoed the positive emphasis on motherhood that characterized black feminist thought in the late 1960s and early 1970s. Alpert may or may not have read the work of Patricia Robinson, Angela Davis, or other black feminists who attempted to redefine "matriarchy." More to the point, Alpert, like the radical women who "discovered" motherhood through their support for the imprisoned Panther women, had a long history of involvement with those on the Left who believed that blacks, as the more oppressed group, should constitute the vanguard of the movement.[39] While a fugitive, Alpert maintained contact with well-known writer and activist Robin Morgan, who had also emerged angrily from the Left into a feminist stance that included among its goals rapprochement with black women.[40] Morgan, and then Alpert, expressed in their writing the desire to seek "sisterhood" with women of color.[41] Both owe an unspoken debt to those very "sisters" for providing some of the earliest language and imagery of a fully reconstructed, positive view of mothering.

White feminists had also begun to explore the meaning of matriarchy for women, although their explorations, in the early 1970s, remained more tentative than African American women's concerted and immediate discursive struggle. As early as 1968, at the Lake Villa Conference and in meetings of New York Radical Women, women expressed interest in learning about historical matriarchies and in championing the maternal values supposed to have ruled ancient societies.[42] In 1971, theorist Elizabeth Gould Davis published *The First Sex,* citing archaeological "proof" of an ancient period of matriarchal rule.[43] Two years later, Anchor Press reprinted Helen Diner's *Mothers and Amazons,* a book originally published in German in 1932, also claiming the existence of a historical matriarchy and exploring the symbolic importance of the powerful, even deified, mother figure.[44]

Surprisingly, members of The Feminists had become early adherents of matriarchist beliefs. After Ti-Grace Atkinson left the organization, members began to study ancient matriarchy and mother-worshiping religions and ultimately evolved their own religious ritual in which they chanted "Momma" while dismantling the effigy of a naked man![45]

Cell 16, which rivaled The Feminists for its early critique of motherhood and its separatist stance, also began to shift early on from a virulent contempt for anyone male or male-influenced to what historian Alice Echols calls a "revaluation of femininity."[46]

The group's leading theorist, Roxanne Dunbar, began to write words of praise for what she now saw as desirable "maternal" traits: "a certain consciousness of care for others, flexibility, non-competitiveness, cooperation, and materialism."[47] These traits had been inscribed upon women by "the oppressor," but in the end they would be used to defeat the reigning "masculine ideology." Dunbar concluded that "by destroying the present society, and building a society based on feminist principles, men will be forced to live in the human community on terms very different from the present."[48]

Echols attributes these separatists' interest in matriarchy and eternal feminine traits to their deep-seated essentialism, which led them to view men and women as irrevocably different biologically and thus temperamentally, with women's bodies as the locus of all that is good and life-giving. She finds it not unreasonable that such a view would, in time, lead these groups to reconsider their earlier, negative view of women's procreative capacity.[49]

These groups also faced the dilemma that confronted Jane Alpert and all radical feminists intent on pursuing a strict gender analysis in the face of actual differences between women: They wanted to extend the feminist movement beyond the vanguard to reach "the masses," but were unable to reach a community of women suffering from the false consciousness of "male-identification." In the face of this dilemma, Cell 16, The Feminists, Jane Alpert, and numerous other white feminists posited a primeval time of primal bonding. Ultimately, feminists could bond with other women, and against men, by looking backward for a model of the "female principle" in ancient matriarchies. Mythical maternalism became the key to sisterhood. Whatever a woman's current conditioning, her common descent from the Great Mother made her a sister. All women had something in common with each other, and virtually nothing in common with men.[50] In the context of essentialist thought, it is not surprising that these feminists expressed the metaphorical connectedness they sought through umbilical imagery.

Other white feminists in search of a united sisterhood, but not intent on finding it through historical or religious matriarchy, had also moved closer to Alpert's vision by the early 1970s. Inspired not so much by their analysis of male-female relations as by their distress over intramovement disputes, a number of feminist writers in the early 1970s had ventured that women worldwide possessed a common "culture."

Occasional declarations of a women's culture based on essential "feminine" traits appeared in the feminist press in its earliest years. A woman writing under the name Starr asserted in the Bay Area journal *It Ain't Me, Babe* in 1970 that "women do have a common way of thinking; our ideology has been unspoken because we live in a male culture that is not ours and denies our culture its expression."[51] In the same issue two authors identified only as Peggy and Dianne defined "woman's culture" as a "culture of feelings, of intense communication, of breaking out of isolation."[52] In recognition of that alleged culture, Ann Forfreedom wrote in the journal *Lesbian Tide,* following the West Coast Lesbian Conference of April 1973, that the disputes between women in the movement paled in comparison to the "love and energy" that eventually united the conference participants, as they swayed to the music of the band Family of Woman, melded into "one great moving, twisting, ecstatic mass of womankind."[53] Only one "being-with-a-penis" disrupted the weekend-long conference, Forfreedom wrote, and thus the "reborn female culture" prevailed over the hostility that so often overshadowed "sisterhood" in the women's movement.[54] Unlike the more widely known radical feminist analysis, which sought to eradicate "patriarchy" and equalize the power relations between women and men, thereby freeing women to develop into liberated, actualized people, this type of analysis prefigured cultural feminism in its supposition of an a priori "female culture" or set of traits that would reemerge if the (male) obstacles were simply removed.

Other early writings made more explicit the link between women's culture and women's biology, a link crucial to the feminist theory later articulated by Jane Alpert. "The Fourth World Manifesto," arguably the most prominent early example of cultural feminism, was written by a group of feminists in protest of what they saw as the covert "male Left," as opposed to truly feminist, agenda of a women's liberation conference for North American and Indochinese women in 1971.[55] Printed in *Notes from the Third Year* for a wide feminist audience, the manifesto blamed the male Left for insinuating false divisions between women and declared that all women—more fundamentally than blacks or Third World peoples—had been "colonized" by all men—"And the territory was and remains our women's bodies."[56] Because of this "colonization," women worldwide needed to struggle together for their freedom as women, rather than siphoning off their energy in internecine dispute or in male-led anti-imperialist or nationalist movements. With the recognition that "the Female Liberation Movement must cut across all (male-imposed) class, race, and national lines," women needed to identify their common traits, perhaps forged through oppression, but now the basis of a distinct female "culture."[57] The original source of that separate culture lay in women's childbearing capacity and child-rearing role; over time it evolved into "the female culture of emotion, intuition, love, personal relationships, etc."[58] Now, the authors claimed, only the proud assertion of the "female principle" would bring about a "truly human society."[59]

Robin Morgan, who had the most direct impact on Alpert, was also one of the foremost proponents of total sisterhood, in the name of the female body and its ties to "nature," to emerge in the early 1970s. In her often-reprinted rejection of the male Left, "Goodbye to All That," first published in 1970, she stated that "white males are most responsible for the destruction of human life and environment on the planet today."[60] All women, on the other hand, are "unavoidably aware of the locked-in relationship between humans and their biosphere—the earth, the tides, the atmosphere, the moon."[61] Women must therefore band together, "Sisters all, with only one real alternative: to seize our power into our own hands, all women, separate and together, and make the Revolution the way it must be made."[62] In her address to the West Coast Lesbian Feminist Conference, Morgan declared that "all women have a right to each other as women. All women have a right to our sense of ourselves as a People."[63] Therefore, she said, "if we can open ourselves *to* ourselves and each other, as women, only then can we begin to fight for and create . . . a real Feminist Revolution, a proud gynocratic *world* that runs on the power of women."[64]

By the time "Mother Right" appeared in August 1973, all of its major points had been raised repeatedly by other feminists. Nevertheless, Alpert pioneered the compilation of these disparate strands of feminist essentialism, universalism, and spiritualism, under the guise of maternalism, at a moment when the women's movement was in a state of particular disarray. Her theory, pacific and totalizing, promised a new chance for feminist community, in terms that preserved most of the values of the cultural left even as it rejected contact with the organized political Left.

Cultural Feminism: Motherhood As a Mask for Difference

The ideas of Alpert and other fledgling cultural feminists did not simply overtake the women's movement. "Mother Right," and Alpert herself, generated controversy within the movement for several years. Many feminists dissented from the totalizing views of cultural feminism, remaining committed to community-based activism, to race and class analysis, and to sexual liberation. These women continued to fight for reproductive rights and day care; their understanding of motherhood remained materialist, their politics activist.[65] However, large segments of the women's movement shifted toward an essentialized, universalized, and spiritualized understanding of women's nature, and this understanding frequently rested on a view of women as "mothers," in Alpert's abstract definition. Despite dissent from socialist feminists, old-style radical feminists, and many African American feminists, cultural feminism by 1976 became an important force within the women's movement.

After an initial flurry of excitement in the feminist press over Alpert's communique, with letters in support, letters in dispute, and a general increase in the discussion of matriarchy, motherhood, and women's essential, maternal nature, Alpert herself became an object of scandal.[66] Soon after she surrendered to federal authorities in November 1974, rumors began to spread in leftist and leftist-feminist circles that she had informed the government of the whereabouts of another fugitive, Pat Swinton. That alleged transgression seemed unforgivable to those on the Left who felt increasingly besieged by *agents provocateurs* and overt police attack. Feminists divided sharply in their support or condemnation of Alpert. To Ti-Grace Atkinson and others, Alpert was a privileged white woman who had betrayed her comrade in struggle, and who ought to be ostracized from the movement. To others, particularly the well-known feminists who would soon become leading proponents of cultural feminism, Alpert was a strong, even heroic, feminist.[67] If anyone in the movement had missed the publication of "Mother Right" itself, they could not fail to learn of Alpert's plight, or the ideas she stood for, from the controversy surrounding her after her surrender.

While much of the controversy about Alpert had to do with feminism's relationship to the Left, Alpert's views themselves also generated detractors. Not all feminists accepted her theory of universal femaleness. Some radical feminists were distressed over the drift of the movement toward spiritualism, unexamined universalism, essentialism, matriarchalism, and desexualized maternalism. Two well-known socialist feminists, Heather Booth and Naomi Weisstein, made a powerful plea to the feminist community in 1975 to stay cognizant of the many problems requiring social activism, and not mysticism, as a curative. Labeling cultural feminism as a form of "ghost dancing," Booth and Weisstein wrote, "Believing that things are true because we want them to be true won't save us. Our amulets and tarot cards, our runes and signs and tea leaves, the ancient craft of Wicce, the current astrology, lost matriarchies, Mother Rights, won't protect us. Mysticism will divert us from the real struggle at hand; it will accelerate our defeat."[68] A presupposed "women's consciousness" could neither heal actual rifts between women in the movement nor lead to material improvement in women's lives.[69] Similarly, Brooke Williams of Redstockings wrote that the growing obsession with matriarchy among feminists did not translate into actual power for mothers or other women, because the focus on matriarchy "promptly mythologizes the idea of power, bases it on morality, and sets it in the past."[70] Karen Lindsey, a radical feminist writer and activist, decried the deradicalization of the discussion of childbearing, stating that "control over one's own body and one's own life is the real political question."[71] Such materialist views persisted, but were increasingly uncommon in a movement that leapt at the image of all women as incipient mothers. Cultural feminism gained strength, but not complete hegemony, in the mid-1970s.

African American women in particular rejected the erasure of difference that cultural feminism entailed. While white cultural feminists were gathering steam in the name of a revalorized view of motherhood that black women had helped to formulate, African American feminists were attempting to solidify a nationwide black feminist organization. After the first Eastern Regional Conference on Black Feminism met in New York City in November 1973, Alice Walker wrote to *Ms.* magazine that she and the four hundred other women present had felt "freed at last to speak to ears that would not automatically begin to close."[72] To Walker and others, the predominantly white women's movement, for all its talk of sisterhood, still failed to address the specific concerns of black women. Theories of women's sameness incorporated rather than challenged racism. Black women needed, more than ever, to focus on their own "sisters," as one conference participant wrote, because their "needs were being shoved in the background, if recognized at all, by white feminists and black men alike."[73]

Within the predominantly white segments of the women's movement, however, cultural feminism began to take hold. The trickle of articles in the feminist press, prior to the publication of "Mother Right," about a female consciousness, matriarchy, feminist spirituality, and maternalism became a torrent by 1974. Often without direct reference to Alpert, many writers began to recapitulate her ideas. For instance, an article entitled "Energizing the Feminine Principle Today" in the July 1974 *Big Mama Rag* stated that "the feminine principle of life, nurturance, balance, and harmony is the principle of the earth itself."[74] Echoing Alpert, the author continued, "This feminine principle—that which is maternal, materialist and peaceful (noncompetitive)—must, for the survival of us all, be reasserted at all levels of interaction. It is woman, the biological female, who can reaffirm this principle through her own self-knowledge."[75] Through the experience of mothering, in other words, women can know themselves, know each other, and exist in harmony with nature.[76]

In a prescient article written in 1974, poet and philosopher Susan Griffin, who would soon emerge as a prominent cultural feminist author, wrote movingly of her own experiences as a mother. Like Alpert, she saw great power in the maternal role. Couched in reminiscences of the everyday events of child rearing, Griffin's tentatively preferred theory of motherhood endows the mother/daughter bond with transcendent power. In tending to her daughter, Griffin gains a deeper understanding of herself. Motherhood becomes a route to self-healing and, above all, to understanding and identifying with other women.

And yet I take the part of the child, too. The wild child. I remember my fury at the constrictions placed upon me as a child. I remember the look of innocence on my daughter's face, and how I wanted her life to be perfect; how I wanted her to suffer nothing that I suffered. . . . And that when I realized that I had given birth to a girl child my heart opened to myself and all the suffering of women seemed unreasonable to me.[77]

Motherhood affords literal communion between mother and child, while on a symbolic level it allows women to commune with each other, and with the inner, unhealed, unmothered, childlike aspects of themselves. The feminist longing for community is transmuted here into a highly personal and psychological form of bonding.

With remarkable prolificness, feminist writers began to treat motherhood as a symbolic, idealized paradigm for a wide range of relationships and experiences. In the article "Who Was Rembrandt's Mother?" Jackie St. Joan wrote that she intended to "examine motherhood as a model of feminist leadership." [78] Another writer invoked the maternalist myth of Demeter and Persephone to assert that women, as nurturers, understood the "sentience of plants," whereas men exploited and plundered nature, creating destruction while women generated life. [79]

In perhaps the most striking development of this period, writer after writer joined the growing feminist spirituality movement, in which the Great Mother, now conceived of as a goddess as well as a historical matriarch, became both a deity and a role model for contemporary women. [80] This aspect of cultural feminism drew in many women early on, as evidenced by the throngs in attendance at the first national conference on women's spirituality, held in Boston in 1976, and devoted to "the goddess." As early as 1968, feminist theologian Mary Daly had contrasted the holistic, communalistic potential of a female-centered religion with the alienating and destructive thrust of patriarchal religions. In 1973, when she published *Beyond God the Father,* her ideas found a wider feminist audience. [81] Popular variations of her theology saturated the women's movement by the mid-1970s, as writers redefined feminism as "a resurgence of woman power and attunement to the cycles and harmonies of our mother, the earth, as we listen through our bodies to that unity." [82] From reinvigorated explorations of matriarchy to paeans to belly dancing—historically a "preparation for childbirth as well as a celebrant's homage to the ancient archetypal 'Earth Mother' deity"—symbolic renditions of motherhood flooded feminist writing. [83]

These trends in feminist thinking reached their peak in *Of*

Woman Born: Motherhood As Experience and Institution by poet Adrienne Rich.[84] Published in 1976, Rich's work combed the fields of history, anthropology, mythology, psychology, literature, and feminist theory to arrive at the bold conclusion that "the repossession by women of our bodies will bring far more essential change to human society than the seizing of the means of production by workers."[85] A complex, far-reaching meditation on the meaning of motherhood, *Of Woman Born* cannot be categorized blithely, for the text also contributes powerfully to a feminist discourse of maternal ambivalence and anger. Nevertheless, a cultural feminist analysis inheres.

Patriarchy, Rich asserted, had alienated women from the powerful potential with which their procreative capacity endowed them. Under centuries of patriarchal rule, motherhood had been distorted into an oppressive, or at best vapid, institution. In agreement with the women's health movement, Rich wrote that the medicalization of birth had denied women an unalienated sense of their own bodies. Psychology and psychiatry had pathologized the mother-child relationship, leaving guilt and violence in the place of a joyful bond. Motherhood as a current institution had little to commend it. But motherhood, freed from the contortions through which patriarchal society put it, could also be the locus of female self-actualization. In ancient history—when women ruled actual, not mythical, "gynarchies," when people worshiped beneficent goddesses of fertility rather than vengeful, angry gods, when women controlled their own birthings—motherhood had been a positive force. Women knew their own bodies. From that knowledge emanated personal and collective strength. The goal for women today, Rich argued, must be to recover that bodily sense of self. Rich asserted that "female biology—the diffuse, intense sensuality radiating out from clitoris, breasts, uterus, vagina; the lunar cycles of menstruation; the gestation and fruition of life which can take place in the female body—has far more radical implications than we have come to appreciate."[86] Those implications applied to all women; like Alpert, Rich stressed the immanent bodily potential for motherhood, rather than the physical production of children. If women could be free to "touch the unity and resonance of our physicality, our bond with the natural order, the corporeal ground of our intelligence," if women could learn "*to think through the body*," then by reclaiming motherhood as experience rather than institution they could better their own lives, bond with each other, and ultimately alter the course of human history.[87]

In Rich's writing, as in the work of many feminist theorists of motherhood of this period, the language and the longings of the counterculture of the 1960s linger palpably. The belief that the body, unmediated by the effects of technology or social institutions, possesses the key to self-knowledge, communion with nature, and connection to other people, had been a major tenet of countercultural thought. The spiritual and sensual transcendence promised by Rich's vision of uncompromised motherhood resembles strongly the holistic, nonalienated existence sought by countercultural communards and naturalists. The promise of joyful unification, of organic community, without the striations of difference imposed by a corrupt culture, is at heart the same promise in cultural feminism's view of motherhood as in the cultural left's reconceptualization of family and community.

But just as the counterculture ignored the significance of gender in order to combine the prizing of nature and the search for community with the pursuit of sexual liberation, cultural feminism's vision of motherhood could not reconcile a lusty acceptance of sexuality with its romance of the body and nature and its plaintive call for community among women.[88] In the work of Alpert, Daly, Griffin, Rich, and the many other theorists who helped to reconceptualize feminism in strongly maternalist terms, sexuality is either downplayed, ignored, or, more commonly, redefined as a diffuse sensuality more akin to spiritual ecstasy than to the customary pleasures of the flesh.[89]

Some writers explain the erasure of sexuality from cultural feminist theories of motherhood as a residual effect of a deep, psychologically based cultural bias against maternal sexuality.[90] Of at least equal importance, however, are the social and political exigencies of the women's movement that spawned cultural feminism. Many of the tensions within the movement coalesced around questions of sexuality, which led cultural feminists to seek palliative solutions. Thus, the cultural feminist emphasis on desexualized motherhood has often been understood as a strategy, more or less deliberate, to neutralize the tensions between lesbians and heterosexual women in the movement.[91] Among those feminists who were receptive to its message, cultural feminism did indeed act as a salve by rendering sexuality symbolic and incorporating the sexual into the spiritual and the maternal. If neither heterosexuals nor lesbians are defined by their specific sexual interests, it becomes more obvious, in cultural feminist terms, that they possess in common an a priori physicality, energized by an immanent, sensually rich maternity. As women, they are more alike than estranged.

Numerous theorists began to define lesbianism in this way in the mid-1970s, thereby rendering the concept less threatening to heterosexuals. Lesbianism became "a life that draws its strength, support and direction from women."[92] Men, wrote Rita Mae Brown, "because they can only think of women in sexual terms, define Lesbian as sex between women."[93] This dilution of the meaning of the sexual is suggested in Rich's theory, which likens the "diffuse" sensuality of the clitoris and vagina to the unity of body, spirit, mind, and community enabled by motherhood in its nonpatriarchal form. In an even more explicit redefinition of sexuality, Sue Silvermarie described lesbian sex itself as a series of explorations into the meaning of motherhood:

In loving another woman I discovered the deep urge to both be a mother to and find a mother in my lover. . . . It is most clear in lovemaking, when the separation of everyday life lifts for awhile. When I kiss and stroke and enter my lover, I am also a child re-entering my mother. I want to return to the womb-state of harmony, and also to the ancient world. I enter my lover but it is she in her orgasm who returns. I see on her face for a long moment, the unconscious bliss that an infant carries the memory of behind its shut eyes. Then when it is she who makes love to me, I feel myself opening and opening, wanting more and more for her to come inside. When the rush begins, I say "push," and I mean in but the intensity is also a pushing out, a borning! She comes in and is then identified with the ecstasy that is born. I have at once the fulness of being impregnated with her and the emptiness of giving birth. So I too return to the mystery of my mother, and of the world as it must have been when the motherbond was exalted.[94]

Though still in the terrain of kissing, touching, and orgasm, the sex described here is at heart comforting and safe, deriving its emotional power primarily from its similarity to the birth process; the woman experiences physical pleasure, but more important, on a symbolic level she is born, gives birth, bonds with her own mother, and glimpses the "ancient world." As Sally Gearhart and Peggy Cleveland wrote in an equally vivid transposition of lesbian sex into spiritualism and maternalism, "The sexual and spiritual functions of our lives are potentially a unity."[95] Patriarchal society had separated the two functions, causing a disease called "Stilps." The cure for "Stilps" could only be found in "woman-love," defined by Gearhart and Cleveland as "remembering our mothers, inventing our daughters, claiming our histories and moving to touch and mend the hurts of other women."[96] A less sexual or more maternalistic definition of lesbianism would be difficult to imagine.

When the debate over pornography polarized the women's movement in the late 1970s, with antipornography advocates deploying the cultural feminist vision of diffuse, symbolically maternal sexuality as the only acceptable form of female sexuality, numerous "pro-sex" feminist critics traced the elision of sexuality from feminist discourse to the search, however misguided, for a cure for the lesbian/straight divide in the movement. But perhaps equally important, cultural feminists' deployment of the desexualized mother figure targeted *racial* rapprochement as strongly as it sought to unify the movement in other ways. If the lesbian/straight split in the movement seemed vitriolic in the early 1970s, racial tensions pervaded the movement with as much tenacity by the time Alpert published "Mother Right" in 1973. Arguably, the cultural feminist vision of a universally bonded womanhood based on biologically immanent motherhood promised to unite black and white women as strongly as it promised to unite lesbians and heterosexuals—perhaps more so, because black women themselves often stressed motherhood as a central feature of women's lives. If sexuality presented an obstacle to the bonding of white women of differing sexual orientations, it represented an equally severe impediment to an interracial sisterhood. Cultural feminism's ultimate sacrifice of sexuality was intricately intertwined with racial politics.

White feminists seldom wrote about the heterosexual rivalry between black and white women. Their silence, perhaps born of guilt, perhaps of ignorance, is conspicuous compared to the frequency and fury of black women's condemnation of sexual relations between black men and white women. While white feminists asked, ever ingenuous, why black women would not "join" the feminist movement, many black women rejoined furiously that they could not unite with the very women who were "stealing" their men.

These grievances began to be articulated in the Civil Rights movement in the mid-1960s. When the "freedom summer" project drew hundreds of white student activists to Mississippi in 1964, black women in SNCC began to decry the ease with which black men and white women were entering into sexual relationships. A male SNCC leader remarked that white women spent that summer "on their backs, servicing not only the SNCC workers but anybody else who came." [97] To some observers, it seemed that the white women flaunted their sexuality, making themselves too readily available to any and all black men. To others, it seemed that many black men, long accustomed to regarding white women as "forbidden fruit," took advantage of young white women too afraid of the charge of racism to refuse sex with a black man. [98] As Mary King, a veteran white SNCC staffer, wrote, "Sexual dalliances were one way for a volunteer to prove she was not racist and I'm certain any number of black men manipulated this anxiety."[99] The net result, whatever the impetus, was a tremendous build-up of tension between black and white women in the organization. As King wrote, many black women "working side by side with black male colleagues all day, found that after hours some of the latter sought the company of the white women volunteers."[100] Many black women in the organization reported feeling betrayed; in SNCC, as in the wider society, they were encouraged to work as the equals of men, while white women were idealized for their beauty, their sexual desirability, and their "femininity."[101] King feels that black women's anger about this form of rejection helped to push SNCC toward its eventual black separatist stance.[102]

The Black Power movement of the 1960s adopted the slogan "black is beautiful." Young African Americans released their hair into Afros, wore African dashikis, and tried to reconstruct a concept of beauty that did not derive from a European norm. Many black women hoped that black men in the movement would challenge the damaging historical construction of the white woman as the object of romantic choice, the "flower of womanhood." The sanctification of white womanhood had caused black men and women unspeakable pain for centuries: The alleged rape by black men of white women had served as the excuse for thousands of lynchings; black women had been sexualized and raped by white men during and since slavery; and black men, susceptible to the vilification of black women so prevalent in American culture, had often prized white women's beauty above that of black women. The movement toward black pride promised an "Afrocentric" definition of desirability.[103] Male Black Power advocates wrote odes to their "African queens," predicting that with black liberation, the black woman would "define herself" and "love her images."[104] To many black women, such expressions of admiration promised to soothe deep and longstanding wounds.

When some black men, in the height of the sexual revolution, and in spite of their professed devotion to "black pride," openly dated white women, many black women responded with anger and dismay. In a few instances, they directed their dismay toward the black men involved, as when poet June Jordan wrote, "let that white girl go." [105] Cellestine Ware wrote in 1970 that Julius Lester, then working at the New York radio station WBAI, "states very calmly that if he dies an unnatural death, it will probably be at the hands of a black woman enraged by his having a white wife." [106]

Much more commonly, however, black women expressed anger at the white women involved. Black sociologist Robert Staples reported, with understatement, in his 1973 book *The Black Woman in America,* that "one barrier to an effective coalition between Black and white women is their competition for Black men." He continued:

The sight of a Black man and white woman engaged in a romantic relationship has produced feelings of hostility and rage among Black women. Many Black women feel that Black men are being treated as stylish possessions or some "modish" prop of white women. . . . At a recent conference of Black women in Chicago, it was reported that the women present could not move to other concerns of the liberation of Black people because of the issue of Black men and white women. [107]

Many black women expressed the same ideas with passionate fury. At a symposium titled "The Black Woman: Myths and Realities," held at Radcliffe College in May 1973, Sheila Okpaku stated very clearly "why Black women have shunned women's lib. We are simply reluctant to align ourselves with the perennial enemy: THE WHITE WOMAN." [108] Ware reported that "all over New York, there have been actual battles between white women and black women over black men." [109] Joyce Ladner wrote that "one must note that very often it is the white woman who makes the sexual advances toward Black men." [110] And Abbey Lincoln seared the page in her essay, "Who Will Revere the Black Woman?": "We are the women whose bars and recreation halls are invaded by flagrantly disrespectful, bigoted, simpering, amoral, emotionally unstable, outcast, maladjusted, nymphomaniacal, condescending white women . . . in desperate and untiring search of the 'frothing-at-the-mouth-for-a-white-woman, strongbacked, sixty-minute hot black.' Our men." [111]

White feminists seldom wrote of this source of racial animosity among women, opting instead to focus on ways to gear the women's movement more precisely to black women's material needs, by fighting sterilization abuse or working to set up day care centers. However, the writings of a few white women indicate that there was some awareness within white feminist circles of these sexual tensions. [112] Within the framework of radical feminism, however, which often prized individual sexual liberation as highly as sisterhood, no easy solution emerged. Mired in racial guilt, fighting for their own sexual freedom, and trying in vain to "invite" black women into the movement, early white radical and socialist feminists faced a true dilemma.

When white cultural feminists introduced theories of universal womanhood based on maternal traits, qualities many black women valued highly, were they searching for common ground, for ways to ease racial tensions between women? The erasure of sexuality from cultural feminist thought suggests an attempt—sometimes explicit, sometimes not—to mollify a primary source of black women's hostility toward white women. In the climate of anger that surrounded the issue of lesbianism, and equally potently, the issue of heterosexual interracial sex, the transposition of sexuality into spirituality and symbolic maternalism held out some promise for reconciliation.

Conclusion

Cultural feminism drew many adherents. Feminist spirituality, eco-feminism, and antipornography activism all blossomed in the late 1970s, often in the name of the new maternalism envisioned by Alpert, Rich, and other leading theorists. But if cultural feminism temporarily quieted certain tensions, its ultimate goal of a unitary sisterhood remained elusive. Black feminism emerged in its own right as a major force in feminist thought by the end of the 1970s. Socialist feminists continued to stress race and class analyses and pursue social activism. Feminist psychoanalytic studies of motherhood, though perhaps encouraged by cultural feminists' attention to the topic, pointed the discussion of motherhood in new directions. And debates about sexuality, couched at first in the dispute over pornography, dominated the movement in the late 1970s and into the 1980s, with differing interpretations of motherhood at the very center of debate.

Chapter 5

"Maternal Thinking": Motherhood As Practice and Metaphor

*I*n the late 1970s and early 1980s, feminist writing on motherhood increased in both volume and depth. Trade, academic, and feminist presses all published major books on motherhood during this period, and feminist periodicals continued their intensive focus on the topic.[1] Two distinct yet overlapping trends manifested in the writing of this period.

Feminists began to address concertedly the daily experience of mothering.[2] From the perspective of both mother and daughter, writers began to discuss the feelings, values, and rituals surrounding motherhood. Assuming, as almost all feminists did by this point, that what mothers do is important, these writers took on the task of making mothering visible and then analyzing its minute yet significant aspects. In psychoanalytic studies, in personal narratives, and through the analytic and discursive mesh of a host of academic disciplines, writers affirmed and furthered the centrality of motherhood to feminist theory.

Concurrent with this energized attention to the material and psychological aspects of mothering, many feminists, in the pattern established by Jane Alpert, Adrienne Rich, and others, extrapolated the symbolic meanings of motherhood. Often pairing motherhood against sexuality, writers and activists interested in ecofeminism, feminist peace activism, and spiritual feminism, and opposed to pornography, treated mothers and motherhood, in abstract, metaphorical, and symbolic terms, as antidotal to the ills of "patriarchy." Along with feminist psychoanalytic theorists, they focused on differences between men and women, and likenesses among women, as they proposed mothering as the curative for troubled human relations and the erosion of authentic community.[3]

Both of these strands of feminist mothering theory continued to grapple with the profound and unresolved meanings of sexuality and community, as originally embraced by the cultural left. Motherhood, whether considered in concrete or abstract form, served as a cipher for feminist longing for a unified women's movement. In a larger sense, motherhood became a cipher for feminists' desire for "authentic" relationship, for connectedness and community. Early cultural feminists, attuned to women's difference from men and to the dangers intrinsic to that difference, had suggested that female solidarity could be forged through motherhood. As the previous chapter details, these claims to sisterhood in a racially and sexually embattled movement entailed transposing sexuality into "safe" maternalist rhetoric. But not all feminists were willing to accept that transposition. To some, the affirmative value of sexual liberation remained crucial to women's overall liberation, and mothering theory remained a contested terrain through which they pursued not only the search for community, but also the reconciliation of community and sexuality. While these differing resolutions to a shared dilemma polarized feminists in the late 1970s and early 1980s, causing many tentative alliances to devolve into absolute acrimony, they also highlight the continuity of countercultural discourse in feminist thought: Intent on an ideal of community, feminists explored the ways in which that ideal could be mediated through the flesh. Mothering theory, presented in widely divergent terms, became a way to discuss that mediation.

New Influences

Although feminist writers had paid close attention to the topic of motherhood since the 1960s, by the late 1970s that attention increased noticeably. While intramovement ideological and political struggle continued to motivate many feminists to foreground motherhood, other factors became particularly relevant to feminist mothering theory in this period. The aging of the baby boom generation, the entry of more feminists into the academy, the changing structure of feminist publishing, and the proliferation of "profamily" views at the right, left, and center of the political spectrum all influenced the scope and the content of feminist discourses on motherhood.

Many observers use demographics to explain the turn of the feminist pen toward motherhood. In the American population as a whole, but most particularly in the educated white middle class into which most women's liberationists fit, birth rates dropped during the early to mid-1970s. The overall American birth rate slid from 23.7 per thousand women in 1960 to 18.4 in 1970, and then continued to decline to 14.8 in 1975.[4] Demographers attribute this dip to the wide availability of birth control and abortion and to the widened options, especially higher education, available to women.[5] Some observers have asserted that the feminist critique of motherhood further dissuaded many women's liberationists from bearing children.[6] According to this reasoning, both economically and culturally, many middle-class women did not *have* to marry young and begin to rear children in the 1960s and 1970s, and so they did not. Yet most middle-class American women of this era did eventually bear children. Many delayed childbearing but did not, in the numbers suggested earlier in the 1970s, forego childbearing altogether. In short, as more middle-class women entered their thirties and completed their education, their sagging birth rate began to lift.[7] While it is difficult to parse out the birth rates of self-professed feminists versus non-feminists, in terms of generation, class, and educational level, most women's liberationists fall into the category of women who began, after a delay, to bear children in the mid-1970s. Because that trend coincides with the explosion of feminist writing on motherhood, many commentators see it as causal.

The content as well as the mere presence of one particular genre of feminist writing on motherhood from this period does lend credence to the demographers' hypothesis: In keeping with the radical feminist maxim that "the personal is political," several writers published detailed accounts of their own everyday experiences as new mothers. Adrienne Rich, in *Of Woman Born*, reveals the deep, daily ambivalence of rearing her sons.[8] Jane Lazarre's *The Mother Knot*, the preeminent example of the genre, also presents a close reading of mothering. Lazarre's story is that of a woman struggling to live up to an internalized image of the "good mother," while also fending off the depression and anger that threaten to overpower her as she feels her sense of "self" slipping away. Lazarre acknowledges the societal contribution to the conditions of her mothering—the isolation in which she and her child are locked; the ways in which others deny her many facets, seeing her now as "the mother"—but she emphasizes the interior experience of growth and change facilitated by motherhood. Lazarre assumes implicitly that mothering is so vital, of such immediate importance, that every insight into its meaning demands revelation. Her voice resembles that of a woman in a support group revealing her condition to others similarly situated. Reviewers responded in kind, noting that Lazarre's search for a workable way to mother mirrored and aided their own.[9] And many writers followed Lazarre's lead. Without apology, and with the absolute assumption that their subjective experiences were of broader application, numerous new feminist mothers recounted their everyday experiences in articles and books.[10] Clearly, beginning in the mid-1970s, feminism contained a discourse of motherhood that drew from the immediate, personal, and concrete experience of mothering.

It is simplistic, however, to assume that a demographic shift manifested immediately and transparently as a discursive shift.

Simply because women writers with a feminist perspective began to have children in greater numbers does not ensure that they would all choose to write about that experience, or that they would do so in increasingly favorable terms. In fact, the shift in feminist writing toward a focus on motherhood, and toward a more positive view of motherhood, predates the increase in birth rates.[11] Moreover, not all of the women whose theories of motherhood influenced feminist thought in the mid-1970s were actual mothers.[12] And of those who were, some, like Adrienne Rich, had been mothers for years.[13] Clearly, something more than a new mother's need to express herself induced so many theorists to write about mothering, in the particular terms in which they wrote, at this exact juncture.

The entry of large numbers of feminists into academia in the mid-1970s provided another potent impetus to the surge of feminist publications on motherhood, and also largely shaped the content of these publications. Professionalization enhanced writers' access to publication, but it also dictated a more rigorous approach to the material, as interpreted through the various disciplines. Recognizing motherhood as a feminist concern from their years of movement involvement, feminist academicians brought that interest to their research. As a result, a body of scholarly writing on motherhood began to take shape, with a preponderance of works in the fields of psychology and psychoanalysis, where the topic had long been explored, if not always along feminist lines. In books and articles, feminist scholars began to advance complex theories about motherhood, far removed in style and content from the earlier polemical or descriptive pieces scattered throughout the feminist press.[14] Now the discourse began to form distinct boundaries and to function almost centripetally, as major writers emerged whose work provided a focal point for reviews and commentary.[15]

This shift toward a centralized academic discourse coincided with, and helped to promote, changes in the feminist publishing structure. Some of the movement-driven publications folded, while new university-based feminist academic journals formed. With editorial boards made up of scholars, these journals selected articles that conformed to academic norms, creating a relatively narrow pool of writers and a relatively self-contained body of readers. Moreover, as feminist scholars' desire to build successful academic careers influenced their decisions about where to publish their work, academic publishers began to serve as major outlets for feminist writing. Insofar as this trend characterized feminist scholarship in general, it applied to works on motherhood, which comprised a growing proportion of the total body of feminist scholarship.[16]

Another, much broader influence on the scope, style, and content of feminist mothering theory during this period derived from the profamily rhetoric of the political and intellectual community at large. A renewed focus on traditional family "values" and configurations, while typically viewed as a drift toward the Right in national politics, in fact suffused the rhetoric of all sides of the political spectrum by the late 1970s.[17] On the Right, the Moral Majority and other groups attempted to reforge links between the traditional family and the old list of Cold War objectives. Nothing new in substance, this campaign drew new energy from the religious revivalism to which it attached itself; the rather isolated extremists of a decade earlier constituted a well-funded power bloc by the mid-to-late 1970s.[18] From the center, pundits responded that they, too, had a stake in the preservation of the "traditional" family. In a speech on the "crisis of confidence" afflicting America, President Jimmy Carter called for "strong families" and "close knit communities."[19] On the Left, fierce controversy erupted as several noted scholars began to decry the aimless individualism or "narcissism" of the age. Christopher Lasch led the offensive, citing the lack of a moral center in American life and suggesting that "meaning" could be found through the reestablishment of father-headed households.[20]

Most feminists rejected the profamily arguments of the Right and center outright and engaged in heated debate with scholars like Lasch, but the drift toward a discourse of "corporate" family politics nevertheless had some influence on feminist thought. Betty Friedan and a few other writers in the early 1980s argued that feminists had mistakenly rebuked the "family" in their passion for sexual politics, and that marriage and family must head the feminist agenda of the next decade.[21] In a subtle shift from the radical politics of the 1960s and early 1970s, which insisted upon "decoding" the nuclear family, valorizing the individual and the body, and seeking new forms of "authentic" community, more and more feminists began to treat the "family" as a functional whole, and sought to address the relationships within it.

All of these influences on feminist mothering theory—the presumption of motherhood's cruciality, the attention to its daily qualities, the entry of feminists into academia, and the drift toward "family" politics—are exemplified in the work of Nancy Chodorow, whose 1978 book *The Reproduction of Mothering: Psychoanalysis and the Sociology of Gender* remains one of the central texts of feminist mothering theory and of American feminism in general. Drawing as much from the psychoanalytic tradition as from the feminist, Chodorow engages object relations theory to explain the replication of gender differences across generations. To discuss Chodorow simply as exemplary of a certain stage of feminist thinking about motherhood cannot do justice to the complexity of her views or their embeddedness in their discipline.[22] However, for the project of tracing the development of feminist discourses of motherhood, a few key elements of her work are illustrative.

Chodorow sets out to explain why, across time and location, women perform, and want to perform, the task of "mothering" the young. Critical of both biological and social learning theories, Chodorow turns to psychoanalytic theory to trace how the capacity and proclivity to nurture become embedded in women's personalities from early infancy on. Chodorow argues that girls' identity develops around the continuity of connectedness to a primary female caretaker, whereas boys' identity formation incorporates a differentiation from the mother. Thus, "because women are themselves mothered by women, they grow up with the relational capacities and needs, and psychological definition of self-in-relationship, which commits them to mothering. Men, because they are mothered by women, do not."[23] Chodorow both hails the ability to nurture and rejects the power imbalance that results from the division of labor that ties women to child care. To correct the unevenness of current social relations, Chodorow proposes that men and women share responsibility for "mothering," thereby breaking the heretofore inevitable cycle of replication.[24]

A dramatic contribution to its discipline, Chodorow's work also reflected and helped to shape feminist discourses of motherhood in the late 1970s. Although decidedly aligned with socialist and materialist, rather than spiritualist and cultural, segments of the feminist movement, Chodorow drew legitimacy for her theory in part from the surge of interest that feminists, under the sway of cultural feminism, placed on motherhood. Yet, concentrating, as one strand of new mothering theory did, on the concrete, daily interactions of mother and child, Chodorow sought ultimately to critique and change the family structure that generated gender oppression. And alongside her socialist critique, developed in part through her own years of feminist activism, Chodorow filtered her views through the language and reasoning of psychoanalytic theory.[25] Her work thus reflected not only the general incorporation of feminist theory into academic discourse, but also, in the particular, the reification of the nuclear family upon which psychoanalysis so clearly rests. Not unlike Sigmund Freud, Chodorow posits a two-parent, heterosexual family structure within which an infant establishes its object relations. Therefore, in Chodorow's analysis, if child rearing arrangements within the family as currently structured produce problems in gender relations, then restructured they will also provide the solutions. This turn to the family exemplifies both the shift of feminist theory toward traditional disciplines and the shift within feminism, as throughout the wider society, toward a functionalist view of the "corporate" family.[26] By the late 1970s, alternatives to the nuclear family, such as communes or extended families, garnered less attention in practice or in theory.

Old Agendas

While feminists in this period as in others reacted to demographic, professional, and political shifts outside the women's movement itself, the enduring ideological and political dilemmas that had been part of feminist discourse since the late 1960s remained vital to the development of theory. Feminists' slip into "profamily" rhetoric, for example, reveals as clearly the utopian search for community as the rightward pull of national politics. The tensions over sexuality and the disputes about the universality of "female-ness" that polarized feminists in the late 1970s echo earlier disputes and underscore the tenacity of the troubling legacy of the counterculture. That feminists continued to grapple with these issues through the screen of motherhood attests to the centrality of motherhood to feminist thought, a centrality born of political struggle.

No theorist furthered the themes of both the counterculture and cultural feminism more clearly than Dorothy Dinnerstein, whose 1976 book *The Mermaid and the Minotaur: Sexual Arrangements and Human Malaise* drew a wide and enthusiastic feminist audience. Dinnerstein, like Chodorow, views current "sexual arrangements" as dysfunctional. Even more convinced that the experiences of infancy shape people for life, Dinnerstein writes of the primal tragedy of all human relations: separation from the mother. The first source of all pleasure to the infant, the mother, in the course of normal individuation and development also becomes the first source of pleasure lost, of frustration and discomfort. A looming figure in both capacities, the mother becomes, for both male and female infants, the object not only of attachment, but also of rage. Because women worldwide have sole responsibility for the care of infants, they become the objects of the unspent infantile rage of adult men who experienced that early loss. Irrational and aggrieved, men dominate and abuse women as they seek out the all-comforting mother, and then lash out when she proves, again, to be inconsistent. Like Chodorow, Dinnerstein concludes that shared parenting presents the only way out of this relational morass; disappointment will always be the lot of the infant, she says, but the resultant rage should be absorbed by both sexes.[27]

While Dinnerstein expresses support for the overall goals of women's liberation, she does not claim direct involvement with "the movement."[28] Many feminists, however, embraced her work fervently. Feminist journals and newspapers, scholarly and non-scholarly, reviewed *The Mermaid and the Minotaur* in largely positive terms.[29] And her own disclaimers aside, Dinnerstein's thought was indeed consonant with a number of trends within feminism in the mid-1970s. By ostensibly presenting her extraordinarily wide-ranging views as a theory about motherhood, Dinnerstein both found a ready audience among feminists of this period and helped to consecrate motherhood as the symbolic center of a discourse that in fact sought the wider reconciliation of sexuality and community, of individual and shared liberation.

Dinnerstein did share with other feminist writers the belief that an understanding of human existence necessitated a thoroughgoing analysis of motherhood. As in the writing of Jane Alpert, Adrienne Rich, and many other authors, motherhood is not only important for Dinnerstein, it is potentially life-saving or life-destroying. Dinnerstein, like the cultural feminists, converts generational and existential problematics into gender terms and burdens motherhood with the task of resolution. While this heavy emphasis on motherhood, both positive and negative, resonates throughout the psychoanalytic tradition from which Dinnerstein draws, it was also a principal discursive mechanism of feminist universalism in the mid-1970s.

Moreover, like the feminists who hail her, Dinnerstein's view of the human condition is profoundly catastrophic. Civilization seems on the brink of extinction in Dinnerstein's work: Old patterns of mortification and rage, always directed against the body of woman, as identified with nature, are now threatening to ravage the entire planet. Ecological disaster is the final outcome of psychic distress. Advanced technology, with its many poisonous byproducts, is transforming a timeless psychological tension into an imminent crisis. Change must occur now.

Interestingly, Dinnerstein's work began to be canonized by the very feminists who veered away from materialist treatments of motherhood, and who presented the most symbolic and metaphorical treatments of the topic. These were the feminists who began, in the early to mid-1970s, to concentrate on the imminent and global dangers facing women. Their view, like Dinnerstein's, was catastrophic and generalized: *All* women face danger from *all* men. As discussed in previous chapters, many feminists saw motherhood as a promising agent of unification for women. Dinnerstein's work helped to solidify that view by reemphasizing the dangers women faced in a world in which men and women, at the deepest levels of interactional capacity, were *different*. Although Dinnerstein calls ultimately for the mollification of difference, the bulk of her argument comprises an exegesis of difference and danger, centered around the body of the mother. That aspect of her work validated strong themes in recent feminist writing and served as a springboard for new theories of universal gender difference.

The "difference feminism" to which Dinnerstein contributed and from which she drew had roots in the earliest radical feminist analyses.[30] Radical feminism had always engaged the supposition of difference based on gender, venturing a range of theories about the causation and perpetuation of that difference. But by the mid-1970s, radical feminists had begun to hone their recognition of gender inequality to a distinct focus on the worst forms of oppression suffered by women as a group. Often neglecting to differentiate among women in terms of class, race, or region of residence, a significant body of feminist writing began to detail the many forms of abuse to which women were vulnerable at the hands of men. Concurrent with their establishment of rape crisis centers, battered women's shelters, and other self-help institutions, feminists began to produce a sizable literature on the topics of rape, incest, battering, and eventually, pornography. In keeping with the cultural feminist supposition of universal female traits, many writers began to focus on the *universal* perils facing women; thus, they wrote, in recognition of danger, as in more positive forms of communion, all women could and should unite. As these feminists exposed what seemed to them unspeakably pervasive violence against women, they declared that women needed, first, to recognize their fundamental difference from men, and then to protect themselves and create alternatives.[31]

Dinnerstein's book, less transparent in its gender separatism because its psychoanalytic slant automatically postulates separate developmental tracks for boys and girls, falls squarely into this feminist discourse of catastrophe, dread, and difference. Because our sexual arrangements are as they are, Dinnerstein argues, men and women have become dissimilar in a way that allows and invites men to harm women. We all emerge from infancy damaged, but the damage done to men turns into the compulsions of sexism in adulthood. As Dinnerstein says, "The boy can start to despise femaleness as he grows toward competent membership in the male fraternity."[32]

On a much deeper level, however, Dinnerstein's work tapped a utopianism still central to feminist thought in the mid-to-late 1970s. *The Mermaid and the Minotaur* reiterates the communalist themes of the 1960s: the longing to find "authenticity" and connectedness through the body; and the belief that motherhood, reconceptualized, can provide a detour around "alienation." These themes, though difficult to grasp, still struck a chord among feminists. After all, the desire to forge a less factionalized women's movement—an "authentic" community—had been central to the formulation of cultural feminism in the mid-1970s. When Dinnerstein presented a theory ostensibly concerned with *gendered* violations of the human spirit, feminist reviewers and readers were able to seize upon this accessible "danger" trope, while also, through the metaphor of motherhood, responding to the profound, rather ungendered, global plan for human interconnectedness at the heart of Dinnerstein's work. Reconstructed motherhood, as metaphor, became a way for Dinnerstein and many other feminists in the late 1970s to speak of the ideal of loving community.

Dinnerstein, unlike the feminist writers who followed, spoke in the *unrevised* language of counterculturalist utopianism. She relied heavily on the theories of radical psychoanalyst Norman O. Brown, whose books *Life against Death* and *Love's Body* had galvanized the cultural left in the 1960s toward truly transcendent expectations of the flesh.[33] Like Brown, Dinnerstein argued that the infant's blissful immersion in the pleasures of the flesh ends brutally with the development of a sense of separateness, a sense of "self." The infant gains that sense as its physical connection to its mother's flesh becomes more and more attenuated and it must meet more of its own physical needs. Frustrated desires generate a keener and keener awareness of the infant's own body. This awareness, at once the genesis of selfhood and achievement in the world, also marks a mournful moment, for the realization of separateness carries the realization of mortality. The infant yearns for the maternal flesh that seemed to defy death, but furiously suppresses its yearning for this flesh that made false promises. It reviles the female body that had the power to confer such joy, such pain. Finally, in denial of the power of the flesh, the adult "infant" cuts off its feelings for the body, trying instead to escape its feelings of powerlessness by "mastering" the environment. While Brown laments the loss of the flesh per se, Dinnerstein notes that it is the woman's body, in particular, that is reviled. In either case, the loss is tremendous, for Brown and Dinnerstein both hold the holism of spirit and flesh sacred: as long as we deny the body, we deny our capacity to experience life fully; if we can reembrace the physical, we can love ourselves, love each other, and live in a relationship of harmony with, rather than mastery of, the environment.[34]

Dinnerstein diverges from Brown when she reframes the counterculture's celebration of interpersonal connectedness and reverence for the body in terms of mothering. In Dinnerstein's view, while rejection of the flesh, male and female, ultimately comes to characterize the human dilemma, the primal rift occurs between mother and infant. The way connectedness and separation get negotiated at the earliest stage of life bears the potential to alter the course of civilization. Separation must occur if the infant is to become a "person," but the goal of individuation as Dinnerstein sees it is to preserve as much of the holistic bond between mother and child as possible. That bond alone, of all human relationships, rests on an adoration of the woman's body; merged and beatific, the infant has not yet learned to rage against, hate, and hurt women. If the separation from mother can be diffused, then perhaps the memory of the cherished maternal flesh can remain vital, sustaining the capacity for pleasure, the acceptance of the flesh, and consequently, the ability to live in harmony with other people and with the environment.[35]

Although Dinnerstein's vision points ultimately to a reinvigorated heterosexuality in which fathers learn to "mother," many feminists drew a different message from her book. From the standpoint of a feminism that already valorized a desexualized motherhood as a way to build community, they extended both global and deeply personal interpretations of her theory. Ecofeminists and feminist peace activists in this period developed further the theory implicit in Dinnerstein's writing: Women, who have been identified with nature, and rebuked for that identification, *are* in fact closer to nature, if for no other reason than that their life-producing bodies defy the drive to deny the power of the flesh and the earth. That denial, now named as the source of violence and destruction, must be countered by theory and practice that honors the maternal body, and thus respects the earth. Through connectedness, modeled on the primal connection of mother and infant, the intense spirit of hopefulness that infused the counterculture can be retrieved. Replacing the 1960s vision of sexual connection, in nature, among friends, many feminists now envisioned unfettered intergenerational connection, a bond unsurpassable in its closeness to nature. Mother and infant, cocooned in unruptured, protected, rapturous bodily communion, became the model for all human relations.[36]

The ecofeminist and feminist peace movements that endorsed theories such as these blossomed in the late 1970s. They were part of a larger, rapidly growing ecology movement in the United States and Europe in the 1970s, which from its inception incorporated the counterculture's vision of holism and community.[37] The ecology movement claimed as its first modern text Rachel Carson's *Silent Spring*, published in 1962. Carson decried the pollution of the environment with DDT, while more generally condemning the ills of an overly technological society. She warned of the destruction of modern society, which seemed blind to the "web of life," the interconnectedness of humans and other species on their shared planet. Carson's holism found a ready audience among counterculturalists, who also counterposed nature and technology, holding up babies and flowers against the establishment's guns. This naturalist ethos within the counterculture grew eventually into ecological activism, pioneered by Earth Day in 1970 and developed into ongoing, organized opposition to nuclear power and the arms race.[38]

Ecofeminism, which began to be articulated as a distinct philosophy in the late 1970s, grew organizationally and conceptually from the wider ecology and feminist movements. Echoing early radical feminists' gendered critique of the counterculture, ecofeminists noted that "human" destructiveness was in fact male destructiveness. Feminist writers had been expounding on the earth-saving potential of women's sensibilities since the mid-1970s, citing women's nurturing behavior as salutary to both the human young and the environment.[39] Susan Griffin gave these themes their fullest treatment in *Woman and Nature: The Roaring Inside Her*, published in 1978. Detailing the ways in which men had identified women with nature since ancient times, and then trampled both, Griffin's treatise of extreme gender difference exhorted women to reclaim their connectedness to nature, for there lay women's sentience and strength: "I know that I am made from this earth, as my mother's hands were made from this earth, as her dreams came from this earth and all that I know, I know in this earth."[40]

In 1979, following the accident at the Three Mile Island nuclear reactor in Pennsylvania, numerous feminists informed by theory such as Griffin's, and experienced in ecological and antinuclear activism, began to talk of the need for an explicitly feminist ecology and peace movement.[41] In March 1980, the Conference on Women and Life on Earth at the University of Massachusetts at Amherst drew over 800 participants.[42] In November 1980, feminist peace and ecology activists regrouped to stage the Women's Pentagon Action, in which 2,000 women, through street theater, civil disobedience, and other nonviolent action, demonstrated their "fear for the life of this planet, our Earth, and the life of the children who are our human future."[43] Four thousand women returned to the Pentagon the next year, as the ecofeminist and feminist peace movements grew rapidly.[44] In 1983, modeling themselves after the British Women's Peace Camp at Greenham Common, an ongoing "encampment" protesting NATO's positioning of cruise missiles there, American feminists initiated a "permanent protest" against U.S. militarism, with the Women's Encampment for a Future of Peace and Justice, near the Seneca Army Depot at Seneca Falls, New York.[45] Throughout the 1980s, this branch of feminist theory and activism flourished.

As philosophy and movement ecofeminism had strong ties to feminist peace activism and to the feminist spirituality movement, and all three made copious use of maternalist rhetoric and imagery.[46] Drawing attention to the perils to which male domination had subjected women, the earth, and all living things, activists and theorists in these three overlapping movements asserted that women, whether by nature or by conditioning, possessed a sensibility geared toward the preservation of life. Mary Daly and many other writers theorized that "male" religion rested on nefariously dualistic thinking: God and devil, spirit and flesh, nature and culture, and so on. Goddess religion, on the other hand, according to its latter-day proponents, had integrated all these categories, or never formulated them, adhering instead to a holistic world view that honored connectedness rather than division; in worshiping the Great Mother, one deified the source of life, thus honoring the connections between generations, among people, between people and the earth, and among the various forms of life on earth. One's position as subject in a world so configured was not unlike that of the merged infant described by Dinnerstein; a culture premised on a mother-centered ontology promised, most profoundly, an embrace of safety in sameness.[47]

This premise of interconnectedness, a gendered restating of the counterculture's holism, undergirded all ecofeminist and feminist peace activist theory. Frequently, the analysis of women's propensity for seeing connection where men saw rupture, for "embedding" action in relationship, circled back to women's mothering functions. Feminists wrote that whereas the "rape" of the earth in the name of progress, or the slaughter of the enemy in the name of war, requires the ability to see oneself as entirely separate from the "other," mothering requires a constant identification with another person. In anticipating a child's needs, in offering care and protection, mothers demonstrate an alternative mode of relating. Ecology and peace require the ethic of care and connection that mothering so amply demonstrates. If that ethic, or mode of relating, could be harnessed to the movements for ecology and peace, the world might have a chance for survival. According to Sara Ruddick, in the influential article "Maternal Thinking," mothering behavior, at its best, can be characterized by the desire to preserve life and foster growth, and can thus serve as a blueprint for human interaction.[48] According to Grace Paley, in the Unity Statement endorsed by the participants of the Women's Pentagon Action in 1980, women have a particular "sense," or "ecological right," gained in large part through the physical and emotional work of caring for children:

We understand that all is connectedness. We know the life and work of animals and plants in seeding, reseeding and in fact simply inhabiting this planet. Their exploitation and the organised destruction of never to be seen again species threatens and sorrows us. The earth nourishes us as we with our bodies will eventually feed it. Through us, our mothers connected the human past to the human future.[49]

These views, although clearly linked to the maternalist rhetoric of earlier peace movements and to cultural feminists' early deployment of motherhood as a universalizing issue, also represent a shift in feminist thought. Cultural feminists had initially stressed women's common capacity for mothering as a basis for feminist solidarity, as a salve for divisions within the movement, and as an organizing tool to attract "the masses." While purporting to honor mothers, past, present, and future, this view in fact diverted attention from actual mothers to a set of immanent qualities labeled as "motherly." Many feminists hoped that a community centered around these principles could succeed. Theorists of the late 1970s and early 1980s, however, began to examine the demonstrated activities of mothering, and to extrapolate from those activities a constellation of values and behaviors that seemed to succeed in fostering meaningful relationship. Again treating actual mother-child relationships as paradigmatic rather than material, this view also strove for community based on mothering principles; but whereas cultural feminists had begun by trying to influence women to actually interact like mothers, they now said that the model of mother-child interaction should inspire feminists to ecological and peace activism. What began as an essentialized and universalized view of mothering became more remote and symbolic, as it suffused feminist discourse more fully.

Pornography versus Motherhood

As part of the development of "difference" feminism in the mid-to-late 1970s, many activists seized upon pornography as the most glaring example, and perhaps the cause, of men's violence toward women. Not all feminists concurred, however, and in what would become the most rancorous debate yet among feminists, various camps began to devise highly discordant analyses of pornography and of women's sexuality in general. Through these "sexuality debates," which convulsed the movement well into the 1980s, dissenting radical and socialist feminists contested cultural feminists' fragile theories of female connectedness.

Through ecofeminism and feminist spirituality, as well as more ideologically inchoate expressions, cultural feminists had been straining for the sense of community, now gendered, articulated a decade earlier by counterculturalists. However, their critics pointed out, in striving for a universal, nurturing, and safe community based on "maternal" principles, cultural feminists both refused to grapple with differences among women and often sacrificed the other high principle of the cultural revolution: sexual liberation.[50] Although the countercultural ideal of community remained vital for all feminists, an increasingly vocal group of dissenters rejected the premise of a safe community based on "motherly" sameness, if that community were pitted against full sexual liberation and the acknowledgment of difference among women. Thus the debate over pornography reached to the core of feminist belief and longing, bringing the dual desires for sexuality and community into question again, as many feminists rejected the shallow "unity" achieved through the deployment of symbolic renderings of motherhood.

Although numerous feminists had condemned pornography since the late 1960s, often criticizing the male Left for its use of pornographic images in the underground press, the feminist antipornography movement as such did not mobilize until the mid-1970s.[51] In 1976, a group of California women protested a billboard that depicted a chained and battered woman accompanied by a caption reading, "I'm black and blue from the Rolling Stones and I love it." The following year, feminists demonstrated against *Snuff,* a hardcore pornographic film rumored to depict the actual torture and murder of a woman. A new nationwide organization, Women Against Violence in Pornography and Media, drew hundreds of members and in November 1978 sponsored a national conference, "Feminist Perspectives on Pornography." In

New York, a group called Women Against Pornography led women on tours of the Times Square red light district. Meanwhile, the "Take Back the Night" movement sponsored marches through many cities across the nation in protest of violence against women.[52]

In addition to their direct activism, antipornography feminists produced a large body of writing in the late 1970s and early 1980s. Highly attuned to the prevalence of male violence against women, some of this literature treated pornography as a cause of that violence, while some treated it as merely correlative. In either case, theorists surmised that the presence of pornographic images, and most particularly those that combined explicit violence with erotic images, reinforced and glamorized the degradation of women. Susan Griffin, in an extension of her earlier work, wrote that pornography, in its vilification of the female body, represents the undistilled intent of Western patriarchal culture to silence both women and nature.[53] Andrea Dworkin, soon to become both a leading antipornography theorist and a fierce supporter of legal sanctions against pornographers, barely skirted biological explanations of male violence when she characterized pornography as the most transparent expression of transhistorical and cross-cultural male violence against women. Citing pornography as both cause and effect of men's violent nature, Dworkin argued unequivocally for its eradication.[54] Kathleen Barry, in *Female Sexual Slavery,* a wide-ranging treatise on sexual violence, minimized distinctions between the worst cases of forced prostitution, the "ideology of cultural sadism" expressed in pornography, and the everyday exploitation endured by women in marriage, arguing that all stem from the male propensity to depersonalize and objectify others.[55] Laura Lederer wrote in her introduction to the widely read anthology *Take Back the Night* that "pornography is the ideology of a culture which promotes and condones rape, woman-battering, and other crimes of violence against women."[56] And Robin Morgan coined the aphorism "Pornography is the theory, and rape the practice."[57]

In contrast to the version of sexuality they saw portrayed in pornography, antipornography feminists posited a "female" eroticism characterized by mutuality, nurturance, and non-genitally focused sensuality. Gloria Steinem claimed that there was a clear and objective difference between pornography and "erotica."[58] Many feminist writers concurred, describing nonviolent, comforting, caressive encounters between familiar, exclusive partners as the true expression of female sexuality. Implying that pornography expressed a core (though perhaps alterable) aspect of male sexuality, many theorists saw lesbian relationships as the only currently available arena for nonexploitive sexuality, because women, by nature, saw, felt, and expressed things differently. Male-dominated, Western, dualistic thinking, in sexuality as elsewhere, separated subject and object, always hierarchically and exploitively. In Kathleen Barry's words, "*Where there is any attempt to separate the sexual experience from the total person, that first act of objectification is perversion.*"[59] In contrast, Barry wrote, by endorsing a woman-centered sexuality, "we are really going back to the values women have always attached to sexuality, values that have been robbed from us, distorted and destroyed as we have been colonized through both sexual violence and so-called sexual liberation. They are the values and needs that connect sex with warmth, affection, love, caring."[60]

The woman-centered sexuality described by antipornography feminists linked several strands of cultural feminist thought with symbolic understandings of motherhood at their discursive center. Maintaining allegiance to the countercultural philosophy of holism that had inspired feminism throughout, cultural feminists had sought since the early 1970s to minimize differences among women, both within and outside the women's movement. Drawing on the positive emphasis on motherhood in both African American feminism and the counterculture, cultural feminists had based their first pleas for a unified women's movement on an exegesis of women's immanent motherly potential. Because sexuality was deeply implicated in many of the tensions among women on the Left and within the women's movement, these feminists had quickly recast sexuality as spirituality, as tenderness, and as motherly attentiveness, in an effort to forge a simple peace within the movement. But cultural feminist theory, as it evolved, reified what had been largely a strategic emphasis on desexualized motherly traits. With a heightened recognition of danger and gender difference, numerous writers by the late 1970s compared woman's pacific *nature* with man's violent *nature*. The antipornography movement made the comparison most clearly: men, in their relentless pursuit of sex, violated women and nature and prevented the creation of authentic community; women, in their urge to establish connection, an urge modeled on the ethic of care evident in mothering, embodied the spirit of holistic community. Community, then, depended on an emphasis on sameness and connectedness, which in turn depended on a recasting of sexuality as the reaffirmation of a "maternal" ethic of care and protection.[61]

Numerous antipornography feminists described the kind of sex that they considered authentically erotic. Notably, these descriptions echoed those offered by Sara Ruddick, Adrienne Rich, and others, of the type of unfettered mothering that could alter human relations, ultimately fostering planetwide peace and ecology. New mothering theory presented a model of interpersonal connectedness and caring in a world fragmented by individualism and depersonalization: The mother, because of her attentiveness to the minute needs of her child, and because of her protective stance, identifies her child's needs with her own in a way unparalleled in modern society. Mothers create a net of safety. Mothering, in this view, of all human interactions comes closest to erasing boundaries between individuals, thereby leaving the least space for the depersonalization that invites violence.[62] Similarly, according to antipornography theorists, true eroticism fosters identification with another. It closes the gap between individuals, revealing deep commonalities and allowing the self to merge with another. Woman-defined eroticism, in the words of Audre Lorde, allows "the sharing of joy, whether physical, emotional, psychic or intellectual, forms a bridge between the sharers which can be the basis for understanding much of what is not shared between them, and lessens the threat of their difference." [63] That sharing, according to Barry, *"must be based in intimacy.* Sexual experience involves the most personal, private, erotic, sensitive parts of our physical and psychic being—it is intimate in fact." [64] Like the ideal of motherhood, this ideal of eroticism is based on erasing impersonality and difference and creating a safe haven for personal and interpersonal growth.

Dissent, Sexuality, and Difference

Many feminists disagreed with the antipornography analysis, arguing that it affirmed a traditional, constricted view of women's sexuality, threatened to compromise the civil and First Amendment rights of all sexual minorities, and stifled efforts to grapple with differences among women in the movement. Soon after antipornography activists began to organize publicly, "pro-sex" or "anti-antipornography" feminists began to speak out. Pro-sex feminists argued that critics of pornography generalized too freely, and, in particular, conflated consensual lesbian sadomasochistic (SM) fantasy and sexual practice with heterosexual rape and violent pornography, when the element of consent and the relative balance of power among women made these scenarios fundamentally dissimilar. Recalling the sexual liberationist agenda of early radical feminism, defenders of lesbian SM, along with other feminist pro-sex advocates, insisted that feminists should not align themselves with the Right in dictating one acceptable mode of sexuality for women. Worse, they said, the safe, "feminine," maternal view of sexuality emerging from the antiporn movement replicated the views of the Right not only in its restrictiveness, but in its actual content. Radical feminists, they said, had worked to expand the definition of sexuality for women. Apparently, the climate of fear pervading feminism since the mid-1970s had made such exploration seem too frightening to many. With feminists' attention riveted to the ubiquitous, variegated forms of violence directed against women by men, the notion that differentials in power could be manipulated willingly for erotic purposes had become too dangerous an idea. But wishing that entire arena of fantasy and desire into nonexistence neither eradicated it in actuality nor made women "safe"; as with other cultural feminist declarations of female sameness, the antipornography description of "true" female sexuality could not stamp out actual difference. In fact, pro-sex feminists declared, a defense of sexual difference was crucial to the vitality of the feminist movement itself. Sexual orthodoxy, or a misguided universalism relating to women's sexual "nature," would cause the movement to fall apart on the very grounds on which cultural feminists sought unity. The feeling of connectedness and cohesive community sought by so many in the movement could not succeed if it stifled individuality, here expressed as sexual heterodoxy. True community, these feminists argued, recognized and made lively use of power and difference. The antipornography/cultural feminist camp simply did not have a workable answer to feminists' enduring desire for connectedness in the face of difference.[65]

Pro-sex activists both critiqued the feminist antipornography movement and presented alternative views of women's sexuality. Samois, a San Francisco-based lesbian SM group, formed in 1979 and soon published *What Color Is Your Handkerchief?* and *Coming to Power,* edited collections of essays and erotica espousing pro-sex and lesbian SM views. Pat Califia, an outspoken member of Samois, published *Sapphistry,* with graphic descriptions of SM practice and fantasy and the article "Among Us, Against Us—The New Puritans," attacking the sexual censoriousness of the women's movement. These publications and others created an uproar in the movement. Some women's bookstores refused to sell them, and feminist journals seethed with debate. Anger peaked in 1982, when members of Women Against Pornography (WAP) protested the Scholar and the Feminist Conference at Barnard College, that year devoted to the topic of sexuality and slanted toward pro-sex views. WAP's protest included the distribution of literature condemning

the views espoused by conference participants and, more contro-
versially, naming particular participants as transgressors of the
"feminist" sexual code. A pro-sex group called The Lesbian Sex
Mafia held a counterdemonstration the day after the conference.
Fury filled the feminist media for months.[66]

Just as cultural feminists had paired race with sexuality in complex
ways when they first fashioned the theories that would peak in the
rhetoric of the antipornography movement, dissenters from this
rhetoric emphasized racial difference as well as sexual difference.
While many individual women of color opposed pornography,
agreed with the basic premises of ecofeminism, developed a feminist theology, and in all these cases invoked the beneficence and
power of the maternal with at least as much vigor as white cultural
feminists, few participated alongside white women in the movements that grew around these causes.[67] Perceiving an intransigent
racism among white feminists, and believing strongly that women
of color needed to organize on their own behalf, many African
American, Latina, Asian, and Native American women formed
separate feminist organizations in the late 1970s and early 1980s.
Through works such as *This Bridge Called My Back: Writings of
Radical Women of Color,* and through organizations such as the
Combahee River Collective, a group committed to black liberationist, lesbian feminist, and socialist principles, feminists of color
articulated radical theories of gender and race attendant to their
own specific experiences, and antithetical to the erasure of difference sought by cultural feminism.[68] Beyond declining to "join"
white feminist causes, a number of black and Chicana feminists
asserted that the "sameness" celebrated by cultural feminists silenced voices of racial diversity as surely as those of sexual diversity. A small but influential group of Third World feminists began
to theorize that the two types of silencing were interrelated.[69] As
writers uncovered these interrelations, some also began to rework
the symbolism of motherhood, important to virtually all feminisms
by this point. Several writers defied the white cultural feminist

appropriation of "the mother" and articulated a sexual and racial politics centered around identification with their own mothers.

In the early 1980s, writer and activist Cherríe Moraga emerged as a strong critic of feminist universalism, reasoning that her racial and sexual identities, as filtered through her identification with her mother, made her, a Chicana lesbian, fundamentally unlike those white cultural feminists who described a unitary female experience. Moraga had often struggled with her mother, through childhood and beyond, for autonomy, for recognition of her worth in a family that gave preference to males, and for acceptance of her difference. Yet she felt ultimately that to understand herself as a woman and relate to other women she needed to come to terms with the impact of her bond with her mother, not only as a woman, but as a person of color. As the child of an Anglo father and a Chicana mother, Moraga wrote, "My brother's sex was white. Mine, brown." [70] An inner psychology, and a women's movement, that failed to see the suffusive influence of race or cultural identity on the development of sexuality could only bring the imperialism of the dominant culture into the bedrooms of women of color. Sexual imperialism within feminism was no longer acceptable, Moraga said; theory based on white women's experiences would not suffice as explication of the experiences of Chicanas, or African American women, or anyone else. The restrictive views of female sexuality emerging from the feminist antipornography movement, Moraga pointed out, silenced sexual diversity in ways that had to be understood as racial as well as sexual. Her own engagement in butch/femme role-playing, for example, helped her gain access to aspects of her sexuality that were particularly hidden by her upbringing as a Chicana; a feminist sexual politics that denied her that access made racial as well as gendered assumptions about "women's nature." Moraga wrote that "the only hunger I have ever known was the hunger for sex and the hunger for freedom and somehow, in my mind and heart, they were related and certainly not mutually exclusive." [71] The goal of a meaningful feminist politics would be that of "feeding people in all their hungers." [72]

Conclusion

The energized attention to motherhood in feminist writing of the late 1970s and early 1980s took several forms. Sometimes validating the everyday experience of mothering, feminist theory at other times abstracted the symbolic meanings of motherhood while paying little attention to actual mothers and children. Continuing the cultural feminist agenda of the mid-1970s, many feminists persisted in viewing women's potential mothering capacity as grounds for creating a unified women's movement. Never an untroubled assertion, this claim began to unravel as it achieved greater prominence in the movement and received closer scrutiny. Feminist psychoanalytic theory, ecofeminism, feminist peace activism, feminist spirituality, and feminist antipornography theory all explored differences between men and women, and similarities among women, each foregrounding in some way women's functions as mothers, actual or symbolic, as the key to enhanced human relations and the building of authentic community.

But just as counterculturalists had struggled to reconcile individual difference, expressed most piquantly as the quest for sexual liberation, with their quest for community, feminists in pursuit of "unity" found that these questions still rankled. Maternal imagery and rhetoric and the supposition of a shared female ethic of caring or a propensity to embed action in relational context could not silence powerful voices within feminism demanding that difference, desire, and power be accounted for in the quest for "sisterhood." Feminist mothering theory since the early 1980s has continued to grapple with this dilemma, at times in the terms set up in the movement's first fifteen years, though increasingly in relation to the specific quandaries posed by reproductive technology, and through the analytic prisms of postmodernism and feminist jurisprudence.

Epilogue

Feminists, like other thinkers, build layers of theory and then pause to examine what they have built. Feminist writers have now begun to create a "metadiscourse" of mothering theory that examines trends within feminist thinking.[1]

As part of the current retrospection about feminism and motherhood, these pages constitute an exploration into causation: *Why* have feminists devoted so many words to understanding motherhood? And *why* have their ideas clustered in particular formations? These questions lead to the heart of modern feminism, for since the earliest stirrings of the second wave in the 1960s, American feminists have written widely and prolifically about motherhood.

In the broadest sense, these writings reveal an evolution within feminist thought toward more and more positive views of mothering. In both tone and content, some early feminist texts rejected motherhood, characterizing it as part of the rubric of a traditional domesticity that bolstered ideological conformity and squelched individual, creative, and sexual expressiveness. Yet even as many early feminists drew a critical view of mothering and the nuclear family from the New Left, they also registered the promotherhood views of the counterculturalists and radical black activists of the 1960s and 1970s. Seeking the sense of holism, "authenticity," community, and sexual liberation lauded by the counterculture, early women's liberationists began to shape a discourse of motherhood geared toward the mediation of those divergent goals. Women's health movement activists and writers joined forces with counterculturalists and other proponents of natural childbirth to promote midwifery and breastfeeding as curative of many of the troubles of an overly technological and male-dominated culture.

The feminist writing that emerged from this union of interests presented pregnancy and motherhood in extremely positive terms.

Feminist discourses of motherhood have also evolved along trajectories more complex than that of the negative to the positive. In a movement fraught with internal strife over matters of "difference," in class, race, political analysis, and sexual orientation, motherhood soon became a symbolic screen onto which some feminists projected their desire for gender unity. Many feminists argued that the potential for motherhood made all women alike in some way and urged women, on the basis of that likeness, to join together in a unified feminist movement. Moreover, with a clear awareness of the centrality of motherhood to black feminist thought, some white feminists presented these declarations of "sameness in motherhood" as an antidote to racial strife within the movement.

Though never hegemonic, the tendency to foreground motherhood as a universalizing issue gained momentum in the late 1970s and early 1980s, as feminist theory itself increased in quantity and complexity. In works of psychoanalytic feminism, ecofeminism, and spiritual feminism, theorists began to suggest that mothering held more than the key to a unified women's movement. As a relational model, motherhood had the potential to reshape human interaction on a global scale. Ostensibly based on nonexploitive, life-sustaining, and peaceful imperatives, motherhood represented an alternative to ecological disaster, war, and various forms of interpersonal exploitation.[2]

But even by the late 1970s, motherhood, as symbol and screen, had been overburdened with the tasks of fostering unity within the women's movement and providing an arena within which feminists could mediate their conflicting desires for community and sexual liberation. Many feminists dissented volubly from a unitary, hyperbolic understanding of the meaning of motherhood. Dissent crystalized most clearly in the "sex debates" that shook the feminist movement from the late 1970s well into the 1990s. "Pro-sex" feminists objected to the sanitized, maternal version of female sexuality advanced by feminist antipornography theorists.[3] Dissent also came from feminists committed to a materialist politics focused on such problems as sterilization abuse, the need for viable day care options, the erosion of mothers' custody rights, and the stigmatization of "bad" mothers.[4]

Old Agendas, New Forms

Dissent notwithstanding, several aspects of earlier feminist mothering theory remain in place to this day. First, feminists have maintained their intensive focus on motherhood, and many continue to attempt to sort out fundamental questions of human sameness and difference, connectedness and individuality, through their theories of motherhood. Moreover, essentialist views of the body, and of the maternal body as especially "natural," still color many feminists' treatment of motherhood.

New approaches and topics have also shaped feminist mothering theory of the past dozen years. For instance, as American feminist theory, like many intellectual forums in this country, has shifted markedly toward a postmodernist, deconstructionist stance, feminist mothering theory has registered this influence deeply. Most profoundly, postmodernist French feminists' delvings into Lacanian psychoanalytic thought have influenced many American feminists to reconsider the importance of the preoedipal phase of development, in which the boundaries between mother and infant are less rigid than in later phases.[5] Similarly, as the American legal system has struggled with the complications of various reproductive technologies, feminists have grappled with the troubling implications of in vitro fertilization, surrogate motherhood, and related topics.[6]

Many feminists continue to approach these newest of topics and analyses with an ideological agenda first set in the 1960s. Still suspicious of technology, they remain drawn to the notion of community as mediated through "nature" or the body. At times, this persistent countercultural strain in feminist thought converges oddly with new developments on the American intellectual and political landscape. Perhaps feminist discussion of the Baby M. case best epitomizes this. In this legal case, "surrogate" mother Mary Beth Whitehead sought to revoke a contract relinquishing to sperm donor William Stern her parental rights to the baby Stern paid her to conceive, carry, and deliver. While many feminists decried the economic exploitation of Mary Beth Whitehead, a working-class woman hired as a "baby vehicle" for a wealthy but infertile couple, others focused on the legal system's attempt to rupture a "sacred bond" between biological mother and child. Because legal discourse does not deal in the "sacred," but rather in the language of individual and contractual "rights," many feminists were forced to place what they saw as a natural relationship in a litigational framework. In other words, they tried to transpose a deeply held belief in the interconnectedness of biological mother and child into a legal analysis of the joint *interests* of these two parties. To make that argument, many feminists found themselves conflating the interests and rights of mother and child, and thus entering tricky terrain long populated by antiabortion activists who sought to *enforce* a physical and legal connection between mother and fetus.[7]

Indeed, the convergence of a feminist discourse of motherhood with antiabortion discourse can no longer be considered an anomaly. In one notable example, feminist author Judith Arcana, writing in defense of reproductive choice, argues that "abortion is a motherhood decision":

Choosing to abort a child is like choosing to send it to one school and not another, choosing whether or not to allow it to sleep with you in your bed, choosing whether—or when—to tell it you are a lesbian, choosing whether or not to send it to Hebrew school, to catechism, to meeting; in magnitude, this choice is most similar to choosing whether to have it institutionalized or keep it at home when its retardation or physical disability is an enormous burden; certainly, deciding whether or not to give it to adoptive parents, an orphanage, or foster care is a similar decision for a mother. Choosing to abort a child is a profoundly made life choice for that child, a choice made by a woman or a girl who is already a mother, no matter how ignorant, angry, sad, hopeful, or frightened she may be.[8]

By referring to the fetus as a "child," Arcana reproduces the literal imagery and language of the antiabortion movement. Like the antiabortion movement, she associates the significance of "choice" with the body of the fetus, rather than with the body of the woman carrying the fetus. Labeled a "mother" from the moment she conceives, the woman finds her life choices paired with those of a valorized fetus. Strikingly, this feminist discussion of abortion focuses not on bodily self-determination and autonomy, but rather on the human interconnectedness of maternity.[9]

It is precisely this notion of motherhood as a means to deeper human connectedness that links earlier feminist views to much current theory. From the utopian strains of the early women's health movement, through the metaphoricizing tendencies of cultural feminism, to the naturalizing arguments of contemporary feminists opposed to reproductive technologies, American feminism has imbued motherhood with the power to build "community," to reduce individual isolation and alienation, to resolve irreconcilable differences. Early on, "community" meant, quite literally, groupings of people involved in cooperative endeavor. Motherhood, feminists thought, could bring women together as midwives and friends. It could unite the women's movement in common understanding of a universal female potential. But by the late 1970s, much feminist mothering theory sought not to unite women in the name of motherhood in a literal sense, but rather to use the perceived dynamics of the mother-child relation as a *model* of "community," of untroubled human interaction. Still seeking the interconnectedness or "holism" postulated by the counterculture, many feminists now held up mother and child, joined by a "sacred bond," as the actualized ideal of "community."

Perhaps the strongest evocation of the holistic ethos that links contemporary feminist mothering theory to its origins in the cultural left can be found in the writing of feminist sociologist Barbara Katz Rothman. In *Recreating Motherhood: Ideology and Technology in a Patriarchal Society,* Rothman describes at length the problems of "technological society." She then writes,

And against this we have motherhood, the physical embodiment of connectedness. We have in every pregnant woman the living proof that individuals do not enter the world as autonomous, atomistic, isolated beings, but begin socially, begin connected. And we have in every pregnant woman a walking contradiction to the segmentation of our lives: pregnancy does not permit it. In pregnancy the private self, the sexual, familial self, announces itself wherever we go.[10]

Here, at last, is motherhood as *communion.*

Because feminist theory is multivalent and complex, there is still much to be addressed in mothering theory. Recent works, for instance, call attention to childlessness, infertility, and the death of children. They focus, too, on the range of mothering experiences, from adoption to single parenting to the paid labor of mothering other peoples' children. Eschewing the universalizing assumptions of earlier writers, many scholars now venture culturally specific and comparative studies.[11]

American feminists have long and vigorously debated the many issues that lie at the heart of motherhood. They might disagree over whether the bath is half empty or half full, but they have most decidedly not thrown the baby out with the bathwater.

Notes

Notes to the Introduction

1. Sylvia Ann Hewlett, *A Lesser Life: The Myth of Women's Liberation in America* (New York: Warner, 1986), 184–85. Hewlett, of course,
is not alone in characterizing feminists as antifamily or antichild. Such
views continue to be expressed in the popular media; for two recent
examples, from all over the political map, see Joan Walsh, "The Mother
Mystique," *Vogue* 183, no. 8 (1993): 96; and Mona Charen, "Feminism
Accounts Payable," *The Human Life Review* 20, no. 4 (1994): 73.

2. Hewlett, *A Lesser Life,* 50.

3. Ibid., 109 and passim; see also, as cited in Hewlett, Select Committee on Children, Youth and Families, *U.S. Children and Their Families:
Current Conditions and Recent Trends* (Washington, D.C.: U.S. Government Printing Office, 1983), 6. According to the *Boston Globe,* September
13, 1990: 1, the United States, as of 1988, ranked "25th in the world in
infant mortality."

4. Robin Morgan, "A Maddening Take on Our Movement," *Ms.* 14,
no. 9 (March 1986): 74, 76; Morgan, in this review of Hewlett, writes
that Hewlett's approach is "a bit like blaming the victim." See also Rose
Laub Coser, "The Women's Movement and Conservative Attacks," *Dissent* 34 (September 1987): 259–62; Sylvia A. Law, "Having It All Is Too
Much: Review of Sylvia Ann Hewlett, *A Lesser Life,*" *New York Times
Book Review,* March 30, 1986: 10. Analytical accounts of the women's
movement's roots, development, theory, and accomplishments are growing
in number. The most detailed history to date is Alice Echols, *Daring to Be
Bad: Radical Feminism in America, 1967–1975* (Minneapolis: University
of Minnesota Press, 1989). Other useful sources include Maren Lockwood
Carden, *The New Feminist Movement* (New York: Russell Sage Founda-
tion, 1974); Barbara Sinclair Deckard, *The Women's Movement: Political,
Socioeconomic, and Psychological Issues,* 2d ed. (New York: Harper and
Row, 1979); Josephine Donovan, *Feminist Theory: The Intellectual Tradi-
tions of American Feminism* (New York: Frederick Ungar, 1985); Hester
Eisenstein, *Contemporary Feminist Thought* (Boston: G. K. Hall, 1983);

Sara Evans, *Personal Politics: The Roots of Women's Liberation in the Civil Rights Movement and the New Left* (New York: Vintage, 1979); Myra Marx Ferree and Beth B. Hess, *Controversy and Coalition: The New Feminist Movement* (Boston: Twayne, 1985); Judith Hole and Ellen Levine, *Rebirth of Feminism* (New York: Quadrangle, 1971); Alison Jaggar, *Feminist Politics and Human Nature* (Totowa, N.J.: Rowman and Allanheld, 1983); Batya Weinbaum, *The Curious Courtship of Women's Liberation and Socialism* (Boston: South End Press, 1978).

5. Tom Hayden, writing for Students for a Democratic Society in "The Port Huron Statement" (1962), penned one of the most enduring and succinct statements of New Left philosophy. The document is reprinted in James Miller, *"Democracy Is in the Streets": From Port Huron to the Siege of Chicago* (New York: Simon and Schuster, 1987). Among the many sources on 1960s cultural and political radicalism that I have found useful are: Judith Clavir Albert and Stewart Albert, eds., *The Sixties Papers: Documents of a Rebellious Decade* (New York: Praeger, 1984); Wini Breines, *The Great Refusal: Community and Organization in the New Left: 1962–1968* (New York: Praeger, 1982); Clayborne Carson, *In Struggle: SNCC and the Black Awakening of the 1960s* (Cambridge, Mass.: Harvard University Press, 1981); Todd Gitlin, *The Sixties: Years of Hope, Days of Rage* (New York: Bantam, 1987); and Sohnya Sayres, Anders Stephanson, Stanley Aronowitz, and Fredric Jameson, eds., *The Sixties without Apology* (Minneapolis: University of Minneapolis Press, 1984).

6. Echols is particularly forceful in this assertion; see especially chapter 3 of *Daring to Be Bad* .

7. For black women's "double jeopardy," see Frances Beale, "Double Jeopardy: To Be Black and Female," in Robin Morgan, ed., *Sisterhood Is Powerful: An Anthology of Writings from the Women's Liberation Movement* (New York: Vintage, 1970), 382–96.

8. This line of argument marks the beginning of what Alice Echols and Ellen Willis, following the lead of the radical feminist group Redstockings, label as "cultural feminism." According to Echols, cultural feminism "was a countercultural movement aimed at reversing the cultural valuation of the male and the devaluation of the female. . . . [Cultural feminists] were generally essentialists who sought to celebrate femaleness" (*Daring to Be Bad,* 6). See also Ellen Willis, "Radical Feminism and Feminist Radicalism," in Sayres et al., eds., *The Sixties without Apology;* and Brooke Williams, "The Retreat to Cultural Feminism," in Redstockings, eds., *Feminist Revolution* (New Paltz, N.Y.: Redstockings, 1975). Many cultural feminist works deal with motherhood in some way, either explicitly

or as an organizing metaphor. Jane Alpert's "Mother Right" (*Ms.* 2, no. 2 [August 1973]: 52–55, 88–94) opened the dam.

9. David Hollinger, "Historians and the Discourse of Intellectuals," in John Higham and Paul K. Conklin, eds., *New Directions in American Intellectual History* (Baltimore: Johns Hopkins University Press, 1979), 42–43.

10. This is a (slight) paraphrase of the definition of feminism given by Linda Gordon in "The Struggle for Reproductive Freedom: Three Stages of Feminism," in Zillah Eisenstein, ed., *Capitalist Patriarchy and the Case for Socialist Feminism* (New York: Monthly Review Press, 1979), 107n. Gordon defines feminism as "an analysis of women's subordination for the purpose of figuring out how to change it."

11. Tillie Olsen, *Silences* (New York: Delacorte, 1978); Adrienne Rich, *On Lies, Secrets and Silence* (New York: Norton, 1979).

12. This is, of course, true of American intellectual discourse in general. As always, there are exceptions, and I treat "international" texts to the extent that they influenced American feminist thought. For example, American ecofeminists and peace activists have identified closely with their British and, to some extent, German counterparts.

13. Betty Friedan, *The Feminine Mystique* (New York: Dell, 1963).

14. Carden, *The New Feminist Movement;* Ginette Castro, *American Feminism: A Contemporary History* (New York: New York University Press, 1990); Flora Davis, *Moving the Mountain: The Women's Movement in America since 1960* (New York: Simon and Schuster, 1991); Deckard, *The Women's Movement;* Ferree and Hess, *Controversy and Coalition;* Friedan, *The Feminine Mystique* and *It Changed My Life: Writings on the Women's Movement* (New York: Random House, 1976).

15. As Wini Breines argues convincingly in *Young, White, and Miserable: Growing Up Female in the Fifties* (Boston: Beacon, 1992), the stage for feminists' preoccupation with the body, for instance, had been set by the sexual and other cultural ambiguities of the fifties. This argument is not disconsonant with mine, but does offer a more gendered tracing of the angst of the fifties, which then informed subsequent cultural revolts. Interestingly, Breines's account shifts from detailed discussion of the fifties to the feminist revolt of the later 1960s, leaving rather untouched the gendered nature of the earlier periods of the New Left and counterculture. I make the same jump. In other words, both of our studies follow the lead of our subjects, picking up the issue of gender inequity in the cultural left by tracing women's growing articulation of discontent. What remains for scholars to think about is how the cultural contradictions that made girls

of the fifities "ready" to be feminists in the late sixties infused the cultural left long before women could give them a name.

Another important set of questions inheres in the comparison of first- and second-wave feminism on the "motherhood" question. Although the radical and socialist feminists of the 1960s and beyond do not hold organizational ties, or even claim much ideological lineage, to earlier feminisms in this regard, second-wave feminism, particularly since the mid-1970s, sometimes echoes first-wave feminism in its use of maternalist themes. These similarities bear scholarly examination, especially in light of recent scholarship on early twentieth-century maternalist politics as an aspect of state-building. Can any of the insights from that scholarship shed new light on late twentieth-century deployments of maternalism? While it is beyond the scope of this study to take up these questions, and while I question attempts to find "roots" of modern feminism in earlier, discontinuous movements, I eagerly await a comparative study of earlier and later feminist maternalisms. On maternalism, see Linda Gordon, *Pitied But Not Entitled: Single Mothers and the History of Welfare, 1895– 1935* (New York: Free Press, 1994); Seth Koven and Sonya Michel, eds., *Mothers of a New World: Maternalist Politics and the Origins of Welfare States* (New York: Routledge, 1993); Molly Ladd-Taylor, *Mother-Work: Women, Child Welfare, and the State, 1890–1930* (Champaign: University of Illinois Press, 1995).

16. Sara Ruddick, "Maternal Thinking," *Feminist Studies* 6, no. 2 (Summer 1980): 342–67.

17. Rhoda Linton, "Seneca Women's Peace Camp: Shapes of Things to Come," in Adrienne Harris and Ynestra King, eds., *Rocking the Ship of State: Toward a Feminist Peace Politics* (Boulder, Colo.: Westview, 1989), 239–61.

18. While my periodization does not reflect its influence, I was pleased to see that Ann Snitow's periodization of feminism and motherhood is not dissimilar to my own. Snitow names three main phases of feminist attention to motherhood: 1963–1975, 1976–1979, and 1980–1990. See Ann Snitow, "Feminism and Motherhood: An American Reading," *Feminist Review* 40 (Spring 1992): 32–51. In many spots, Snitow's analysis is consonant with mine, as well; I note these instances throughout this work. Snitow published a similar piece in *Ms.*, "Motherhood—Reclaiming the Demon Texts," *Ms.* 1, no. 6 (May/June 1991): 34–37.

19. A number of works have influenced my conceptualization of these categories. Foremost is probably Echols, *Daring to Be Bad*, passim. See also Eisenstein, *Contemporary Feminist Thought*, passim; Maggie Humm,

The Dictionary of Feminist Theory (Columbus: Ohio State University Press, 1990), 41–42, 183–84, 212–14; Alison Jaggar and Paula Rothenberg, eds., *Feminist Frameworks: Alternative Theoretical Accounts of the Relations between Women and Men* (New York: McGraw-Hill, 1978), passim.

20. This summary draws from many sources; see especially Gitlin, *The Sixties,* passim, and Miller, *"Democracy Is in the Streets,"* passim. It should be noted, too, that there were often tensions between the New Left and the counterculture over political strategy, emphasis, and interpretation. And each segment of the cultural left underwent its own transformations throughout the 1960s. This study focuses on the tactics and philosophies that had evolved by the late 1960s.

Notes to Chapter One

1. On the New Right, see Linda Gordon and Allen Hunter, "Sex, Family and the New Right: Anti-feminism As a Political Force," *Radical America* 11/12, nos. 6 and 1 (November 1977/February 1978 combined issue): 9–25; Rosalind Pollack Petchesky, "Antiabortion, Antifeminism, and the Rise of the New Right," *Feminist Studies* 7, no. 2 (Summer 1981): 206–47; Zillah Eisenstein, "Antifeminism in the Politics and Election of 1980," *Feminist Studies* 7, no. 2 (Summer 1981): 187–205; Rebecca Klatch, "Coalition and Conflict among the Women of the New Right," *Signs* 13, no. 4 (Summer 1988): 671–94; Susan Harding, "Family Reform Movements: Recent Feminism and Its Opposition," *Feminist Studies* 7, no. 1 (Spring 1981): 57–75. On revisionist feminism, see Betty Friedan, *The Second Stage* (New York: Summit Books, 1981); Jean Bethke Elshtain, *Public Man, Private Woman: Women in Social and Political Thought* (Princeton: Princeton University Press, 1981); Alice Rossi, "A Biosocial Perspective on Parenting," *Daedalus* 106, no. 2 (Spring 1977): 1–31. For analyses of this phenomenon of antifeminist "feminists," see Judith Stacey, "The New Conservative Feminism," *Feminist Studies* 9, no. 3 (Fall 1983): 559–83; Wini Breines, Margaret Cerullo, and Judith Stacey, "Social Biology, Family Studies, and Antifeminist Backlash," *Feminist Studies* 4, no. 1 (February 1978): 43–67; Deborah Rosenfelt and Judith Stacey, "Second Thoughts on the Second Wave," *Feminist Studies* 13, no. 2 (Summer 1987): 341–61.

2. I will refer to the period from 1968 to 1973 as the "early" feminist period. The 1968 starting date marks the first year in which radical and

socialist feminist writing really began to appear in print. The 1973 closing date is looser, and many works overlap the "early" period and what I later label the period of transition to cultural feminism. In August 1973, Jane Alpert's essay "Mother Right: A New Feminist Theory" appeared in *Ms.* magazine, marking the transition to a positive, even idealized, view of mothering among many white feminists. In chapter 4 I show how Alpert's theory drew from a range of feminist theory that preceeded it, but I retain the periodization that identifies her piece as the seminal work of the cultural feminist period because the article was so widely read and was thought of at the time as a harbinger of a new feminist attitude toward mothering. On Alpert and the shift from "radical" to "cultural" feminism, see Echols, *Daring to Be Bad,* 247–54 and passim; see note 1 to chap. 4 below for a fuller situating of my work in relation to Echols's.

3. Although the radical and socialist feminists of the late 1960s who are the subjects of this study have been credited most often with an antimotherhood stance, Betty Friedan actually launched the feminist attack on conventional domesticity in 1963, with the publication of *The Feminine Mystique.*

4. Christopher Lasch, *Haven in A Heartless World: The Family Besieged* (New York: Basic Books, 1977), chaps. 2, 4, 6, 7, and passim. See also Theodore Adorno et al., *The Authoritarian Personality* (New York: Norton, 1969); Geoffrey Gorer, *The American People: A Study in American Character* (New York: Norton, 1949); Kenneth Keniston, *The Uncommitted: Alienated Youth in American Society* (New York: Dell, 1965); David Potter, *People of Plenty: Economic Abundance and the American Character* (Chicago: University of Chicago Press, 1954); David Riesman, *The Lonely Crowd: A Study of the Changing American Character* (New Haven: Yale University Press, 1950); Philip Slater, *The Pursuit of Loneliness: American Culture at the Breaking Point* (Boston: Beacon, 1970).

5. Philip Wylie, *Generation of Vipers* (New York: Rinehart, 1942).

6. Theodore Lidz, Stephen Fleck, and Alice R. Cornelison, *Schizophrenia and the Family* (New York: International Universities Press, 1965); see also David M. Levy, *Maternal Overprotection* (New York: Columbia University Press, 1943); Joseph C. Rheingold, *The Fear of Being a Woman: A Theory of Maternal Destructiveness* (New York: Grune and Stratton, 1964). I was directed to this literature by David Spiegel, "Mothering, Fathering, and Mental Illness," in Barrie Thorne and Marilyn Yalom, eds., *Rethinking the Family: Some Feminist Questions* (New York: Longman, 1982), 95–110. Lasch, *Haven in a Heartless World,* 152–55, also discusses these theories.

7. Among the most illustrative examples is Dan Greenburg, *How to*

Be a Jewish Mother: A Very Lovely Training Manual (Los Angeles: Price Stern Sloan, 1965). For a discussion of the popular psychological literature of mother-blaming, see Paula Caplan, *Don't Blame Mother: Mending the Mother-Daughter Relationship* (New York: Harper and Row, 1989).

8. Philip Roth, *Portnoy's Complaint* (New York: Random House, 1969).

9. Barbara Ehrenreich, *The Hearts of Men: American Dreams and the Flight from Commitment* (Garden City, N.Y.: Doubleday, 1983), chap. 5.

10. Jack Kerouac, *On the Road* (New York: New American Library, 1957). See also Allen Ginsberg, "The Green Automobile," in *Collected Poems* (New York: Harper and Row, 1984), 83.

11. Ehrenreich, *Hearts of Men,* chap. 4.

12. Ibid., passim; Lasch, *Haven in a Heartless World,* passim. Breines, *Young, White, and Miserable,* also discusses ways in which young *women's* discontent, if usually unarticulated as such, helped lay the groundwork for the undermining of 1950s domesticity.

13. Recent works on post-Freudian angst and mothering include Caplan, *Don't Blame Mother,* and Jane Swigart, *The Myth of the Bad Mother: Parenting without Guilt* (New York: Avon, 1991).

14. Ellen Peck and Judith Senderowitz, eds., *Pronatalism: The Myth of Mom and Apple Pie* (New York: Crowell, 1974), 2–4 and passim. Aside from providing the examples of pronatalism listed here, Peck and Senderowitz offer a broad definition of pronatalism as a "social force."

15. U.S. Bureau of the Census, *Historical Statistics of the United States, Colonial Times to 1970* (Washington, D.C.: U.S. Government Printing Office, 1975), Part 1, pp. 19, 49, 64 and 133; Elaine Tyler May, *Homeward Bound: American Families in the Cold War Era* (New York: Basic, 1988), 221.

16. May, *Homeward Bound.* I use the term "containment" in May's dual sense throughout this work.

17. Ibid., 208–18. May hints at this analysis but ends her study with the close of the 1950s. My analysis of the relationship of the New Left and counterculture to the domestic and Cold War ideology of the 1950s is an extension of May's thesis, although nothing in her work suggests that she, too, would emphasize the essentialism of the cultural left.

18. Gitlin, *The Sixties,* passim. See bibliography for the dozens of sources on the New Left and the counterculture.

19. Tom Hayden, "The Port Huron Statement," in Miller, *"Democracy Is in the Streets,"* 332.

20. Ibid.; 332; Breines, *The Great Refusal,* passim; Gitlin, *The Sixties,* passim.

21. Jerry Rubin, *Do It! Scenarios of the Revolution* (New York: Simon and Schuster, 1970), 17.

22. Ibid.

23. Ibid.

24. Ibid., 18.

25. Ibid.

26. Herbert Marcuse, *Eros and Civilization* (Boston: Beacon, 1955) and *One Dimensional Man: Studies in the Ideology of Advanced Industrial Society* (Boston: Beacon, 1964). On Marcuse and his influence on the cultural left, I referred especially to Theodore Roszak, *The Making of a Counter Culture: Reflections on the Technocratic Society and Its Youthful Opposition* (Garden City, N.Y.: Doubleday, 1969), 84–123; and Richard King, *The Party of Eros: Radical Social Thought and the Realm of Freedom* (Chapel Hill: University of North Carolina Press, 1972), 116–56. On Reich, see Wilhelm Reich, *The Function of the Orgasm: Sex-Economic Problems of Biological Energy* (New York: Farrar, Straus, and Giroux, 1961), *Sex-Pol Essays, 1929–34*, ed. Lee Baxandall (New York: Vintage, 1972), and *The Sexual Revolution; Toward a Self-Governing Character Structure* (New York: Orgone Institute Press, 1945); and King, *The Party of Eros*, 51–77.

27. All of the sources on the counterculture deal with these themes; see bibliography. For all its paeans to bellbottoms and other excesses, Charles Reich's *The Greening of America* (New York: Random House, 1970) still stands as the most explicit explication of the ideals of the counterculture; my own isolation of particular strands of thought within the counterculture was influenced by Reich early on, and reflects that influence, perhaps in ways that I can no longer even identify. Raymond Mungo, *Total Loss Farm: A Year in the Life* (New York: E. P. Dutton, 1970), 148, describes "the modern family who are holding together for right-now and forever, because they choose to, and because they are having fun." Roszak has insight into the meaning of drugs and the ideal of community in the counterculture, in *The Making of a Counter Culture*, 155–77, 200–204.

28. May, *Homeward Bound*, 208–26.

29. R. D. Laing, *The Divided Self: An Existential Study in Sanity and Madness* (Harmondsworth, Eng.: Penguin, 1960); Spiegel, "Mothering, Fathering, and Mental Illness," in Thorne and Yalom, eds., *Rethinking the Family*, 101–2.

30. Reich, *The Greening of America*, 271–74; Hayden, "Port Huron Statement," 232 and passim; Gitlin, *The Sixties*, passim; Roszak, *The Making of a Counter Culture*, 200–204. The desire to reconcile personal

autonomy and community had, of course, been long present in American culture; this discussion seeks only to locate a specific historical generation of that desire. For a wider discussion of the dilemma, see John Hewitt, *Dilemmas of the American Self* (Philadelphia: Temple University Press, 1989).

31. "SNCC Founding Statement," in Massimo Teodori, ed., *The New Left: A Documentary History* (Indianapolis: Bobbs-Merrill, 1969), 99–100; Evans, *Personal Politics,* 36–37 and passim.

32. Hayden, "Port Huron Statement"; Breines, *The Great Refusal,* 1–8 and passim; Evans, *Personal Politics,* passim; Gitlin, *The Sixties,* 112–26 and passim; Roszak, *The Making of a Counter Culture,* passim.

33. Reich, *The Greening of America;* Roszak, *The Making of a Counter Culture,* passim; Gitlin, *The Sixties,* 206–14.

34. For some examples of mainstream ideas about gender on "hippie" communes, see Vivian Estellachild, "Hippie Communes," *Women: A Journal of Liberation* 2 (Winter 1971): 40–43; Richard Fairfield, *Communes USA: A Personal Tour* (Baltimore: Penguin, 1972), passim; and Keith Melville, *Communes in the Counterculture: Origins, Theories, Styles of Life* (New York: Morrow, 1972), 153–54. In "Communes for All Reasons," *Ms.* 3, no. 2 (August 1974): 64, Rosabeth Moss Kanter remarks on the sexism of many countercultural communes. See also Gitlin, *The Sixties,* 430; Robin Morgan, "Goodbye to All That," *The Rat,* February 9–23, 1970, reprinted in *Going Too Far: The Personal Chronicles of a Feminist* (New York: Random House, 1978), 121–30, and "Barbarous Rituals," in Morgan, ed., *Sisterhood Is Powerful,* 181–88.

35. Pat Mainardi, "The Marriage Question," in Redstockings, *Feminist Revolution: An Abridged Edition with Additional Writings* (New York: Random House, 1978), 120; Morgan, "Goodbye to All That," 121–30.

36. Mainardi, "The Marriage Question," 120.

37. See, e.g., "Women's Workshop on Sexual Self-Determination," *It Ain't Me, Babe,* December 1, 1970: 5. Other strong feminist endorsements of the Left's critique of the nuclear family, its communalism, its call for sexual liberation, and its overall commitment to "revolutionary changes" in everyday life are in Barbara McKain and Michael McKain, "Building Extended Families," *Women: A Journal of Liberation* 1, no. 2 (Winter 1970): 24–25; and Bread and Roses, "Bread and Roses Declaration: The Rights of Women," *Old Mole,* March 16–19, 1970: 3.

38. See Michelle Rosaldo and Louise Lamphere, eds., *Women, Culture and Society* (Palo Alto, Calif.: Stanford University Press, 1974), passim;

and especially Sherry Ortner, "Is Female to Male As Nature Is to Culture?" in Rosaldo and Lamphere, *Women, Culture and Society,* 67–87. See also Eisenstein, *Contemporary Feminist Thought,* 22–26; Humm, *The Dictionary of Feminist Theory,* 155–56.

39. Ortner, "Is Female to Male As Nature Is to Culture?" 67–87. Gayle Rubin, in the mid-1970s, was also influential in formulating a theory of gender as socially constructed. Rubin spoke of kinship systems as arenas for the symbolic exchange of women, and did not give biologistic explanations of this exchange. See Gayle Rubin, "The Traffic in Women: Notes on the Political Economy of Sex," in Rayna Reiter, ed., *Toward an Anthropology of Women* (New York: Monthly Review Press, 1975), 157–210. For a discussion of these theories, see Eisenstein, *Contemporary Feminist Thought,* 15–26, and Humm, *The Dictionary of Feminist Theory,* 155–56, 195.

40. Eisenstein, *Contemporary Feminist Thought,* 22.

41. For a very clear endorsement yet questioning of the goals of the Left, with explicit discussion of the views of Reich and Marcuse and the problem of women's sexual repression, see the pamphlet by Laurel Limpus, *Liberation of Women: Sexual Repression and the Family* (Boston: New England Free Press, n.d.) The pairing of the terms "pleasure" and "danger" is from the book by that title, Carole Vance, ed., *Pleasure and Danger: Exploring Female Sexuality* (Boston: Routledge and Kegan Paul, 1984).

42. For example, many of the feminist groups and theorists who have glorified motherhood and who have spoken in terms of a transhistorical, cross-cultural community of women have also deemed sexuality as expendable. See chap. 4 below.

43. On feminism and utopianism generally, see Eisenstein, *Contemporary Feminist Thought,* xiii–xiv and passim.

44. Juliet Mitchell, "Women: The Longest Revolution," *New Left Review* 40 (November–December 1966): 11–37, and *Woman's Estate* (New York: Pantheon, 1971).

45. Mitchell, "Women: The Longest Revolution," and *Woman's Estate.* See also Eisenstein, *Contemporary Feminist Thought,* chap. 2 and passim.

46. Socialist feminists, beginning with Mitchell, have been quick to add that only then will children be reared in a liberated way. While Chodorow would develop this point much further, there is already in Mitchell the notion that an upheaval in the social relations of child rearing could revolutionize society even on the level of personality formation.

This account of socialist feminist ideas relies on Jaggar, *Feminist Politics and Human Nature*, 310–15 and passim; and Eisenstein, *Contemporary Feminist Thought*, 17–19. Aside from Jaggar, Eisenstein, and Mitchell, I have drawn from the following sources for this summary of socialist feminist thought about motherhood: Zillah Eisenstein, "Some Notes on the Relations of Capitalist Patriarchy," in Eisenstein, ed., *Capitalist Patriarchy*, 41–55; Nancy Chodorow, "Mothering, Male Dominance and Capitalism," in Eisenstein, ed., *Capitalist Patriarchy*; 83–106; Ann Foreman, *Femininity As Alienation: Women and the Family in Marxism and Psychoanalysis* (London: Pluto Press, 1977); Heidi Hartman, "The Unhappy Marriage of Marxism and Feminism: Towards a More Progressive Union," in Lydia Sargent, ed., *Women and Revolution: A Discussion of the Unhappy Marriage of Marxism and Feminism* (Boston: South End Press, 1981), 1–41; Ann Ferguson and Nancy Folbre, "The Unhappy Marriage of Patriarchy and Capitalism," in Sargent, ed., *Women and Revolution*, 313–38; and Ilene J. Philipson and Karen V. Hansen, "Women, Class, and the Feminist Imagination: An Introduction," in Karen V. Hansen and Ilene J. Philipson, eds. *Women, Class, and the Feminist Imagination: A Socialist-Feminist Reader* (Philadelphia: Temple University Press, 1990), 3–40.

47. Shulamith Firestone, *The Dialectic of Sex: The Case for Feminist Revolution* (New York: Bantam, 1970). Firestone was a member of the radical feminist groups New York Radical Women, Redstockings, and New York Radical Feminists. See Echols, *Daring to Be Bad*, 381.

48. Firestone, *The Dialectic of Sex*, passim.

49. Mitchell, *Woman's Estate*, 87–91. Eisenstein cites this charge in *Contemporary Feminist Thought*, 17.

50. See, e.g., Michele Barrett, *Women's Oppression Today: Problems in Marxist Feminist Analysis* (London: Verso Editions and NLB, 1980); Lise Vogel, "Marxism and Feminism: Unhappy Marriage, Trial Separation, or Something Else?" in Sargent, ed., *Women and Revolution*, 195–217. Eisenstein, *Contemporary Feminist Thought*, 15–18, cites and discusses the above works.

51. The Left, the counterculture, and early feminists all evidenced ambivalence on this point. For all their valorization of nature, they all at times endorsed the use of birth control, which involved varying degrees of technological engineering in its production. They rationalized the contradiction by framing the discourse in terms of self-determination: Technology as a mere tool in the service of the essential self, choosing freely, could be simplified, naturalized, and ultimately reclaimed. Firestone's endorse-

ment of reproductive technology was stated in more or less these terms, but she opened herself to criticism because she placed technology at the very center of her utopianist plan, thus highlighting the contradictions of the cultural left's position.

52. Echols, *Daring to Be Bad*, 103–37, gives a detailed account of this split from the Left. Also, I am aware that this analysis of Firestone as a feminist-from-the-1960s-counterculture threatens to dethrone Germaine Greer, author of *The Female Eunuch* (London: McGibbon and Kee, 1970), the usual recipient of that title. The difference between the two is that Firestone attempts to conjoin a feminist analysis with the Left's view. Greer essentially restates the Left's sexual liberation theme.

53. Firestone, *The Dialectic of Sex,* 240.

54. Ibid. Snitow, "Feminism and Motherhood," 36, also sees Firestone's text as a 1960s-style "example of utopian writing," misunderstood as a "mother-hating book."

55. On these debates within the Left and the women's movement, see Echols, *Daring to Be Bad,* chap. 3 and passim.

56. Joanne Cooke, Charlotte Bunch-Weeks, and Robin Morgan, eds., *The New Women: A MOTIVE Anthology on Women's Liberation* (Greenwich, Conn.: Fawcett Publications, 1970), 17.

57. Women's Liberation, Berkeley, Calif., "Let's Liberate Women!" 1969: 1, in "Women's Liberation, Berkeley, California" file, Schlesinger Library.

58. "Letter," *It Ain't Me, Babe,* September 17, 1970: 4.

59. See, e.g., Beverly Jones, "The Dynamics of Marriage and Motherhood," in Morgan, ed., *Sisterhood Is Powerful,* 49–66; and Anonymous, "Them and Me," in Shulamith Firestone and Anne Koedt, eds., *Notes from the Second Year: Women's Liberation* (New York: Notes from the Second Year/Radical Feminism, 1970), 67. Ann Snitow remarks briefly that the youth of early feminist writers might have contributed to their lack of interest in mothering, in "Feminism and Motherhood," 37.

60. Carol Hanisch, "The Personal Is Political," in Firestone and Koedt, eds., *Notes from the Second Year,* 77; Morgan, *Going Too Far;* Echols, *Daring to Be Bad,* 76, 97.

61. Abbie Hoffman, *Revolution for the Hell of It* (New York: Dial, 1968).

62. "No More Miss America: Ten Points of Protest," in Morgan, ed., *Sisterhood Is Powerful,* 521–24; Echols, *Daring to Be Bad,* 92–101.

63. Morgan, *Going Too Far,* 74; Echols, *Daring to Be Bad,* 97–98.

64. Echols, *Daring to Be Bad,* 170. The primary source on this action

is Susan Rennie and Kirsten Grimstad, *The New Woman's Survival Catalogue* (New York: Coward, McCann and Geoghegan, 1973), 209.

65. Morgan, *Going Too Far*, 71–75; Echols, *Daring to Be Bad*, 92–101.

66. "The Big Letdown," *Newsweek*, September 1, 1969: 49–50. See also Sara Davidson, "An 'Oppressed Majority' Demands Its Rights," *Life*, December 12, 1969: 67–78; Ruth Brine, "The New Feminists: Revolt against 'Sexism,' " *Time*, November 21, 1969: 53–56; Helen Dudar, Judith Gingold, and Nancy Dooley, "Women's Lib: The War on Sexism," *Newsweek*, March 23, 1970: 71–78. In general, reporters gave the heaviest coverage to separatist groups most likely to provide pithy quotes. Ti-Grace Atkinson of The Feminists was probably the media's favorite for antimotherhood quotes; she was quoted in *Life* as saying that "sex is overrated," and that pregnancy is "very painful. It's so immature to grow babies in people's bodies." Reporters tended to pin a "down with motherhood" image on the women's movement, when in fact, as the sympathetic reporters for *Newsweek* wrote, the movement was equally "focused on the liberating possibilities of a network of child-care centers staffed by men and women who will take the drudgery out of child-rearing" (p. 76).

67. Carol Hanisch, "A Critique of the Miss America Protest," in Firestone and Koedt, eds., *Notes from the Second Year*, 87.

68. Hanisch, "A Critique of the Miss America Protest," 87.

69. Cleveland WITCH, "Bury Mother's Day," flyer in "WITCH" file, Schlesinger Library, n.d.

70. Cleveland WITCH, "Bury Mother's Day." Few sentimental occasions escaped the ridicule of WITCH; to wit, from the WITCH "Unwedding Ceremony": "We promise to love, cherish, and groove on each other and on all living things. We promise to smash the alienated family unit. We promise not to obey." ("W.I.T.C.H. Un-Wedding Ceremony," flyer, in "Radical Women" file, Schlesinger Library, n.d.)

71. Hanisch, "The Personal Is Political," 77.

72. Hanisch, "A Critique of the Miss America Protest," 87.

73. The Feminists, "The Feminists: A Political Organization to Annihilate Sex Roles," in Firestone and Koedt, eds., *Notes from the Second Year*, 117; Echols, *Daring to Be Bad*, 167–85.

74. Ti-Grace Atkinson, "Radical Feminism and Love," mimeograph in "Feminism—Addresses, Lectures, Essays" file, Schlesinger Library, April 12, 1969; Atkinson writes that "the oppression of the class of women qua women is stable historically and similar geographically" (p. 1).

75. The Feminists, "The Feminists: A Political Organization to Annihi-

late Sex Roles," 117; Echols, *Daring to Be Bad,* 167–85. See also The Feminists, "Manifesto for a New Women's Liberation Organization in New York," 1969, in "The Feminists—NYC" file, Schlesinger Library.

76. Ti-Grace Atkinson, "The Institution of Sexual Intercourse," in Firestone and Koedt, eds., *Notes from the Second Year,* 43–44.

77. Another example of Atkinson's antisexual emphasis, and her insistence on new forms of community in which children are the responsibility of the whole community rather than of their biological mothers, is in Ti-Grace Atkinson, "Vaginal Orgasm As a Mass Hysterical Survival Response," a speech delivered to the Medical Committee for Human Rights, Philadelphia, April 5, 1968. (Schlesinger Library file, "Feminism—Addresses, Lectures, Essays.")

See also the writings of the Boston-based radical feminist group, Cell 16, for an antisex and antimaternity position; for example, Dana Densmore, "Independence from the Sexual Revolution," in Anne Koedt, Anita Rapone, and Ellen Levine, eds., *Notes from the Third Year* (New York: Notes from the Third Year, 1971), 56–61, and Roxanne Dunbar, "Female Liberation As the Basis for Social Revolution," in Firestone and Koedt, eds., *Notes from the Second Year,* 48–54.

78. Radicalesbians, "The Woman Identified Woman," in Koedt, Rapone, and Levine, eds., *Notes from the Third Year,* 83; Echols, *Daring to Be Bad,* 210–41.

79. Brooke Williams, "The Retreat to Cultural Feminism," in Redstockings, ed., *Feminist Revolution,* 79–83. Echols makes this point about lesbian feminism, its emphasis on "how one lived one's life," and its foreshadowing of cultural feminism, in *Daring to Be Bad,* 240–41.

80. Del Martin and Phyllis Lyons, *Lesbian/Woman* (San Francisco: Glide Publications, 1972); see also, e.g., Lisa Goldberger, "Lesbian Mother Appeal Denied," *The Tide* 3, no. 7 (April 1974): 15; Nancy Williamson, "The Mean Mothers," *Lesbian Tide* 3, no. 5 (December 1973): 10.

81. Williamson, "The Mean Mothers," 10; Ann Davis, "Whose Children Are They? Child Care At the Lesbian Conference," *Lesbian Tide,* June 1973: 11, 18.

82. Carden, *The New Feminist Movement,* 113.

83. I base this generalization on the dearth of books on the topic of lesbian motherhood in this early period, and on the relatively infrequent references to lesbian motherhood in the feminist journals prior to the mid-1970s. Jill Johnston, *Lesbian Nation: The Feminist Solution* (New York: Simon and Schuster, 1974), and Martin and Lyons, *Lesbian/Woman,* discuss lesbians and motherhood. Nevertheless, most references to lesbian motherhood prior to the mid-1970s dealt with the custody (and other

legal) rights of women who had had children in prior heterosexual relationships.

84. Martha Shelley, "Notes of a Radical Lesbian," in Morgan, ed., *Sisterhood Is Powerful,* 344–45.

85. Echols, *Daring to Be Bad,* chap. 4 and passim.

86. Ibid., 187, and more generally, on New York Radical Feminists, 186–98.

87. New York Radical Feminists, "Politics of the Ego: A Manifesto for N.Y. Radical Feminists," in Firestone and Koedt, eds., *Notes from the Second Year,* 125.

88. New York Radical Feminists, "Politics of the Ego," 125–26; Echols, *Daring to Be Bad,* 188–89.

89. New York Radical Feminists, "Politics of the Ego," 125.

90. Redstockings, "Redstockings Manifesto," in Firestone and Koedt, eds., *Notes from the Second Year,* 113. Echols, *Daring to Be Bad,* 139–58.

91. Mainardi, "The Marriage Question," 121.

92. Redstockings, "Redstockings Manifesto," 113.

93. Ibid.

94. Ibid., 112–13.

95. Ibid.

96. "NOW Bill of Rights," item 5, flyer in "NOW" file, n.d., Schlesinger Library.

97. "NOW Bill of Rights," item 4. As in many of its other initiatives, NOW sought changes that would allow women to participate fully in the public life available to men. Radicalized slightly, the organization did specify that child care should be available to poor people as well as rich. On the other hand, critics have maintained that across-the-board income tax revisions might merely help to maintain the status quo because the cost of day care, relative to income, weighs more heavily for poor people than for the middle classes; NOW's equal access approach implied, perhaps falsely, that the same service would meet the needs of diverse groups of people equally.

98. Dunbar, "Female Liberation as the Basis for Social Revolution," 52.

99. The Feminists, "The Feminists: A Political Organization to Annihilate Sex Roles," 117. The Feminists made the further point here that the problems of current mothering arrangements were so intense that it would be preferable to gestate babies outside the uterus; only that way would children become a community responsibility.

100. "Bread and Roses Declaration," *Old Mole,* no. 34 (March 6–19, 1970): 3.

101. Ibid.

102. "The Nature of Change and Political Action—Reform vs. Revolution," in "Women's Liberation, Berkeley, CA." file, Schlesinger Library, 2.

103. Ibid.

104. Ibid.

105. Deckard, *The Women's Movement*, 401–2.

106. The Congress to Unite Women, "What Women Want: For Starters," in Firestone and Koedt, eds., *Notes from the Second Year*, 96.

107. New England Women's Coalition flyer, "help win FREE 24 HOUR CHILD-CARE in Cambridge," n.d., in "New England Women's Coalition" file, Schlesinger Library. A similar effort took place in Chicago; Day Creamer and Heather Booth, "Action Committee for Decent Childcare: Organizing for Power," *Women: A Journal of Liberation* 2, no. 4 (June 1972), 7–9.

108. Deckard, *The Women's Movement*, 401; Hole and Levine, *Rebirth of Feminism*, 420.

109. Rosalyn Baxandall, "Cooperative Nurseries," in Sookie Stambler, ed., *Women's Liberation: Blueprint for the Future* (New York: Ace, 1970), 219.

110. Ibid., 222.

111. Ibid. Baxandall notes, however, that the process of "radicalization" had been slow.

112. One of the more dramatic pieces of evidence for this claim, for the early women's movement, can be found in Susan Rennie and Kirsten Grimstad, *The New Woman's Survival Catalogue*, put out in 1973. A compendium of information relating to the women's movement, put together in the *Whole Earth Catalog* fashion of the time, the book contained a large section on "motherhood," almost entirely devoted to the day care question.

Notes to Chapter Two

1. On the counterculture's complex relationship to the New Left, see Breines, *The Great Refusal*, 20 and passim; Charles DeBenedetti, *An American Ordeal: The Antiwar Movement of the Vietnam Era* (Syracuse, N.Y.: Syracuse University Press, 1990), 76–78, 135–36, 161–62, 223–24; Gitlin, *The Sixties*, 195–221; Rubin, *Do It!*, passim.

2. The historiographical bone that I am picking here is this: While some studies of the women's movement mention briefly its similarity in "style" to the cultural left, they do not elaborate on that point by tracing

the continued impact of countercultural values and beliefs on American feminism. Rather, they proceed to discuss the controversies that erupted within specific New Left organizations, leading to the departure of certain key women from those groups and the establishment, by those women, of the earliest women's liberation groups. While, in an organizational sense, that analysis is invaluable, it does not give a fully robust picture of the cultural and intellectual roots of the women's movement. It presents too linear and rational a transition, with a hefty portion of determinism at the top. I believe that the roots of women's liberation, in a discursive and cultural sense, must be traced more generically to the broad-based cultural protest movements of the 1960s. In this study, I try to illustrate those roots in the limited case of feminist discourse on motherhood, with the belief that the paradigm can be extended fruitfully to explore other aspects of feminist thought. I am much more specific in teasing out the impact of the counterculture, as distinct from the New Left, in this chapter than in chapter 1, because the more "apolitical" branches of the cultural left spearheaded the "back to nature," communal, and sensualist aspects of the 1960s revolution that bear particular relevance to this discussion of "positive" mothering theory. The general critique of the nuclear family that gave rise to the "negative" feminist discourse of motherhood discussed in the previous chapter arose more evenly from the organized and the "apolitical" left. Gitlin, *The Sixties*, 432, suggests, but does not elaborate on, this idea as it pertains to women's liberation generally.

Virtually all general accounts of the women's liberation movement focus on its New Left antecedents; see, for example, Carden, *The New Feminist Movement;* Echols, *Daring to Be Bad;* Evans, *Personal Politics;* Irvin D. Solomon, *Feminism and Black Activism in Contemporary America* (Westport, Conn.: Greenwood Press, 1989); Gayle Graham Yates, *What Women Want: The Ideas of the Movement* (Cambridge, Mass.: Harvard University Press, 1975). When analyzing feminists' views of motherhood and domesticity, in particular, scholars have also looked to the New Left as the principal source of the women's movement's "negative" critique of the nuclear family. See Echols, *Daring to Be Bad,* passim; Edith Hoshimo Altbach, "Notes on a Movement," in Edith Altbach, ed. *From Feminism to Liberation* (Cambridge, Mass.: Schenkman, 1971), 12–14. And likewise, in discussing what became a positive, sometimes utopianist, feminist approach to mothering by the early 1970s, several authors have pointed to the left's critique of authority, its endorsement of bodily self-determination, and its commitment to small, self-run, cooperative ventures in business and service provision; see Echols, *Daring to Be Bad,* chap. 6; Sheryl Burt Ruzek, *The Women's Health Movement: Femi-*

nist Alternatives to Medical Control (New York: Praeger, 1978), 6–64, passim.

3. Roszak, in *The Making of a Counter Culture,* chap. 6 and passim, discusses the utopianism of the cultural left. He cites Paul Goodman as the leading thinker in this vein, but discusses Herbert Marcuse, Norman O. Brown, Allen Ginsberg, Alan Watts, Timothy Leary, and others, as well. Discussion of the topic can be found in most works on the New Left and the counterculture; especially useful to me have been Breines, *The Great Refusal,* chap. 4 and passim; Gitlin, *The Sixties,* passim; Reich, *The Greening of America,* passim; Lyman T. Sargent, *New Left Thought: An Introduction* (Homewood, Ill.: Dorsey Press, 1972), 141–50.

4. Several scholars have discussed the utopianism of feminist thought, although none that I can recall makes an explicit connection to the counterculture. See Eisenstein, *Contemporary Feminist Thought,* xiii–xiv, 148n.

5. Angelika Bammer, *Partial Visions: Feminism and Utopianism in the 1970s* (New York: Routledge, 1991), chap. 3 and passim, discusses the utopian impulse in feminism but focuses on feminist fiction. See also Humm, *The Dictionary of Feminist Theory,* 228–29. Ruzek, in *The Women's Health Movement,* 182, writes, "The influence of the youth culture and hippie movements are also evident in feminism. As in these movements, feminists proclaimed the validity of personal experience over derived knowledge and accorded individual choice supreme status."

5. Roszak, *The Making of a Counter Culture,* chaps. 1, 6, and passim; Reich, *The Greening of America,* esp. chaps. 1 and 12; Gary Snyder, "Buddhism and the Coming Revolution," in Albert and Albert, eds., *The Sixties Papers,* 431–33. Again, most of the vast literature on the counterculture touches on this theme.

6. Jacques Ellul, *The Technological Society* (New York: Knopf, 1964); Marcuse, *Eros and Civilization* and *One-Dimensional Man.* See also Paul Goodman, *Growing Up Absurd; Problems of Youth in the Organized System* (New York: Random House, 1960); Norman O. Brown, *Life against Death: The Psychoanalytic Meaning of History* (Middletown, Conn.: Wesleyan University Press, 1959) and *Love's Body* (New York: Random House, 1966); Keniston, *The Uncommitted.*

7. My understanding of the term "prefigurative politics" is from Breines, *The Great Refusal,* 6–7.

8. Arguably, the project of forging connections, or eliminating divisions in pursuit of holistic experience, subsumed all other aspects of the countercultural philosophy. In every endeavor in which the counterculture held sway, or by which it was swayed, this theme emerges: In education, cultural radicals argued for open classrooms, with walls literally removed,

and with divisions such as tracking eliminated. In psychology, gestaltists urged the reintegration of impulse and intellect, field and ground, mind and body. In architecture, the symmetrical geodesic dome, unencumbered by inner walls or divisions, became popular with counterculturalists. The examples go on.

9. On the primitivism of the counterculture, see Reich, *The Greening of America,* 284, 414, 421, 424. Virtually all works on the counterculture explore or describe these ideas. For works that offer both primary description and some analysis, see, e.g., Fairfield, *Communes USA,* passim; Melville, *Communes in the Counterculture,* passim. For complete immersion in primitivism, there is, of course, Tom Wolfe, *The Electric Kool-Aid Acid Test* (New York: Bantam, 1968), passim; or Peter Rabbit, *Drop City* (New York: Olympia Press, 1971), passim.

10. See Wolfe, *The Electric Kool-Aid Acid Test,* 32. On hippies and their aversion to the "plastic" society, see for example, Lewis Yablonsky, *The Hippie Trip* (New York: Pegasus, 1968), 301; Reich, *The Greening of America,* 246. Again, a reading of any of the primary or secondary literature on the counterculture provides more evidence than I can cite to support these points.

11. Julian Beck, "Notes toward a Statement on Anarchism and the Theatre," in Albert and Albert, eds., *The Sixties Papers,* 408. Again, many writers touch on these themes, but perhaps none as concertedly as Reich, *The Greening of America,* passim. See also, Naomi Feigelson, *The Underground Revolution: Hippies, Yippies and Others* (New York: Funk and Wagnalls, 1970), 38–41.

12. Melville, *Communes in the Counterculture,* 93 and passim; Stephen Diamond, *What the Trees Said: Life on a New Age Farm* (New York: Dell, 1971), passim; Yablonsky, *The Hippie Trip,* chap. 10; Nicholas von Hoffman, *We Are the People Our Parents Warned Us About* (Chicago: Ivan R. Dee, 1989; orig. 1968), 74–77.

13. Allen Ginsberg, *Howl* (San Francisco: City Lights Books, 1956). The literature on the body-consciousness of the counterculture is vast and interwoven with all descriptions of the counterculture. See King, *The Party of Eros,* for a discussion of the major theorists whose work contributed to these views. Reich's discussion in *The Greening of America* captures more of the exuberance of the counterculture's reclamation of the body. In an unsympathetic assessment of the impact of hallucinogens on this body-consciousness, von Hoffman writes that some hippies "live in a condition of dismembered hysteria questing after the parts of their own bodies" (p. 115).

14. Many sources discuss the communalism of the counterculture.

Yablonsky, *The Hippie Trip,* 205, describes the many communal faces of hippies who describe themselves as belonging to a "tribe," "family," or "community." See also Melville, *Communes in the Counterculture,* passim; and Reich, *The Greening of America,* passim. Roszak discusses the intellectual underpinnings of the search for community in *The Making of a Counter Culture,* passim, as does Sargent in *New Left Thought,* 35–55. Von Hoffman gives a vivid picture of the harassment by authorities to which hippie enclaves were subjected. On the communes' lack of an economic base, Fairfield's *Communes USA* speaks eloquently throughout; see also Rabbit, *Drop City,* passim.

15. Wolfe, *The Electric Kool-Aid Acid Test,* 50.

16. Much has been written on hippie mothers, with most primary sources simply describing their presence approvingly, as if the mention of many mothers, with children running around freely, offers de facto proof of the "natural" and wholesome values of the communities in question. See Fairfield, *Communes USA,* 326–27 and passim; Wolfe, *The Electric Kool-Aid Acid Test,* passim; Ina May Gaskin, *Spiritual Midwifery* (Summertown, Tenn.: The Book Publishing Company, 1978; orig. 1975), passim; Gitlin, *The Sixties,* 372. On hippies and the innocence of children, Bennett M. Berger writes in "Hippie Morality—More Old Than New," in Edgar Z. Friedenberg, ed., *The Anti-American Generation* (Chicago: Aldine Publishing Company, 1971), 88–89: "Clearly, the symbols of childhood and innocence are very much in: flowers, ice cream, kites, beads, bells, bubbles and feathers, and sitting on the ground, like Indians, or legs outstretched in front of one, like Charlie Brown and his friends."

17. This critique of modern obstetrical practices is almost identical to that advanced by feminists in the early 1970s. Counterculturalists (some of whom later identified as feminists) voiced these same concerns and sought or created alternatives. The following sources, while chronicling feminist birth activism, also refer to counterculturalists' analyses and actions: Suzanne Arms, *Immaculate Deception: A New Look at Women and Childbirth* (New York: Bantam, 1981; orig. 1975), passim; Margot Edwards and Mary Waldorf, *Reclaiming Birth: History and Heroines of American Childbirth Reform* (Trumansburg, N.Y.: Crossing Press, 1984), 155–64; Gaskin, *Spiritual Midwifery,* 13–15 and passim; Rosabeth Moss Kanter, "Communes for All Reasons," *Ms.* 3, no. 2 (1974): 63–64; Raven Lang, *Birth Book* (Ben Lomond, Calif.: Genesis Press, 1972), passim; "Motherhood . . . Part 1," *Big Mama Rag* 1 (1972): 8–9; Ruzek, *The Women's Health Movement,* 58–59; Deborah A. Sullivan and Rose Weitz, *Labor Pains: Modern Midwives and Homebirth* (New Haven: Yale University Press, 1988), 42–44; Pam Wellish and Susan Root, *Hearts Open*

Wide: Midwives and Births (Berkeley: Wingbow Press, 1987), passim. Barbara Katz Rothman, *Giving Birth: Alternatives in Childbirth* (New York: Penguin, 1982), discusses virtually all of the countercultural and feminist ideas about childbirth analyzed in this chapter, and at times makes connections between the two groups of women. I cite her work explicitly below, but also direct the reader to her for a full comparison between what she labels the "medical" model of childbirth versus the "midwifery" model.

18. Grantly Dick-Read, *Childbirth without Fear: The Principles and Practice of Natural Childbirth* (New York: Harper, 1944). For useful discussions of Dick-Read, see Arms, *Immaculate Deception,* 167–71; and Rothman, *Giving Birth,* 84–89.

19. Rothman, *Giving Birth,* 87–89.

20. Ibid., 89–94; Rothman offers the most succinct discussion of the compatibility of the Lamaze method with American hospital birth. See also Arms, *Immaculate Deception,* 184–85; Boston Women's Health Course Collective, *Our Bodies, Ourselves* (Boston: New England Free Press, 1971), 88–90; Elizabeth Bing and Marjorie Karmel, *A Practical Training Course for the Psychoprophylactic Method of Painless Childbirth* (New York: American Society for Psychoprophylaxis in Obstetrics, 1961).

21. Ruzek, *The Women's Health Movement,* 47, 58–59; Doris Haire, "The Cultural Warping of Childbirth," *International Childbirth Education Association News,* Special Issue (1972): 3–35. On the philosophy of the ICEA, see the ICEA brochure, "About Membership," n.d., at Schlesinger Library, "Childbirth" file.

22. Kaye Lowman, *The LLLove Story* (Franklin Park, Ill.: La Leche League International, 1977); Edwards and Waldorf, *Reclaiming Birth,* 87–90; Rothman, *Giving Birth,* 103–9; Sullivan and Weitz, *Labor Pains,* 29; Lynn Y. Weiner, "Reconstructing Motherhood: The La Leche League in Postwar America," *Journal of American History* 80 (March 1994): 1357–81.

23. Rothman *Giving Birth,* 107–9, remarks on the ways in which La Leche League, though hardly feminist, meshes more readily than other traditionalist groups with its more radical allies.

24. Rothman, *Giving Birth,* 94–98; Ruzek, *The Women's Health Movement,* 196–98.

25. Quoted in Fairfield, *Communes USA,* 264. This theme also runs powerfully through Lang's *Birth Book,* which straddles the countercultural and the feminist analyses.

26. Rothman and Ruzek (see n. 24) chronicle the tensions between the more and less traditional natural childbirth advocates. This split between

traditionalists and counterculturalists would remain true, to some extent, for feminists and traditionalists as well. However, as the feminist women's health movement gained stature in the overall childbirth movement, all groups shifted sharply toward a feminist, self-determinationist position, thereby mollifying some of the tensions.

27. Boston Women's Health Course Collective, *Our Bodies Ourselves,* 130–31.

28. Ibid., 131. On the free clinic movement, see Ruzek, *The Women's Health Movement,* 60–64; and Helen I. Marieskind and Barbara Ehrenreich, "Toward Socialist Medicine: The Women's Health Movement," *Social Policy,* September–October 1975: 34–35.

29. Ruzek, *The Women's Health Movement,* 60–64.

30. Von Hoffman, in *We Are the People Our Parents Warned Us Against,* passim, gives a good sense of the importance of the free clinic to the Haight-Ashbury community in the late 1960s; see also Ruzek, *The Women's Health Movement,* 61.

31. Ruzek, *The Women's Health Movement,* 61. On the formation of the women's health movement, see also Boston Women's Health Course Collective, *Our Bodies, Ourselves;* Davis, *Moving the Mountain,* 227–58; Carol Downer, "Covert Sex Discrimination Against Women as Medical Patients," Address to the American Psychological Association, September 5, 1972, reprinted by Know, Inc., Pittsburgh, Pa.; Carol Downer, "Women Professionals in the Feminist Health Movement," mimeograph by the Feminist Women's Health Center, Los Angeles (1974); Marieskind and Ehrenreich, "Toward Socialist Medicine," 34–42; Colette Price, "The Self-Help Clinic," Feminist Women's Health Center reprint from *Woman's World* 1, no. 4 (March–May 1972); Judith P. Rooks, "The Women's Movement and Its Effect on Women's Health Care," in Leota Kester McNall, ed., *Contemporary Obstetrical and Gynecological Nursing* (St. Louis: C.V. Mosby, 1980), 3–26.

32. Boston Women's Health Course Collective, *Our Bodies, Ourselves,* chap. 5 and passim; Price, "The Self-Help Clinic"; Ruzek, *The Women's Health Movement,* 54, 130.

33. Ruzek, *The Women's Health Movement,* 61.

34. Rennie and Grimstad, *The New Woman's Survival Catalog,* 72.

35. Ruzek, *The Women's Health Movement,* 27–29, notes the apparent contradiction inherent in feminists' complaints about women being identified through the reproductive organs and the concurrent feminist focus on reproductive health care.

36. Ibid., passim.

37. Every comprehensive source on the women's movement discusses

abortion activism. For a particularly incisive discussion of the centrality of the ideology of self-determination to this activism, see Rosalind Pollack Petchesky, "Reproductive Freedom: Beyond 'A Woman's Right to Choose,' " *Signs* 5, no. 4 (Summer 1980): 661–85. For a summary of abortion activism, see Davis, *Moving the Mountain*, 157–83.

38. Linda Gordon, *Woman's Body, Woman's Right: A Social History of Birth Control in America* (New York: Grossman, 1976), 47.

39. See chapter 1 for a full discussion and annotation of this view.

40. On the abortion issue and sexual self-determination, specifically, see Petchesky, "Reproductive Freedom." See also Myrna Lamb, "On the Sanctity of Life," *Second Wave* 2, no. 1 (1972): 9; Deborah Rose, "Lookin' Around: How Women Are Regaining Control," *Second Wave* 2, no. 3 (1973): 23–27. On the centrality of sexual self-determination in a broader sense, a strong and typical statement can be found in "Women's Workshop on Sexual Self-Determination," *It Ain't Me, Babe*, December 1, 1970: 5. Wini Breines, again, in *Young, White, and Miserable*, passim, has insight into why this generation of women had such an intense body focus to start with.

41. The bibliography of early feminist writing on the body and sexuality is too lengthy to give in full. Among the most influential works are: Lucinda Cisler, "On Abortion and Abortion Law," and Anne Koedt, "The Myth of the Vaginal Orgasm," in Koedt and Firestone, eds., *Notes from the Second Year*, 89–93, 37–41; Barbara Ehrenreich and Deirdre English, *Witches, Midwives, and Nurses: A History of Women Healers* (Old Westbury, N.Y.: Feminist Press, 1973); Ellen Frankfort, *Vaginal Politics* (New York: Quadrangle Books, 1972); Barbara Seaman, *The Doctors' Case against the Pill* (New York: P. H. Wyden, 1969).

Ruzek, *The Women's Health Movement*, 30, gives a graphic example of the emphasis early radical feminists placed on the body; she reports that in 1972, twenty-six women artists turned an old house into a symbolic female body, each room representing a body part. She writes, "In the flesh-colored kitchen, sponges fashioned into fried eggs transmuted into human breasts adorned the walls and ceiling."

42. It seems more than incidental that the New Right mislabeled the feminist demand for reproductive freedom as antinatalist, and that it collapsed into the abortion issue the entire feminist discourse of motherhood and the family. Recognizing the centrality of the father-dominated nuclear family to its own politics of containment, the Right set out to reforge the association between domesticity and anticommunism by equating women's demand for abortion and birth control with an abdication of the family in favor of selfish individualism, and by linking the defense

of the family to the defense of America. Samuel Blumenthal, an avid antiabortionist, provides one of the more transparent examples of this way of thinking in *The Retreat from Motherhood* (New Rochelle, N.Y.: Arlington House, 1975). According to Blumenthal, the American birth rate reached a low in 1973 because, in alarming numbers, young, leftist, feminist women chose sex over motherhood. In fact, they devised elaborate "Marxist" theories to prove that the maternal instinct had been invented by men. And they kept insisting, foolishly, on their right to make their own choices, including decisions about abortion. Without question, that was a decision a confused young woman should not be free to make. "Before you can say the words 'mother-love,' her local gynecologist can have the embryo sucked out of her uterus and flushed down the drain" (p. 165). Ultimately, Blumenthal claims, this freedom of choice leaves women unhappy. Misinterpreting an article in which feminist writer Karen Lindsey reveals her bitterness over the false promises of the sexual revolution, but urges women to hold "power-tripping" men and not sex itself culpable, Blumenthal declares that feminists themselves believe that they have taken sexual liberation too far. With the demise of patriarchy, he submits, women are feeling the ill effects of too much freedom. In contemporary sexual relations, what was "missing was the paternal imperative of patriarchy that would have given the guys a sense of responsibility" (p. 78). Reinstate patriarchy and outlaw abortion, and society's troubles will cease; fail to do that, and the course of destruction is clear. Triumphantly, Blumenthal states the Right's worst fear: "It should surprise no one that communist countries have had the lowest birth rates of all. As American society becomes more socialistic . . . children will have even less survival value than they might have had in a free society" (p. 23).

43. Nancy Mills, quoted in Arms, *Immaculate Deception*, 223. Another California midwife expressed the same idea in slightly more stream-of-consciousness fashion: "When my friends began having babies—I don't know—it's all combined with women's liberation—health issues—self-help—I began working with self-help about three years ago—and now there's a strong Women's Health Collective in Santa Cruz—everything just sort of grew up side by side and . . . it needs to be done . . . and . . . I like it" (Jackie Christeve, "Midwives Busted in Santa Cruz," *Second Wave* 3, no. 3 [Summer 1974]: 10). Raven Lang's introduction to *Birth Book* (pp. 2–3) also reveals the conjoined impact of countercultural, New Left, and feminist activism and thinking on the home birth and lay midwifery movement. In the secondary literature, a number of writers have commented on the interplay of movements and ideas that led to a concerted

feminist focus on natural childbirth; several mention the counterculture, or the "holistic" movement, but none fleshes out that argument, showing exactly which ideas from the counterculture influenced feminism and how that influence manifested in feminist thought or practice. I think that the countercultural link is a crucial one for feminist thought about motherhood (and for feminist thought in general, although that wider argument is not my project here), and therefore extend the analysis further than others have. See Edwards and Waldorf, *Reclaiming Birth*, 155, 193–95; Judy Barrett Litoff, *American Midwives: 1860 to the Present* (Westport, Conn.: Greenwood Press, 1978), 143; Marieskind and Ehrenreich, "Toward Socialist Medicine," 34–42; Ruzek, *The Women's Health Movement*, 58–61 and passim; Sullivan and Weitz, *Labor Pains,* 35, 42–45.

44. Boston Women's Health Course Collective, *Our Bodies, Ourselves,* 107, 111. Ruzek, *The Women's Health Movement,* 196, writes that "nearly half the 1971 edition of *Our Bodies, Ourselves* is devoted to pregnancy, prepared childbirth, and the postpartum period."

45. Kathy Linck, "Legalizing a Woman's Right to Choose," in Dorothy Tennov and Lolly Hirsch, coordinators, *Proceedings of the First International Childbirth Conference* (Stamford, Conn.: New Moon Publications, 1973), 26.

46. Tennov and Hirsch, *Proceedings of the First International Childbirth Conference,* passim.

47. For a strong defense of the Santa Cruz midwives, see Jackie Christeve, "Midwives Busted in Santa Cruz," *The Second Wave,* 3, no. 3 (Summer 1974): 5–10. See also *The Monthly Extract* 3 (March–April 1974): 7; Arms, *Immaculate Deception,* 277–80; Ruzek, *The Women's Health Movement,* 59.

48. A leading proponent of this view is Alice Echols, *Daring to Be Bad.* It is not an unreasonable view, given feminists' anger at the male-dominated Left in the late 1960s and early 1970s. See, e.g., Morgan, "Goodbye to All That," 121–30.

49. These themes are touched on by many feminist writers during this period. The most prominent work was Ehrenreich and English, *Witches, Midwives, and Nurses.* See also, e.g., Carol Somer, "How Women Had Control of Their Lives and Lost It," *Second Wave* 2, no. 3 (1973): 5–10, 28; Tennov and Hirsch, *Proceedings of the First International Childbirth Conference,* passim.

50. In addition to the sources listed in notes 51 and 52 below, numerous writers expressed these ideas, many referring to Doris Haire's report, "The Cultural Warping of Childbirth." The Boston Women's Health

Course Collective cautions about doctors' unnecessary interventionism and profit motives, as do Suzanne Arms and Raven Lang.

51. These ideas about the body as a machine, and the connections between the rationalization of birth and the rationalization of labor and the social order would be developed fully later by Barbara Katz Rothman in *Giving Birth* and *Recreating Motherhood: Ideology and Technology in a Patriarchal Society* (New York: Norton, 1989); and by Emily Martin, in *The Woman in the Body: A Cultural Analysis of Reproduction* (Boston: Beacon, 1987). Nevertheless, the major primary sources from the period I am discussing here all touch on these themes. See especially Arms, *Immaculate Deception,* passim; Boston Women's Health Course Collective, *Our Bodies, Ourselves,* passim; Lang, *Birth Book,* passim. In the secondary literature, Ruzek's discussion of these ideas as they emerged in the women's health movement is helpful; see *The Women's Health Movement,* 98–102 and passim.

52. All of these ideas appear in the primary sources of the period, some more emphasized in certain works than others. The transcript of the International Childbirth Conference of 1973 provides a full overview of feminist critiques of established obstetrical practices; each of the criticisms listed here receives direct treatment. See Hirsch and Tennov, *Proceedings of the First International Childbirth Conference.* Arms, *Immaculate Deception,* and Lang, *Birth Book,* also cover all the complaints. Additionally, in the feminist periodical literature of the times, there is frequent mention of these themes. In 1972, mother and daughter Lolly and Jeanne Hirsch helped to found the newsletter *Monthly Extract—An Irregular Periodical;* a reading of the run of this newsletter probably gives the fullest view of the feminist critique of and alternatives to traditional obstetrics during this period. For a few examples from other periodicals, see Sharon de Maehl and Linda Thurston, "Caution: Trusting Your Obstetrician May Be Harmful to Your Health," *Second Wave* 2, no. 3 (1973): 21–23; Joan Haggerty, "Childbirth Made Difficult," *Ms.* 1, no. 7 (January 1973): 16–17; Lorna J. Rogers, "Babies Are Born Not Delivered," *It Ain't Me, Babe,* no. 15 (October 8, 1970): 15; Shirley Streshinsky, "Are You Safer with a Midwife?" *Ms.* 2, no. 4 (October 1973): 24–27. The secondary literature in the field also summarizes this critique; the most thorough review is probably Ruzek, *The Women's Health Movement,* passim.

53. Wellish and Root, *Hearts Open Wide,* 10.

54. Again, these themes and images are reiterated throughout the literature, as, for example, in Arms, *Immaculate Deception,* 240, 383; Dorothy Dobbyn, "A Feminist's Case for Homebirth," *Women: A Journal of Liberation* 4, no. 3 (1976): 20–23; Jeanne Hirsch, "Watching a Childbirth

at Home," in Tennov and Hirsch, *Proceedings of the First International Childbirth Conference,* 18.

55. Kathleen Barry, "How They Turned the Tables on Us," in Tennov and Hirsch, *Proceedings of the First International Childbirth Conference,* 3–4; Somer, "How Women Had Control of Their Lives and Lost It," 8.

56. Deirdre English, "Society Makes Us Sick," in Tennov and Hirsch, *Proceedings of the First International Childbirth Conference,* 4. The broader point about pregnancy as a nondiseased state is brought up repeatedly at the conference; see, for example, the speech by Evelyn Kurtzberg, 10–11.

I should make it clear that feminists were championing the reemergence of the *lay* midwife, not the nurse midwife, who might have straddled the gulf between holistic and orthodox medicine ideologically, but who worked within traditional medical settings. On this distinction, see especially Rothman, *Giving Birth,* 63–77.

57. Boston Women's Health Course Collective, *Our Bodies, Ourselves,* 88.

58. Tennov and Hirsch, *Proceedings of the First International Childbirth Conference,* 17, 19; Rothman, *Giving Birth,* 29, 35, 48, and passim; Lang, *Birth Book,* passim; Sullivan and Weitz, *Labor Pains,* 43–44; Arms, *Immaculate Deception,* passim.

59. Christeve, "Midwives Busted in Santa Cruz," 5.

60. Ibid., 7.

61. Downer, "Women Professionals in the Feminist Health Movement," 3.

62. Rogers, "Babies Are Born Not Delivered," 15; Christeve, "Midwives Busted In Santa Cruz," 6, 10. In the secondary literature, these themes are best summarized by Rothman, *Giving Birth,* passim.

63. Carol Somer, "The Midwife As Witch," in Tannov and Hirsch, *Proceedings of the First International Childbirth Conference,* 2.

64. There was a parallel discussion for breastfeeding. Feminists claimed that mother's milk was nutritionally superior to formula because it contained only natural, not chemical, ingredients. Mother's milk conferred a healthful immunity to the infant, where formula left the baby prey to numerous illnesses. Mother's milk cost less, thus defying the profiteering of the formula companies. Nursing fostered closeness between mother and child, in terms of eye contact, skin to skin contact, and so on. And nursing allowed mother and child to follow an inner, intuitive, natural schedule, rather than submit to some artificial external clock. See, e.g., Sally Wendkos Olds, "Breastfeeding Successfully in Spite of Doctors and Hospitals," Rosalea Fisher, "Why Nurse Your Baby?" Bridget Nozal, "Some

Thoughts on Breastfeeding," and Pattie Harrington, "Nursing a Toddler," all in Tennov and Hirsch, *Proceedings of the First International Childbirth Conference*, 20–22. See also Rothman, *Giving Birth*, chap. 7.

65. Janet Darragh, "Birth at Home," in Tennov and Hirsch, *Proceedings of the First International Childbirth Conference*, 17.

66. Christeve, "Midwives Busted in Santa Cruz," 8.

67. Naomi Lambert Mayer, "The Midwife: Liberating Childbirth," in Tennov and Hirsch, *Proceedings of the First International Childbirth Conference*, 15.

68. Christeve, "Midwives Busted in Santa Cruz": 8.

69. Ibid., 9.

70. Ibid.

71. The most dramatic reference is Arms, *Immaculate Deception*, especially chap. 1, "Your Sister Has a Baby Girl," but most of the sources already cited use this language and imagery.

72. Cheryl Anderson, during open discussion, in Tennov and Hirsch, *Proceedings of the First International Childbirth Conference*, 29.

73. Lang, *Birth Book*, 40.

74. Arms, *Immaculate Deception*, 151.

75. Ibid., 384.

76. Gaskin, *Spiritual Midwifery*, 14.

77. Ibid., 11.

78. Ibid., 52.

79. Ibid., 53; Lang's *Birth Book* contains similar stories.

80. Boston Women's Health Course Collective, *Our Bodies, Ourselves*, 10.

81. Lucille B. Ritvo, "Realizing Women's Special Eroticism in Childbirth and Nursing," in Tennov and Hirsch, *Proceedings of the First International Childbirth Conference*, 7.

82. Christeve, "Midwives Busted in Santa Cruz," 10.

83. Ritvo, "Realizing Women's Special Eroticism in Childbirth and Nursing," 7.

84. Ibid., 6.

85. Nozal, "Some Thoughts on Breastfeeding," 21. Viva made similar sensualist claims for nursing in "Hooked on Weaning," *Ms.* 3, no. 10 (April 1975): 51–54, 90; the responses in the Letters section of the magazine reflect both the countercultural view I am tracing here and statements of horror at the notion of turning nursing into an "orgy." Notably, the strongest disapproval comes from an older woman, who writes, in criticism of what I have identified in a broader sense as the spontaneous, playful ethos of the counterculture, that "there is a time for an adult to act

with childlike spontaneity and fully indulged sexuality. That time is not when a mother is nursing her child, but when one adult is in bed with another adult" ("Letters," *Ms.* 4, no. 2 [August 1975]: 7–8).

86. Again, this is a consistent theme in the feminist literature of childbirth and is perhaps strongest in the most "countercultural" of the sources. See especially Arms, *Immaculate Deception*, passim; Gaskin, *Spiritual Midwifery*, 11; Lang, *Birth Book*, passim.

87. Michele Hoffnung Garskof, "The Psychology of the Maternity Ward: A Study in Dehumanization," in Tennov and Hirsch, *Proceedings of the First International Childbirth Conference*, 12.

88. The most extreme version of these views that I have seen came later, in Rothman, *Recreating Motherhood*. But during the 1968–1974 period discussed here, these views also received wide play among feminists. See, e.g., Hirsch, "Watching a Childbirth at Home," 18.

89. Arms, *Immaculate Deception*, 151.

90. Ibid., 384.

Notes to Chapter Three

1. This analysis in no way implies that black feminisms first emerged in the 1960s, or that the debates over gender issues among African Americans commenced with the Black Power movement. To the contrary, both black feminism and intrarace gender conflict have long, complex histories. For a good summary of both, see Toni Morrison, ed., *Race-ing Justice, En-gendering Power: Essays on Anita Hill, Clarence Thomas, and the Construction of Social Reality* (New York: Pantheon, 1992). See also Deborah K. King, "Multiple Jeopardy, Multiple Consciousness: The Context of a Black Feminist Ideology," in Darlene Clark Hine, ed., *Black Women's History: Theory and Practice*, vol. 1 (Brooklyn, N.Y.: Carlson Publishing, 1990), 331–61; Barbara Omolade, *The Rising Song of African American Women* (New York: Routledge, 1994), chaps. 5, 7, and 11; Jessie M. Rodrique, "The Black Community and the Birth Control Movement," in Kathy Peiss and Christina Simmons, eds., *Passion and Power: Sexuality in History* (Philadelphia: Temple University Press, 1989), 138–54.

2. E. Franklin Frazier, *The Negro Family in the United States* (Chicago: University of Chicago Press, 1939); Bonnie Thornton Dill, "The Dialectics of Black Womanhood," *Signs* 4, no. 3 (1979): 544–46.

3. Daniel Patrick Moynihan, *The Negro Family: The Case for National Action* (Washington, D.C.: U.S. Government Printing Office, 1965).

4. For a summary of the reaction to the Moynihan report, see Lee

Rainwater and William Yancey, *The Moynihan Report and the Politics of Controversy* (Cambridge, Mass.: M.I.T. Press, 1967); see also C. Eric Lincoln, ed., *Is Anybody Listening to Black America?* (New York: Seabury Press, 1968); Joanne Grant, ed., *Black Protest: History, Documents, and Analyses* (New York: Fawcett, 1968).

5. Imamu Amiri Baraka, *Raise Race Rays Raze: Essays since 1965* (New York: Random House, 1971), passim; H. Rapp Brown, *Die Nigger Die!* (New York: Dial Press, 1969), 105–13 and passim. For discussions of sterilization abuse, see Frances Beale, "Double Jeopardy: To Be Black and Female," in Toni Cade, ed., *The Black Woman: An Anthology* (New York: Penguin, 1970), 95–98. (Beale's name is sometimes spelled "Beal"; following the lead of Cade, from whose anthology I cite, I use the former spelling.) Toni Cade, "The Pill: Genocide or Liberation," in Cade, ed., *The Black Woman,* 162–69. On blacks' perception of the general white genocidal impulse, see Samuel F. Yette, *The Choice: The Issue of Black Survival in America* (New York: Putnam, 1971), passim; and Robert Weisbord, *Genocide? Birth Control and the Black American* (Westport, Conn.: Greenwood Press, 1975), passim.

6. Charles V. Hamilton, "Riots, Revolts and Relevant Responses," in Floyd B. Barbour, ed., *The Black Power Revolt: A Collection of Essays* (Boston: Sargent, 1968), 171–78; John E. Johnson, Jr., "Super Black Man," in Barbour, ed., *The Black Power Revolt,* 224–26.

7. William L. Van DeBurg, *New Day in Babylon: The Black Power Movement and American Culture, 1965–1975* (Chicago: University of Chicago Press, 1992), offers a thorough account of the Black Power movement from a cultural perspective. Black nationalism was not new, but rather resurgent, in the 1960s; on earlier black nationalism, see, e.g., George M. Fredrickson, *Black Liberation: A Comparative History of Black Ideologies in the United States and South Africa* (New York: Oxford University Press, 1995); Manning Marable, *Through the Prism of Race and Class: Modern Black Nationalism in the U.S.* (Dayton, Ohio: Black Research Associates, 1980); Bill McAdoo, *Pre–Civil War Black Nationalism* (New York: D. Walker Press, 1983); Wilson Jeremiah Moses, *Alexander Crummell: A Study of Civilization and Discontent* (New York: Oxford University Press, 1989).

8. Quoted in Michele Wallace, *Black Macho and the Myth of the Superwoman* (New York: Verso, 1990; orig. 1979), 8; see also Stokely Carmichael, "What We Want," in Albert and Albert, eds., *The Sixties Papers,* 137–44.

9. Chuck Stone, "The National Conference on Black Power," in Barbour, ed., *The Black Power Revolt,* 195.

10. Ibid.

11. I am not suggesting that the sexism of black radical groups exceeded that of white radical groups, or that the terms in which black radical men expressed sexism were more objectionable. Rather, I am attempting to explain why a black feminist response to sexism within activist groups emerged so strongly as a reworking of the meaning of motherhood, per se, and am suggesting that the pronatalist imperative of a nationalist perspective, located within specific historical circumstances, helped to shape this response. Joyce Hope Scott, "From Foreground to Margin: Female Configurations and Masculine Self-Representation in Black Nationalist Fiction," in Andrew Parker, Mary Russo, Doris Sommer, and Patricia Yaeger, eds., *Nationalisms and Sexualities* (New York: Routledge, 1992), 296–312, makes the point that this is not always the outcome of nationalist struggle; she discusses attitudes toward women in earlier black nationalist movements in the United States, arguing that nineteenth-century collectivism, which embraced women's liberation, gave way to a twentieth-century patriarchalism patterned after that of white America.

12. Eldridge Cleaver, *Soul on Ice* (New York: Dell, 1968), 162. It is worth noting that Cleaver's views on women, at least those expressed publicly, changed over time. In 1969, as Panther minister of information, Cleaver spoke strongly in favor of black women's liberation, stating that if the Panthers wanted to consider themselves a vanguard organization, they would have to set an example of respect for women; see "Eldridge Cleaver on Women's Liberation," *Guardian,* August 2, 1969: 5. For changing Panther views, see also Bobby Seale, "Women's Liberation and the Black Panther Party," *Salt of the Earth* 2, no. 4: 6, 9.

13. Black Unity Party, "Birth Control and Black Children," reprinted in Patricia Robinson et al., "Poor Black Women," New England Free Press, "New England Free Press" file, Schlesinger Library, n.d.

14. Black Unity Party, "Birth Control and Black Children." On male-dominated families, see Combahee River Collective, "A Black Feminist Statement," in Eisenstein, ed., *Capitalist Patriarchy,* 368, especially the segment of the black nationalist pamphlet cited therein: Mumininas of Committee for Unified Newark, *Mwanamke Mwananchi (The Nationalist Woman),* (Newark, N.J.: n.p., 1971), 4–5.

15. Evette Pearson, "White America Today," reprinted from *The Black Panther,* January 4, 1969, in Philip S. Foner, ed., *The Black Panthers Speak* (Philadelphia: J. B. Lippincott, 1970), 26.

16. Baraka, *Raise Race Rays Raze,* 150.

17. A far greater number of women, across the spectrum of Black

Power organizations and ideologies, grappled with the meaning of male dominance, and even the extent of its existence in their movements, than the resultant writings would indicate. "Panther Sisters on Women's Liberation," in G. Louis Heath, ed., *Off the Pigs! The Literature of the Black Panther Party* (Metuchen, N.J.: Scarecrow Press, 1976), 339–50, shows the sense of fluidity around the "woman question." As black reviewers' responses to Wallace's *Black Macho,* as well as recent debates sparked by the publication of Elaine Brown's autobiography and account of the Black Panthers, indicate, the history of women's gender activism within the Black Power movement is controversial and still largely unexplored by scholars. Elaine Brown, *A Taste of Power: A Black Woman's Story* (New York: Pantheon, 1992), and Angela Davis's review, "The Making of a Revolutionary," *Women's Review of Books* 10, no. 9 (1993): 1, 3–4. On the need for black feminists to contend with the "matriarchy" question, see Snitow's brief comments in "Feminism and Motherhood: An American Reading," 37.

18. Beale, "Double Jeopardy," 93.

19. Ibid.

20. Toni Cade, "The Pill: Genocide or Liberation," in Cade, ed., *The Black Woman,* 164. Similarly, a few years later, Pearl Lomax, in "Black Women's Lib?" *Essence,* August 1972: 68, decried the *psychological* damage done to black women by the black movement's pronatalism (and other manifestations of sexism).

21. This analysis raises the very complex matter of the relation between the primarily white counterculture of the 1960s and the cultural aspects of the black liberation movement of that period. Although the two movements shared many values, and some black individuals socialized with white counterculturalists, and vice versa, neither movement was racially integrated in any significant way and the two in fact differed in several fundamental ways. On the cultural aspects of the Black Power movement, see especially Van DeBurg, *New Day in Babylon.* Feigelson, *The Underground Revolution,* chap. 5, discusses the relations between black and white *cultural,* as well as political, radicals in the 1960s. Clayton Riley, "Black Nationalists and the Hippies," *Liberator,* December 1967: 4–7, talks about the tensions between blacks and hippies.

22. Beale, "Double Jeopardy," 93; Linda LaRue, "The Black Power Movement and Women's Liberation," *Black Scholar* 1 (May 1970): 36–42, and Kathleen Cleaver, "Black Scholar Interviews Kathleen Cleaver," *Black Scholar* 3 (December 1971): 54–59, also give versions of the false consciousness explanation for male chauvinism among blacks.

23. Patricia Robinson et al., "The Sisters Reply," in Albert and Albert, eds., *The Sixties Papers,* 479.

24. Ibid., 479–80.

25. The writings in Cade, ed., *The Black Woman,* represent the most cohesive presentation of this critique. Another strong statement is in Patricia Robinson's essay, "Poor Black Women," in the New England Free Press reprint by that title.

26. Robinson et al., "The Sisters Reply," 479.

27. See especially Cleaver, *Soul on Ice,* passim.

28. Beale, "Double Jeopardy," 92.

29. Ibid. See also Pauli Murray, "The Liberation of Black Women," in Mary Lou Thompson, ed., *Voices of the New Feminism* (Boston: Beacon, 1970), 87–102; and, all in Cade, ed., *The Black Woman:* Kay Lindsey, "The Black Woman As Woman," 85–89; Abbey Lincoln, "Who Will Revere the Black Woman?" 80–84; Jean Carey Bond and Patricia Peery, "Is the Black Male Castrated?" 113–18; and Cade, "The Pill: Genocide or Liberation?" 162–69.

30. Bond and Peery, "Is the Black Male Castrated?" 117 (originally published as "Has the Black Male Been Castrated?" *Liberator* 9, no. 5 (May 1969): 4–8.

31. Gwen Patton, "Black People and the Victorian Ethos," in Cade, ed., *The Black Woman,* 147.

32. Toni Cade, "On the Issue of Roles," in Cade, ed., *The Black Woman,* 103–4.

33. Fran Sanders, "Dear Black Man," in Cade, ed., *The Black Woman,* 74. Eleanor Holmes Norton makes the same point, briefly, in Cellestine Ware, "The Black Family and Feminism: A Conversation with Eleanor Holmes Norton," *Ms.,* Spring 1972 Preview Issue: 96.

34. In the years subsequent to the early feminist period described here, scholars have documented the matrifocality of the black family, in an effort to rehabilitate its image and validate its unique coping strategies through centuries of oppression. In spoken or unspoken rebuttal of the Moynihan Report's allegation of a destructive "matriarchy," scholars have tried to show how black women's current manifestations of strength and independence were forged historically, and how they represent a positive force in the black community. In this view, the emphasis in black feminism on motherhood, matrilinearity, and matriarchy flows directly from the material circumstances of black female life over generations.

I emphasize the active, discursive dimension of black feminist thought that occurred in the context of the 1960s debate over "matriarchy," nationalism, and pronatalism. It is in the crucible of that debate that a particular view of black motherhood took form. For Alice Walker, in 1974, to write about the wisdom garnered from her "mother's garden" was to make a finely honed feminist statement, also influenced and given texture by the rich historical fact of matrifocality in her family. Ten years earlier, Walker's words would not have carried the multilayered meaning they imparted after the Moynihan Report. To be sure, black women bonded intergenerationally well before 1968! But in the discursive mediation of that bonding a historically specific feminist analysis emerged.

I belabor this point because I see the collapse of black feminist discourses of motherhood into the "material" circumstances of black life as particularly troubling. It is as if black women create feminist theory with their bodies and their relationships; the primary source becomes the theory, such that the scholarship compares white feminist "theory" with black "life," a dissonant comparison at best. See also bell hooks's discussion of this issue in *Talking Back: Thinking Feminist, Thinking Black* (Boston: South End Press, 1989).

35. Lincoln, "Who Will Revere the Black Woman?" 81–82.

36. Ibid., 82.

37. On earlier black feminisms and maternalism, see Eileen Boris, "The Power of Motherhood: Black and White Activist Women Redefine the 'Political,' " in Seth Koven and Sonya Michel, eds., *Mothers of a New World: Maternalist Politics and the Origins of Welfare States* (New York: Routledge, 1993), 213–45; Evelyn Brooks, "The Feminist Theology of the Black Baptist Church, 1880–1900," in Hine, *Black Women in American History*, vol. 1, 167–95; Lynda F. Dickson, "Toward a Broader Angle of Vision in Uncovering Women's History: Black Women's Clubs Revisited," in Hine, ed., *Black Women's History: Theory and Practice*, vol. 1, 103–19; Gordon, *Pitied But Not Entitled*, chap. 5; Sharon Harley, "Anna J. Cooper: A Voice for Black Women," in Sharon Harley and Rosalyn Terborg-Penn, eds., *The Afro-American Woman: Struggles and Images* (Port Washington, N.Y.: Kennikat Press, 1978), 87–96; Wilson Jeremiah Moses, "Domestic Feminism, Conservatism, Sex Roles, and Black Women's Clubs, 1893–1896," in Hine, ed., *Black Women in American History*, vol. 3, 959–70.

38. Angela Davis, "The Black Woman's Role in the Community of Slaves," *Black Scholar* vol. 3, no. 4 (December 1971): 2–15. Also, Angela Davis, "Prison Interviews," in Angela Davis and Bettina Aptheker, eds., *If They Come in the Morning* (New York: Third Press, 1971), 185–86: "Our enemies have attempted to mesmerize us, to mesmerize Black people, by propounding a whole assortment of myths with respect to the Black

woman. We are inveterate matriarchs, implying we have worked in collusion with the white oppressor to insure the emasculation of our men. Unfortunately, some Black women have accepted these myths without questioning their origin and without being aware of the counterrevolutionary content and effect. They're consequently falling into behind-the-scenes positions in the movement and refuse to be aggressive and take leadership in our struggle for fear of contributing to the oppression of the Black male. . . . As Black women, we must liberate ourselves and provide the impetus for the liberation of Black men from this whole network of lies around the oppression of Black women which serve only to divide us, thus impeding the advance of our total liberation struggle."

39. Davis, "The Black Woman's Role in the Community of Slaves," 3. Wallace writes about Davis and Jackson in *Black Macho,* 160–67; for an important critique of Wallace's interpretation, see Linda Powell, "Black Macho and Black Feminism," in Barbara Smith, ed., *Home Girls: A Black Feminist Anthology* (New York: Kitchen Table Press, 1983), 283–92.

40. Davis, "The Black Woman's Role in the Community of Slaves," 3.

41. Ibid., 7; on Davis's article, see Manning Marable, *Black American Politics: From the Washington Marches to Jesse Jackson* (London: Verso, 1985), 43. I cite Davis's article here for its contribution to this particular discourse. Important criticism of her thesis has been raised as well; see E. Frances White, "Listening to the Voices of Black Feminism," *Radical America* 18, nos. 2–3 (1984): 12–13.

42. Patricia M. Robinson, "A Historical and Critical Essay for Black Women of the Cities (Excerpts)," in Stambler, ed., *Women's Liberation: Blueprint for the Future,* 274–83; Patricia Haden, Donna Middleton, and Patricia Robinson, "A Historical and Critical Essay for Black Women," in Altbach, ed., *From Feminism to Liberation,* 125–42.

43. Robinson, "Historical and Critical Essay for Black Women," 274.

44. Ibid., 278.

45. Ibid., 282–83.

46. Alice Walker, "In Search of Our Mothers' Gardens," in *In Search of Our Mothers' Gardens: Womanist Prose* (New York: Harcourt Brace Jovanovitch, 1984), 237.

47. Ibid., 243.

48. Walker uses the word "womanist," as distinct from feminist. She traces the word to the black folk expression "womanish," which connotes both a commitment to women and an irreverent attitude of "outrageous, audacious, courageous or *willful* behavior," which Walker sees as something positive for black women. Walker, *In Search of Our Mothers' Gardens,* xi.

49. To say that black feminists have focused on motherhood, and that that focus has tended to be "positive," is not to say that it has been monolithic, without nuance, or uncomplicated. See, e.g., Diane Sadoff, "Black Matrilineage: The Case of Alice Walker and Zora Neale Hurston," *Signs* 11, no. 1 (Autumn 1985): 4–26; Sadoff writes that Walker at times "confuses motherhood with sisterhood and idealizes the mother-daughter bond" (p. 12).

50. To some extent, white feminists also bemoaned the absence of working-class or "ordinary" women in the movement. However, the most heated discussion of class came a few years later, when working-class and middle-class (mostly white) participants in the movement began to address issues of classism within the already existing movement. Racism within the movement would also receive separate attention in subsequent years. Here I address the discussion of the recruitment of black women into the movement, rather than the later discussion of relations between black and white feminists already involved in some kind of common endeavor.

51. See, e.g., Echols, *Daring to Be Bad*, 369–77; Cherríe Moraga, in the Preface to Cherríe Moraga and Gloria Anzaldua, eds., *This Bridge Called My Back: Writings by Radical Women of Color* (New York: Kitchen Table/Women of Color Press, 1981), xv; and, especially, bell hooks, *Feminist Theory: From Margin to Center* (Boston: South End Press, 1984), passim. Phylliss Marynick Palmer, "White Women/Black Women: The Dualism of Female Identity and Experience in the United States," *Feminist Studies* 9, no. 1 (Spring 1983): 154, notes the "disjunction between white women's embracing black women as images of strength and pathos and ignoring the realistic needs and interests of these same black women." Sharon Patricia Holland, " 'Which Me Will Survive?': Audre Lorde and the Development of A Black Feminist Ideology," *Critical Matrix*, Special Issue, no. 1 (1988): 2–30, also writes of how white feminists, in the nineteenth century and now, have been guilty of "metaphorizing" black women's lives. Margaret A. Simons, in "Racism and Feminism: A Schism in the Sisterhood," *Feminist Studies* 5, no. 2 (Summer 1979): 384–401, discusses the exclusion of black women from much feminist theory, along with their superfical "inclusion" in other works. The deepest reading of what Adrienne Rich calls "white solipsism" in feminist thought is probably in Elizabeth Spelman, *Inessential Woman: Problems of Exclusion in Feminist Thought* (Boston: Beacon, 1988), chap. 5.

52. Evans, *Personal Politics*, 212–32.

53. A transcript of the proceedings of the Sandy Springs Conference is included in Echols, *Daring to Be Bad*, 369–77; see also Echols's discussion of this episode on pp. 105–7.

54. These same arguments would manifest concerning class and sexual orientation in the women's movement in the 1970s. Largely because of the prominence of the Black Power movement in the late 1960s, and the frequent assertion on the white Left that blacks held the moral high ground, many feminists emerging from New Left involvement ascribed to this belief; see Echols, *Daring to Be Bad*, 46–50, 125–29. For a good example of white leftist thinking about race, see "Following the Panthers . . . the Panthers and Us," *The Mole* 2, no. 4 (March 5, 1971): 3–5.

55. Echols, *Daring to Be Bad*, 370.

56. Beale, "Double Jeopardy," 98. See also Cellestine Ware, *Woman Power: The Movement for Women's Liberation* (New York: Tower Publications, 1970), chap. 2. The interviews with black feminist activists in Brenda Eichelberger, "Voices on Black Feminism," *Quest* 3, no. 4 (Spring 1977): 16–28, though conducted somewhat later, deal retroflectively with this period.

57. Naomi Weisstein used the phrase in the essay "Woman As Nigger," in Leslie B. Tanner, ed., *Voices from Women's Liberation* (New York: New American Library, 1970), 296–303. Weisstein's article, which originally appeared in *Psychology Today* (October 1969), actually dealt with the unrelated topic of psychology's failures vis-à-vis women. Vivian Gornick also expounded at length on the phrase, and made the explicit comparison between the oppression of blacks and of women, in "The Next Great Moment in History Is Ours," in Deborah Babcox and Madeline Belkin, eds., *Liberation Now! The Writings of the Women's Liberation Movement* (New York: Dell, 1971), 25–39. This argument had been used all along in the emerging women's movement, especially by white women civil rights activists, as they began to apply the analysis of that movement to their own situation. The 1965 memo by Casey Hayden and Mary King, "Sex and Caste: A Kind of Memo," reprinted in Albert and Albert, eds., *The Sixties Papers*, 133–36, is a case in point. But the uses of this argument in the later 1960s and early 1970s, to resolve the question of how women's liberation should relate to blacks, differed in that the justification for organizing on the basis of gender oppression had already been established by this point, and now various writers were reverting to the earlier rhetoric. Echols refers briefly to the earlier discussions of this topic in *Daring to Be Bad*, 75.

58. Bell hooks, for example, notes the alienating effect of such rhetoric in *Ain't I a Woman: Black Women and Feminism* (Boston: South End Press, 1981), 8, 142.

59. "Free Our Sisters, Free Ourselves," in Tanner, ed., *Voices from Women's Liberation*, 119–20. See also "Women Support Panther Sisters,"

in Tanner, ed. *Voices from Women's Liberation,* 118. Flax Hermes, "Mass Women's March in Conn.," *Militant* 33, no. 48 (December 5, 1969): 1, 3, gives a detailed account of the demonstration.

60. WITCH, "Pass the Word, Sister," in Tanner, ed., *Voices from Women's Liberation,* 123.

61. Ibid., 122–23.

62. One of WITCH's "covens," for example, explained the WITCH acronym on Mother's Day as standing for "Women Infuriated at Taking Care of Hoodlums," in Morgan, ed., *Sisterhood Is Powerful,* 604.

63. Leading examples include Altbach, ed., *From Feminism to Liberation;* Cooke, Bunch-Weeks, and Morgan, eds., *The New Women: A MOTIVE Anthology;* Morgan, ed., *Sisterhood Is Powerful;* Stambler, ed., *Women's Liberation: Blueprint for the Future;* Tanner, ed., *Voices from Women's Liberation.*

64. Betsy Warrior, "Females and Welfare," in Tanner, ed., *Voices from Women's Liberation,* 277. While not contesting this image of mothers as relentless advocates for their children, Warrior was also cautioning in this article against allowing the political organizations of the male-dominated Left to *use* welfare mothers toward ends that would not benefit women first and foremost.

65. Beale, "Double Jeopardy," 97–98. The essay also appeared in various other anthologies, including Morgan, *Sisterhood Is Powerful,* and Cooke et al., *The New Women.*

66. For example, in *It Ain't Me Babe,* July 1–23, 1970, two adjacent articles, "Abortion Laws; —or—What Happened to Your Civil Rights," and "Caution: Abortion May Be Genocidal!" deal with the question of reproductive rights. The first, by Sharon Judith Simms of the San Francisco group Association to Repeal Abortion Laws, speaks of the need for safe, inexpensive, legal abortions. The second, written by a group of "sisters," recounts a speech given by Judi Claude, a black woman, at a recent proabortion rally, enumerating the ways in which free abortion on demand would be insufficient to end sterilization abuse or to "help women of color control their bodies and their lives."

67. "Program of the Southern Female Rights Union, New Orleans, Louisiana," quoted in Charlotte Bunch, "A Broom of One's Own: Notes on the Women's Liberation Program," in Cooke et al., *The New Women: A MOTIVE Anthology,* 203. Similarly, see the flyer distributed in 1972 by the Women's National Abortion Action Coalition (WONAAC), "International Tribunal on Abortion, Contraception & Forced Sterilization," "Women's Rights Rallies" file, Schlesinger Library. White feminist attention to coercive sterilization practices intensified in 1973, following expo-

sés of involuntary sterilizations of young black women in Alabama and South Carolina; NOW, for example, issued a statement in July of that year citing the Alabama case and declaring that the organization "has always stood for the individual's right to control their own reproductive lives without unwarranted government intrusion" ("Statement of National Organization for Women—July 9, 1973," from "Sterilization" file, Schlesinger Library). On the exposés, see B. Drummond Ayres, Jr., "Racism, Ethics and Rights at Issue in Sterilization Case," *New York Times,* July 2, 1973: 10; Nancy Hicks, "Sterilization of Black Mother of 2 Stirs Aiken, S.C.," *New York Times,* August 1, 1973: 27.

68. "Chicago Women's Liberation Union" file, Schlesinger Library, n.d.; "Chicago Maternity Center in Crisis," *Womankind* 1, no. 10 (June 1972): 2. A few years later, the Committee for Abortion Rights and Against Sterilization Abuse (CARASA) was even more liberal in its use of black feminist analysis and made an explicit effort to attract black women and address their concerns. An internal CARASA draft proposal addressing the issue of child care noted the white bias of an exclusive focus on abortion rights and echoed Beale closely: "The population we have been most interested in doing outreach to—black, hispanic, working-class, third-world (to use all the shorthand refs. I can think of)—are not hostile or indifferent to the issue of reproductive rights, but I think they may see the order of priorities differently. I suggest that they identify reproductive rights as an important issue to them if child caring supports are considered as first need, birth-control and protection from population control measures as next; for more effective outreach by CARASA, we should recognize their priorities and make ourselves prepared to participate in them" ("CARASA and Child Care Politics and Program, Draft Proposal," in "CARASA" file, Schlesinger Library, n.d.) As the above examples suggest, socialist feminist analysis and organizing efforts account for most of the broadly defined feminist reproductive rights activism of the mid-1970s on; see Adele Clarke and Alice Wolfson, "Class, Race, and Reproductive Rights," in Hansen and Philipson, *Women, Class, and the Feminist Imagination,* 258–67.

69. "Oppression of Different Groups of Women, Whether, Why and How Women's Liberation Relates to Them, i.e. Priorities in Organizing," in "Women's Liberation, Berkeley, California" file, Schlesinger Library, n.d., p. 8; and "The Nature of Change and Political Action—Reform vs. Revolution," in "Women's Liberation, Berkeley, CA." file, Schlesinger Library, n.d.

70. Omolade, *The Rising Song of African American Women,* 75–76, 168–69; Combahee River Collective, "A Black Feminist Statement," 362–

72. On the National Black Feminist Organization, see Beverly Davis, "To Seize the Moment: A Retrospective on the National Black Feminist Organization," *Sage* 5, no. 2 (Fall 1988): 43–47; Karla Jay, "Double Trouble for Black Women: An Interview with Margaret Sloan," *The Tide* 3, no. 9 (July 1974): 3, 22–24; Sylvia Witts Vitale, "Black Sisterhood," *National Black Feminist Organization Newsletter* 1, no. 3 (September 1975): 2. Extremely important, too, in the context of feminist reproductive rights activism is the later development of a black women's health movement, in the early 1980s; see Clarke and Wolfson, "Class, Race, and Reproductive Rights," 265.

71. This analysis draws on the work of Echols, in *Daring to Be Bad* and other writings; see below, chap. 4, note 1.

Notes to Chapter Four

1. As throughout this book, I must acknowledge my debt to the writings of Alice Echols. In *Daring to Be Bad*, as well as in two pieces exploring the relation of cultural feminism to the antipornography movement—"The New Feminism of Yin and Yang," in Ann Snitow, Christine Stansell, and Sharon Thompson, eds., *Powers of Desire: The Politics of Sexuality* (New York: Monthly Review Press, 1983), 439–59; and "The Taming of the Id," in Carole Vance, ed., *Pleasure and Danger*, 50–72—Echols advances several of the ideas central to my own thesis and periodization. At the same time, there are many places where our emphases differ, where we attribute causality differently, and, on a few occasions, where our views diverge. It is Echols who most cogently dates the "devolvement" of radical feminism into cultural feminism to the early-to-mid 1970s, and who focuses on Jane Alpert's "Mother Right" as the signal article of the new era. While numerous other writers, including Brooke Williams, Leah Fritz, and especially Ellen Willis (in "Radical Feminism and Feminist Radicalism") also wrote about this shift in feminism, and some noted the centrality of the controversy about Alpert to the shift, Echols broached the first full historical study of the topic. Echols develops the hypothesis that cultural feminism's universalizing tendencies were aimed at easing the internal factiousness of the women's movement in the early 1970s. Additionally, Echols (along with Willis and other writers in the feminist "pro-sex" or anti-antipornography movement) notes that cultural feminists, in their devotion to the antipornography cause, have demonized both male and female sexuality, replacing the latter with a vision of sexless, sometimes maternal, female bonding.

Like Echols, I see in the universalizing theories of the early cultural feminists an attempt to heal an ailing women's movement. While I concur with her assessment of the rift caused by the "gay/straight" split in the movement, I believe that closer attention needs to be given to the issue of race in the women's movement by the early 1970s. I argue that white feminists' desire for rapprochement with black women was a *central* motivating factor in their creation of a universal theory of womanhood. Moreover, because I trace the revaluation of the mother in feminist theory so clearly to the cultural left and to early black feminist thought, I am much more inclined to see continuity where Echols finds cultural feminist rupture with the Left. Finally, while Echols remarks on the intense cultural feminist concentration on motherhood, and notes also the tradeoff made between motherhood and sexuality in cultural feminist theory, she does not question at length why motherhood, of all possible topics, rose to such a position of prominence; that is not the primary intent of her much wider-ranging study. My work is narrower and addresses specifically the causative factors of the trends Echols points out.

The term "false universalism" is from Eisenstein, *Contemporary Feminist Thought,* 132; Eisenstein speaks of the universalizing impulse within feminism in less explicitly political terms than Echols, seeing the tendency as growing "inevitably from the need to establish gender as a legitimate intellectual category." She does, however, acknowledge the concrete and damaging effects of the impulse, particularly in terms of race.

2. Quoted in Joreen, "Trashing: The Dark Side of Sisterhood," *Ms.,* April 1976: 92; also quoted in Echols, *Daring to Be Bad,* 184.

3. Strong accounts of these early divisions can be found in Marlene Dixon, "On Women's Liberation," *Radical America* 4, no. 2 (February 1970): 26–34; Marlene Dixon, *The Future of Women* (San Francisco: Synthesis Publications, 1983), 73–89; Leslie Cagan, "Something New Emerges: The Growth of a Socialist Feminism," in Dick Cluster, ed., *They Should Have Served That Cup of Coffee: Seven Radicals Remember the Sixties* (Boston: South End Press, 1979), 239–58. Echols devotes several chapters to the internal conflicts of the women's liberation movement; *Daring to Be Bad,* chaps. 2–5, passim.

4. There are many accounts of these battles. See, e.g., Robin Morgan's keynote address to the West Coast Lesbian-Feminist Conference, April 14, 1974, "Lesbianism and Feminism: Synonyms or Contradictions," reprinted in *Lesbian Tide* 2, no. 10/11 (June 1973): 30–34; see also Rita Mae Brown, *A Plain Brown Rapper* (Baltimore: Diana Press, 1976), passim; Echols, *Daring to Be Bad,* chap. 5. A reading of feminist or lesbian journals from the period supports my point; *The Furies* and *off our backs* contain dozens of pertinent examples of lesbian infighting.

5. Cagan, "Something New Emerges"; Dixon, *The Future of Women;* Echols, *Daring to Be Bad,* chaps. 2–5; Leah Fritz, *Dreamers and Dealers: An Intimate Appraisal of the Women's Movement* (Boston: Beacon, 1979), 133–37; Gail Paradise Kelly, "Women's Liberation and the Cultural Revolution," *Radical America* 4, no. 2 (February 1970): 19–25; Marilyn Webb, "We Are Victims," *Voice of the Women's Liberation Movement* 6 (February 1969): 1, 4–5, 12; Ellen Willis, "Declaration of Independence," *Voice of the Women's Liberation Movement* 6 (February 1969): 1, 4–5, 14.

6. Joreen, "Trashing"; Echols, *Daring to Be Bad,* 67 and passim; Dixon, *The Future of Women,* 81; Anselma Dell'Olio, "Divisiveness and Self-Destruction in the Women's Movement: A Letter of Resignation," in "Women's Liberation: Criticism" file, Schlesinger Library, 1970.

7. Alice Rossi, "Women: Terms of Liberation," *ADA World Magazine* January, 1971, 8M.

8. Dana Densmore, "On Unity," *No More Fun and Games,* no. 5 (July 1971): 53–63.

9. "The Women's Page," *It Ain't Me, Babe* August 6, 1970: 15.

10. Of the many discussions of this issue, some of the clearest are in Brown, *A Plain Brown Rapper;* Charlotte Bunch, *Passionate Politics: Feminist Theory in Action* (New York: St. Martin's, 1987); Echols, *Daring to Be Bad,* 204–10, 235–37.

11. This quote is often attributed to Jill Johnston, although Johnston credits Ti-Grace Atkinson with the thought, if not the exact words; remarking on Atkinson's speech to a Daughters of Bilitis audience, Johnston writes, in *Lesbian Nation: The Feminist Solution* (New York: Simon and Schuster, 1973), 117, that "she even said that lesbianism was a practice and feminism a theory."

12. There are many accounts of Friedan's early stand on lesbianism. See, e.g., Carden, *The New Feminist Movement,* 113.

13. Female Liberation, "From Us," *Second Wave* 2, no. 3 (1973): 2–4; on lesbians as the truest feminists, see Charlotte Bunch, "Lesbians in Revolt," in Nancy Myron and Charlotte Bunch, eds., *Lesbianism and the Women's Movement* (Baltimore: Diana Press, 1975), 29–37.

14. For a few references, see "Racism/Sexism," *It Ain't Me, Babe,* 1, no. 7 (May 21–June 10, 1970): 13; Cory Logan, "From a Black Sister," *Women: A Journal of Liberation* 1, no. 3 (Spring 1970): 46–47; Stephanie Jenkins, Karen Kennedy, Barny McGee, Karen Burke-Redman, and Billie Warden, "From Survival: For Our Times, For Our Movement," *Women: A Journal of Liberation* 3, no. 4: 58–60; Cellestine Ware, "The Relationship of Black Women to the Women's Liberation Movement," in *Woman*

Power, 75–99; Joyce Ladner, *Tomorrow's Tomorrow: The Black Woman* (Garden City, N.Y.: Doubleday, 1971), 270–88.

15. Bread and Roses, "The Rights of Women," *Old Mole,* no. 34 (March 6–19, 1970): 3.

16. Densmore, "On Unity," 63. Densmore originally delivered this speech to the Conference to Unite Women, held in Washington, D.C., in October 1970.

17. This was part of the wider struggle between those radical feminists who saw as primary women's oppression "as women," as Densmore put it, and those radical and socialist feminists who sought a more complex analysis. See Echols's discussion of these tensions, *Daring to Be Bad,* chaps. 4 and 5, passim. See also Dixon, *The Future of Women,* 73–89.

18. Stacey Fulton, "Letter," *Lesbian Tide* 3, no. 1 (August 1973): 18.

19. "Black Caucus Position," *Lesbian Tide* 2, no. 10/11 (June 1973): 19.

20. Karla Jay, "Double Trouble," 3, 22–24; "Letters," *Ms.* 3, no. 2 (August 1974): 4–13.

21. Gordon and Hunter, "Sex, Family and the New Right"; Petchesky, "Antiabortion, Antifeminism, and the Rise of the New Right"; Echols, *Daring to Be Bad,* 244–45.

22. Jane Alpert, "Mother Right: A New Feminist Theory," *Ms.* 2, no. 2 (August 1973): 52–55, 88–94. The article was published in several other feminist periodicals as well, but Alpert wrote to Gloria Steinem that she wanted *Ms.* as her major mouthpiece because she wanted her article to "reach all those thousands of women who read 'Ms.' alone among the feminist press" (p. 53).

23. On the increasing violence and vanguardism of the Left, see Gitlin, *The Sixties,* 384–408; Miller, *"Democracy Is in the Streets,"* 311–13.

24. Jane Alpert, *Growing Up Underground* (New York: Morrow, 1981), chaps. 14–16. For other accounts of Alpert, see Echols, *Daring to Be Bad,* 247–62; Fritz, *Dreamers and Dealers,* 133–50.

25. Samuel Melville, *Letters from Attica* (New York: Morrow, 1972); Alpert, "Mother Right," 88.

26. Alpert, "Mother Right," 89.

27. Ibid., 90.

28. This response characterizes most of radical feminist theory in the late 1960s and early 1970s. See especially Firestone, *The Dialectic of Sex;* Firestone writes that women's biological tie to childbearing is the key to women's oppression, and that that tie must be broken.

29. Alpert, "Mother Right," 91.

30. Ibid.

31. Ibid., 92.

32. Ibid., 93. It is interesting to note that Alpert refers to a potential "new" split in the movement: "between mothers and childless women." In fact, that division had already been noted by many women, although with less fury than the racial, class, or gay/straight splits. See Sandra, "Mothers and Non-Mothers," *It Ain't Me, Babe,* August 21–September 3, 1970: 15; Alice Abarbanel, "Letter," *It Ain't Me, Babe,* October 8, 1970: 15.

33. Alpert, "Mother Right," 92.

34. Ibid., 93.

35. Ibid., 94. On Alpert's religious interpretation of feminism, see Echols, *Daring to Be Bad,* 251–52.

36. The editorial pages and letters of many of the feminist periodicals in late 1973 are sprinkled with reaction to Alpert's theory. *Ms.,* at Alpert's request, devoted a large "letters" section to response to "Mother Right"; see "Forum: Dear Jane Alpert," *Ms.* 2, no. 8 (February 1974): 58–60, 100, 104–6. See also "Jane Alpert Talks about the Left and Feminism," *Big Mama Rag* 3-A, no. 2 (March 1975): 8, 9, 13.

37. Echols, *Daring to Be Bad,* 253.

38. Alpert, *Growing Up Underground,* 315–16, and chap. 16, passim; Echols, *Daring to Be Bad,* 247–62.

39. Alpert, *Growing Up Underground;* Echols, *Daring to Be Bad,* 123–30; Gitlin, *The Sixties,* 384–401.

40. On Alpert's relationship with Morgan, see Alpert, *Growing Up Underground,* chaps. 12–16, passim. See also Alpert, "Mother Right"; and Echols, *Daring to Be Bad,* 247–62. Morgan sent Alpert a copy of Elizabeth Gould Davis's *The First Sex,* which Alpert quotes at length to support her thesis that mothers of ancient times transposed their immanent biological potential into political power; see *Growing Up Underground,* 315. But Morgan's intense interest in matriarchy, it must be noted, followed chronologically that of the black women who rescued the concept from infamy. On Morgan and "rapprochement," see, all collected in Morgan, *Going Too Far,* "The Media and the Man," 90–93; "The Wretched of the Hearth," 94–106; "Goodbye to All That," 121–30.

41. Alpert, "Mother Right," 93; Morgan, "The Media and the Man," "The Wretched of the Hearth," "Goodbye to All That." As in Alpert's later use of the concept, African American women's transposition of matriarchy from a damaging epithet into a source of personal and communal strength had sometimes led to spiritualized or mythologized views of motherhood that obscured the lines of material difference between women. In the African American case, the universalization did not attempt to erase racial distinctions, but it did tend to blur past and present, Africa

and the United States, poor women and middle-class women, and mothers and nonmothers.

42. Echols, *Daring to Be Bad,* 113.

43. Elizabeth Gould Davis, *The First Sex* (New York: Putnam, 1971).

44. Helen Diner, *Mothers and Amazons* (Garden City, N.Y.: Anchor, 1973; orig. 1932).

45. Echols, *Daring to Be Bad,* 183. Although The Feminists' twist in focus surprised a few in the early 1970s, it follows that with their penchant for rules, they would choose to worship the mother figure, a mythic being fixed by the hierarchical rules of kinship in a dominant position over her daughters. There need be no wrangling over star status when that status is vested in the mythical past!

46. Ibid., 161.

47. Dunbar, "Female Liberation As the Basis for Social Revolution," 53.

48. Ibid.

49. Echols, *Daring to Be Bad,* 185.

50. Ibid., 165.

51. Starr, "Unspoken Culture," *It Ain't Me, Babe* 1, no. 5 (April 7, 1970): 14.

52. Peggy and Diane, "Witches Brew," *It Ain't Me, Babe* 1, no. 5 (April 7, 1970): 5.

53. Ann Forfreedom, "Lesbos Arise!" *Lesbian Tide,* June 1973: 14.

54. Ibid., 5. The "being-with-a-penis" referred to a male-to-female, still-preoperative transsexual, who was scheduled to sing at the conference. Enormous controversy erupted around this individual, and around the larger issue of transsexualism.

55. Barbara Burris, "in agreement with Kathy Barry, Terry Moon, Joann DeLor, Joann Parent, Cate Stadelman," "The Fourth World Manifesto," in *Notes from the Third Year,* 102–19; Echols, *Daring to Be Bad,* 245–47.

56. Burris et al., "The Fourth World Manifesto," 109.

57. Ibid., 107.

58. Ibid., 118.

59. Ibid.

60. Morgan, "Goodbye to All That," 123.

61. Ibid., 126. "Gina," in the article, "Nature: Our Sister In the Struggle?" *It Ain't Me, Babe,* May 21–June 10, 1970: 5, also made broad assertions about women's "nature" and the positive ecological promise of women's liberation.

62. Morgan, "Goodbye to All That," 128.

63. Robin Morgan, "Lesbianism and Feminism: Synonyms or Contradictions?" *Lesbian Tide,* June 1973: 34.

64. Ibid.

65. For just a few examples, see Christeve, "Midwives Busted in Santa Cruz," 5–10; "Lesbian Mother Appeal Denied," *The Tide* 3, no. 7 (April 1974): 15; Carol Hille, "Indian Women Sterilizations Seen As Genocide," *Big Mama Rag* 3-A, no. 3 (1975): 3; Susan Bram, "Women and Children First; or How Pop Planning Fucked Over Mom," *Heresies* 2, no. 2 (Summer 1978): 65, 67, 69, 71, 73.

66. For a good sampling of the immediate reaction to Alpert, see *Ms.* Readers, "Forum: Dear Jane Alpert." Alpert requested that *Ms.* serve as an open forum for discussion of her ideas, because as a fugitive she had little opportunity to speak openly with other feminists. As the editors wrote, "Her theory drew more reader reaction than any other piece we have published" (p. 58).

67. Accounts of the turmoil over Alpert can be found in Alpert, *Growing Up Underground,* chap. 16; Echols, *Daring to Be Bad,* 257–62; and Fritz, *Dreamers and Dealers,* 133–50. Fritz, writing in 1979, elevates Alpert to a high hero status indeed: "The risk Alpert took was not the hero's risk of alienating the authorities . . . but the much greater risk of speaking truth to her own people. The risk that kept Moses out of the promised land, that left Jesus without comfort on the cross" (p. 142).

68. Naomi Weisstein and Heather Booth, "Will the Women's Movement Survive?" *Sister* 4, no. 12 (1975): 5.

69. Ibid., 1–6.

70. Brooke, "The Retreat to Cultural Feminism," in Redstockings, eds., *Feminist Revolution,* 81; see also Rita Mae Brown, "It's All Dixie Cups to Me," in *A Plain Brown Rapper,* 196–97.

71. Karen Lindsey, "The Politics of Childlessness," *Second Wave* 3, no. 3 (Summer 1974): 12–13.

72. Alice Walker, in "Letters," *Ms.* 3, no. 2 (August, 1974): 4.

73. Ashaki Habiba Taha, in "Letters," *Ms.* 3, no. 2 (August 1974): 6. While black feminists did not rush to join white feminist organizations during the reign of cultural feminism any more than in earlier years, a great deal of black feminist thought and writing also shifted toward essentialism, mysticism, matriarchalism, and a generalized romanticization of the mother-daughter bond. These themes were stated in "black" terms, however, as in Alice Walker's wish, in the letter cited here, that African American women would "begin reclaiming their mothers and grandmothers." Whereas white cultural feminists saw "Mother Right" as a way to break down barriers between women based on race, class, and sexual

preference, most black feminists who endorsed similar theories deployed a mystified view of motherhood as a way to break down barriers between black women, not between black women and white women.

As in the wider feminist movement, numerous black feminists maintained a materialist and activist stance throughout this period. See, for the culmination of this strand of black radical, feminist, materialist thought, in one of its earliest manifestations, The Combahee River Collective, "A Black Feminist Statement."

74. Linda Fowler, "Energizing the Feminine Principle Today," *Big Mama Rag* 3, no. 1 (July 1974): 13.

75. Ibid.

76. Ibid., 13–14.

77. Susan Griffin, "On Wanting to Be the Mother I Wanted," *Ms.* 5, no. 7 (January 1977): 98. Griffin writes, in preface, "What follows was written in 1974 for MOMMA, the newspaper for single mothers, in answer to a request for a feminist theory of motherhood."

78. Jackie St. Joan, "Who Was Rembrandt's Mother?" *Quest* 2, no. 4 (Spring 1976): 67.

79. Mary Rice, "Daughters of Demeter: Women and Plants," *Second Wave* 3, no. 2 (Spring 1974): 19–21. On all of the above themes, see also the well-known article by Barbara Starrett, "I Dream in Female: The Metaphors of Evolution," *Amazon Quarterly* 3, no. 1 (1974): 13–27.

80. The full blossoming of the feminist spirituality movement occured in the late 1970s. In the mid-1970s, however, many articles on spirituality began to appear in the feminist periodical press. See, e.g., Judy Davis and Juanita Weaver, "Dimensions of Spirituality," *Quest* 1, no. 4 (Spring 1975): 2–6; Peggy Kornegger, "The Spirituality Ripoff," *Second Wave* 4, no. 3 (Spring 1976); Susan Rennie and Kirsten Grimstad, "Spiritual Explorations Cross-Country," *Quest* 1, no. 4 (Spring 1975): 49–51. A measure of the growth of interest in these topics can be found in the changes between the 1973 and 1975 editions of Rennie and Grimstad's *New Women's Survival Sourcebook*. The later edition contains a whole chapter on "Religion and Spirituality," whereas the earlier edition makes no mention at all of these topics.

81. Mary Daly, *The Church and the Second Sex* (New York: Harper and Row, 1968) and *Beyond God the Father: Toward a Philosophy of Women's Liberation* (Boston: Beacon, 1973); Echols, *Daring to Be Bad*, 253.

82. Linda Fowler and Jacqueline St. Joan, "The Spiritual Revolution: Becoming Whole," *Big Mama Rag* 3, no. 6 (January 1975): 1.

83. On matriarchy, see, e.g., Esther Newton and Paula Webster, "Ma-

triarchy and Power," *Quest* 2, no. 1 (Summer 1975): 67–72; on bellydancing, Daniela Gioseffi, "The New Dance of Liberation," *Ms.* 4, no. 7 (January 1976): 68–69. On goddess religion, the strongest source is Merlin Stone, *When God Was a Woman* (New York: Dial Press, 1976).

84. Adrienne Rich, *Of Woman Born: Motherhood As Experience and Institution* (New York: W. W. Norton, 1986; orig. 1976).

85. Ibid., 285.

86. Ibid., 39–40.

87. Ibid., 40, 284. I gained added insight into Rich's work from Eisenstein, *Contemporary Feminist Thought*, 69–78. For a sense of the reception of Rich's book among feminists, see, e.g., Kathy Barry, "Reviewing Reviews—*Of Woman Born*," *Chrysalis*, no. 2 (1977): 8–9; Elizabeth Janeway, "Review of *Of Woman Born*," *Chrysalis*, no. 2 (1977): 132–35.

88. On the counterculture's opportunistic blindness to gender, which I have discussed in chapters 1 and 2, a graphic example can be found in Melville, *Communes in the Counterculture*, 153–54. Melville writes about a commune in Taos, New Mexico: "Hanging over the counter next to the stove was a sign-up list for kitchen chores and laundry, with the names of several of the *girls* listed opposite the jobs. 'We don't believe in laying down too heavy a structure here,' explained Allen. 'So there is just one list. Somehow everything else *seems to get done* sooner or later' " (italics mine). Of course, the speaker went on to say how the women got the things done!

89. Alpert, "Mother Right"; Daly, *Beyond God the Father*; Susan Griffin, *Woman and Nature: The Roaring inside Her* (New York: Harper and Row, 1978); Rich, *Of Woman Born*.

90. Nancy Chodorow and Susan Contratto, "The Fantasy of the Perfect Mother," in Thorne and Yalom, eds., *Rethinking the Family*, 54–71; Susan (Contratto) Weisskopf, "Maternal Sexuality and Asexual Motherhood," *Signs* 5, no. 4 (Summer 1980): 766–82.

91. Alice Echols has been the leading proponent of this idea. See Echols, "The Taming of the Id"; Echols, *Daring to Be Bad*, epilogue; Ann Snitow, "Retrenchment vs. Transformation: The Politics of the Antipornography Movement," in Kate Ellis et al., eds., *Caught Looking: Feminism, Pornography and Censorship* (New York: Caught Looking, Inc., 1984). All of these analyses came out of the anti-antipornography movement, which began to mobilize in response to the feminist antipornography movement of the late 1970s through the present; Echols, Snitow, and others, such as Kate Ellis and Ellen Willis, argue that the feminist reaction to pornography has a great deal to do with the debates within feminism

about sexuality, and is connected as well to the sense in the movement of "losing ground," in terms of the ERA and other battles. Antiporn feminists, these theorists argue, constructed an asexual mother image against what they saw as the frighteningly sexualized woman constructed not only by pornography, but by radical feminist sexual liberationists.

92. Rita Mae Brown, "The Shape of Things to Come," in Myron and Bunch, eds., *Lesbianism and the Women's Movement,* 69.

93. Ibid.

94. Sue Silvermarie, "The Motherbond," *Women: A Journal of Liberation* 4, no. 1 (Winter 1974): 27.

95. Sally Gearhart and Peggy Cleveland, "On the Prevalence of Stilps," *Quest* 1, no. 4, (Spring 1975): 53.

96. Ibid., 63.

97. Evans, *Personal Politics,* 80. Echols, *Daring to Be Bad,* 29–30, also discusses these tensions.

98. Evans, *Personal Politics,* 78–82; Mary King, *Freedom Song: A Personal Story of the 1960s Civil Rights Movement* (New York: Morrow, 1987), 464–65.

99. King, *Freedom Song,* 464.

100. Ibid., 465.

101. Ibid., 464–65; Evans, *Personal Politics,* 81.

102. King, *Freedom Song,* 465. On the racial and sexual tensions in the Freedom Summer projects, see also Mary Aickin Rothschild, *A Case of Black and White: Northern Volunteers and the Southern Freedom Summers, 1964–1965* (Westport, Conn.: Greenwood Press, 1982).

103. Wallace, *Black Macho and the Myth of the Superwoman,* passim, speaks to this set of issues, as do most of the authors in the Cade anthology, *The Black Woman.*

104. Don L. Lee, " 'blackwoman:' and 'BLACKWOMAN,' " in Mel Watkins and Jay David, eds., *To Be a Black Woman: Portraits in Fact and Fiction* (New York: Morrow, 1970), 272.

105. June Jordan, "Getting Down to Get Over Poem: Dedicated to My Mother," in Doris J. Mitchell and Jewel H. Bell, eds., *The Black Woman: Myths and Realities: Selected Papers from the Radcliffe Symposium* (Cambridge, Mass.: Radcliffe College, 1973), 39.

106. Ware, *Woman Power,* 92.

107. Robert Staples, *The Black Woman in America* (Chicago: Nelson-Hall, 1973), 170–71.

108. Sheila Okpaku, "Black Male and Female Relationships," in Mitchell and Bell, eds., *The Black Woman: Myths and Realities,* 99.

109. Ware, *Woman Power,* 92

110. Ladner, *Tomorrow's Tomorrow,* 281.

111. Lincoln, "Who Will Revere the Black Woman?" 84. For other strong statements by African American writers on this topic, see Inez Smith Reid, *"Together" Black Women* (New York: Emerson Hall Publishers, 1972), 79–87; Jeanne Noble, *Beautiful, Also, Are the Souls of My Black Sisters: A History of the Black Woman in America* (Englewood Cliffs, N.J.: Prentice-Hall, 1978), 316–25; Nathan Hare and Julia Hare, "Black Women 1970," in Lee Rainwater, ed., *Black Experience: Soul* (New Brunswick, N.J.: Transaction Books, 1971), 98–101.

112. Two examples, particularly interesting for this study because the discussion of race occurs in connection with mothering biracial children, are Cecile, in *It Ain't Me, Babe* 1, no. 12 (August 21–September 3, 1970): 14; and Jane Lazarre, *The Mother Knot* (New York: McGraw-Hill, 1976), passim. Lazarre's book actually straddles the 1973–1976 transition to cultural feminism and the 1976–1980 period of full-blown feminist focus on motherhood; I discuss the book at greater length in chapter 5. See also Rosemary Santini, "Black Man: White Woman," *Essence,* July 1970: 12; Santini, a white woman, acknowledges the resentment of black women when she appeared in public with her black lover.

Notes to Chapter Five

1. The complete list of feminist works on mothering from this period is too lengthy to reproduce here; see the bibliography for a full listing. Major works include: Judith Arcana, *Our Mothers' Daughters* (Berkeley: Shameless Hussy Press, 1979); Nancy Chodorow, *The Reproduction of Mothering: Psychoanalysis and the Sociology of Gender* (Berkeley: University of California Press, 1978); Dorothy Dinnerstein, *The Mermaid and the Minotaur: Sexual Arrangements and Human Malaise* (New York: Harper and Row, 1976); Jane Flax, "The Conflict between Nurturance and Autonomy in Mother-Daughter Relationships and within Feminism," *Feminist Studies* 4, no. 2 (June 1978): 171–89; Nancy Friday, *My Mother/ Myself: The Daughter's Search for Identity* (New York: Delacorte Press, 1977); Lazarre, *The Mother Knot;* Rich, *Of Woman Born;* Rossi, "A Biosocial Perspective on Parenting"; Ruddick, "Maternal Thinking." Several leading feminist journals published special "motherhood" issues; see *Feminist Studies,* June 1978; *Frontiers,* Summer 1978; *Women's Studies Quarterly,* Winter 1983.

2. See, e.g., Rich, *Of Woman Born.* I was pleased to see, when Ann Snitow's chronology of feminism and motherhood was published in 1992, as "Feminism and Motherhood: An American Reading," that she, too,

sees roughly the same time period (1975–1979) as "the period in which feminism tried to take on the issue of motherhood seriously, to criticize the institution, explore the actual experience, theorize the social and psychological implications" (p. 34).

3. Echols, *Daring to Be Bad*, 288–91, mentions briefly the connections between ecofeminism, feminist peace activism, and feminist antipornography activism, noting that all proceed from assumptions of gender *difference*.

In "The Fantasy of the Perfect Mother," published in 1982, in Thorne and Yalom, eds., *Rethinking the Family*, 54–71, Nancy Chodorow and Susan Contratto note feminists' intensifying interest in motherhood since the late 1960s; detecting a tendency to exaggerate the power of the mother, for better or for worse, Chodorow and Contratto conclude that the writings reveal "unprocessed," infancy-based fantasies and expectations of mothers and suggest that feminists need to move from "drive" to "relational" theories to achieve a more realistic assessment of mothers and mothering.

4. Andrew Hacker, ed., *U/S: A Statistical Portrait of the American People* (New York: Viking, 1983), 51–52. The black birth rate dipped during this period as well, but was always higher than that of whites; see Carrel Peterson Horton and Jessie Carney Smith, eds. *Statistical Record of Black America* (Detroit: Gale Research Inc., 1990), 628, 630.

5. William H. Chafe, *The Unfinished Journey: America since World War II*, 2d ed. (New York: Oxford University Press, 1991), 436–37.

6. See, e.g., ibid.; Hewlett, *A Lesser Life*, chap. 8. A feminist-bashing version of the same argument was made by Ben J. Wattenberg, *The Birth Dearth* (New York: Pharos Books, 1987); Susan Faludi takes these arguments to task in *Backlash: The Undeclared War against American Women* (New York: Crown Publishers, 1991), passim.

7. By 1980, according to Bureau of the Census estimates, only 10 percent of American women remained childless by age forty-four (Hewlett, *A Lesser Life*, 420 n. 11). See also Hacker, ed., *U/S*, 58, who reports that whereas, in 1970, 44.2 percent of first babies born to women in the 30–34 age group had college-educated mothers, in 1979, that rate had risen to 67.9 percent.

8. Rich, *Of Woman Born*, passim.

9. Lazarre, *The Mother Knot*. For reviews of Lazarre, see Annie Gottlieb, "Feminists Look at Motherhood," *Mother Jones*, November 1976: 51–53; Jane Shapiro, "To Tell the Truth: Jane Lazarre's *The Mother Knot*," *Ms.* 4, no. 12 (June 1976): 93–95; Louise Bernikow, "Review of *The Mother Knot*," *New York Times Book Review*, March 21, 1976: 26.

10. Prominent examples include Phyllis Chesler, *With Child: A Diary of Motherhood* (New York: Crowell, 1979); Ronnie Friedland and Carol Kort, eds., *The Mothers' Book: Shared Experiences* (Boston: Houghton Mifflin, 1981); Barbara Holland, *Mother's Day: Or, The View from in Here* (Garden City, N.Y.: Doubleday, 1980); Beverly Salpin, *The Magic Washing Machine: A Diary of Single Motherhood* (Mesquite, Texas: Ide House, 1983). This was largely a literature about heterosexual mothers. A parallel lesbian literature emerged a few years later; see, e.g., Jan Clausen, "A Flommy Looks at Lesbian Parenting," *Off Our Backs* 16 (August–September 1986): 16–17; Sandra Pollack and Jeanne Vaughn, eds., *Politics of the Heart: A Lesbian Parenting Anthology* (Ithaca, N.Y.: Firebrand Books, 1987). These experiential accounts differ somewhat from the advocacy literature about lesbian parenting, which appeared early on and grew in quantity and depth throughout the 1970s and 1980s; important works include Gifford Guy Gibson, *By Her Own Admission: A Lesbian Mother's Fight to Keep Her Son* (Garden City, N.Y.: Doubleday, 1977); Gillian E. Hanscombe and Jackie Forster, *Rocking the Cradle: Lesbian Mothers: A Challenge in Family Living* (Boston: Alyson Publications, 1982); Donna Hitchens and Ann Thomas, eds., *Lesbian Mothers and Their Children: An Annotated Bibliography of Legal and Psychological Materials* (San Francisco: Lesbian Rights Project, 1980); Mary Stevens, "Lesbian Mothers in Transition," in Virginia Vida, ed., *Our Right to Love: A Lesbian Resource Book* (Englewood Cliffs, N.J.: Prentice-Hall, 1978), 207–11; Francie Wyland, *Motherhood, Lesbianism and Child Custody* (Toronto: Wages Due Lesbians, 1977).

11. The birth rate began to shift upward slowly, beginning in 1977 (15.4 per 1000). See Hacker, ed., *U/S*, 52.

12. To even list the mothers and nonmothers among feminist writers seems absurdly essentialist, but, for example, Jane Alpert had no children when she wrote "Mother Right."

13. It is notable that no one speaks with more urgency about the significance of motherhood than Adrienne Rich, who is also very clear in *Of Woman Born* about her distance in time from hands-on mothering.

14. This description clearly applies to the works by Chodorow, Dinnerstein, Flax, Rossi, and Ruddick already cited. Other works include Jane Gallop, *The Daughter's Seduction: Feminism and Psychoanalysis* (New York: Cornell University Press, 1982); Luce Irigaray, "And the One Doesn't Stir without the Other," *Signs* 7, no. 1 (Autumn 1981): 60–67; Joyce Trebilcot, ed., *Mothering: Essays in Feminist Theory* (Totowa, N.J.: Rowman and Allanheld, 1983); Susan (Contratto) Weisskopf, "Maternal Sexuality and Asexual Motherhood," *Signs* 5, no. 4 (1980): 766–82.

15. See, e.g., two review essays in *Signs:* Marianne Hirsch, "Mothers and Daughters," *Signs* 7, no. 1 (1981): 200–222; and Ethel Spector Person, "Review of Jean Baker Miller, *Toward a New Pschology of Women;* Helen Block Lewis, *Psychic War in Men and Women;* and Dinnerstein, *The Mermaid and the Minotaur,*" *Signs* 4, no. 1 (1978): 163–67. See also Judith Lorber, Rose Coser, and Alice Rossi, "On *The Reproduction of Mothering:* A Methodological Debate," *Signs* 6, no. 3 (Spring 1981): 482–514; Dacia Maraini, "On *Of Woman Born,*" *Signs* 4, no. 4 (Summer 1979): 687–94; Jane McCabe, "Review of *Of Woman Born: Motherhood As Experience and Institution,*" *Frontiers* 3, no. 2 (Summer 1978): 77–78; Marcia Westkott, "Mothers and Daughters in the World of the Father," *Frontiers* 3, no. 2 (1978): 16–20.

16. At the same time, many nonacademic feminist journals and small feminist publishing houses, some inspired by the cultural feminist call for "feminist capitalism," became primary outlets for the other strand of newly energized feminist interest in motherhood, which valorized the mother as metaphor and symbol but paid little attention to the material aspects of mothering. The net effect, in part because of the "academization" of a large group of feminists, was a relatively bifurcated publishing structure within feminism. See, for example, *Womanspirit,* which published from 1974–1984; *Sinister Wisdom,* which began publishing in 1976; and *Chrysalis,* which first came out in 1977. Of academic journals, for example, *Signs* began publishing in 1975, *Frontiers* in 1975, and *Feminist Issues* in 1980.

17. Barrie Thorne, "Feminist Rethinking of the Family: An Overview," and Eli Zaretsky, "The Place of the Family in the Origins of the Welfare State," in Thorne and Yalom, eds., *Rethinking the Family,* 1–24 and 88–224. Snitow, "Feminism and Motherhood," 34, notes very briefly that feminism, like the nation at large, shifted "from discussing motherhood to discussing families."

18. Frances Fitzgerald, "The Triumphs of the New Right," *New York Review of Books,* November 19, 1981: 19–26; Gordon and Hunter, "Sex, Family and the New Right."

19. Quoted in Chafe, *The Unfinished Journey,* 453.

20. Lasch, *Haven in a Heartless World.*

21. Feminist critiques of Lasch and other "profamily" views from the Left include Breines, Cerullo, and Stacey, "Social Biology, Family Studies, and Antifeminist Backlash"; Barbara Ehrenreich, "On Feminism, Family and Community," *Dissent* 30, no. 1 (1983): 103–9; Stacey, "The New Conservative Feminism." Also on Lasch, see Marshall Berman, "Review of *Haven in a Heartless World,*" *New York Times Book Review,* January

15, 1978: 15. From the other end of the political spectrum, George Gilder loved Lasch's book; *National Review,* February 17, 1978. Aside from Friedan, in *The Second Stage,* other feminist revisionists included Jean Bethke Elshtain and Alice Rossi. Elshtain, "Feminism, Family and Community," *Dissent* 29, no. 4 (1982): 442–49, criticized feminists' analysis of the family, advocating a "social feminism" in which mothers stay home to rear their children. This view sparked heated debate in feminist and leftist circles; see Ehrenreich, "On Feminism, Family and Community." Rossi's earlier article, "A Biosocial Perspective on Parenting," had created even more controversy; Rossi argues that women's physiology makes them better suited than men to nurture the young, and that the feminist push to eliminate sex roles might be ill-founded. For responses, see Margaret Cerullo, Judith Stacey, and Winnie Breines, "Alice Rossi's Sociobiology and Anti-Feminist Backlash," *Berkeley Journal of Sociology* 22 (1977–1978): 167–77; Nancy Chodorow, "Consideration of a Biosocial Perspective on Parenting," *Berkeley Journal of Sociology* 22 (1977–1978): 179–97; Harriet Engel Gross et al., "Considering 'A Biosocial Perspective on Parenting,' " *Signs* 4, no. 4 (Summer 1979): 695–717.

22. For fuller discussions of Chodorow, see Eisenstein, *Contemporary Feminist Thought,* 87–95; Jane Flax, *Thinking Fragments: Psychoanalysis, Feminism, and Postmodernism in the Contemporary West* (Berkeley: University of California Press, 1990), 157–68; Haunani-Kay Trask, *Eros and Power: The Promise of Feminist Theory* (Philadelphia: University of Pennsylvania Press, 1986), 65–78 and passim; Roger S. Gottlieb, "Mothering and the Reproduction of Power: Chodorow, Dinnerstein, and Social Theory," *Socialist Review* 14, no. 5 (1984): 93–119.

23. Chodorow, *The Reproduction of Mothering,* 209.

24. Ibid., Afterword.

25. On the influences on Chodorow's theory, see Judith Thurman, "Breaking the Mother-Daughter Code: An Interview with Nancy Chodorow," *Ms.* 11, no. 3 (September 1982): 34–38, 138–39.

26. Several critics take Chodorow to task on these grounds; see Pauline Bart, "Review of Chodorow's *The Reproduction of Mothering,*" in Joyce Trebilcot, ed., *Mothering: Essays in Feminist Theory,* 147–52; Eisenstein, *Contemporary Feminist Thought,* chap. 9. Spelman, *Inessential Woman,* chap. 4, presents a cogent and important race and class analysis of Chodorow's work.

27. Dinnerstein, *The Mermaid and the Minotaur,* passim; Eisenstein, *Contemporary Feminist Thought,* 79–86.

Nancy Friday's *My Mother/My Self* also posits an all-powerful mother and charts the disastrous results for the daughter. Although reviewed at times by the mainstream press as a feminist book, feminists did not regard it as such, generally, because of its extreme mother-blaming. See, e.g., Sara Voorhees, "Review of *My Mother/My Self,*" *Frontiers* 3, no. 2 (Summer 1978): 75–77. For an excellent discussion of the "all-powerful" mother—good and bad—in feminist writing of this period, see Chodorow and Contratto, "The Fantasy of the Perfect Mother," 54–75.

28. Dinnerstein, *The Mermaid and the Minotaur,* Preface.

29. For a sampling of feminist reviews of Dinnerstein, see Vivian Gornick, "Review of *The Mermaid and the Minotaur,*" *New York Times Book Review,* November 14, 1976: 5, 70; Jane Lazarre, "Why Everybody Is Talking about *The Mermaid and the Minotaur,*" *Ms.* 6, no. 1 (July 1977): 38–43; Ann Snitow, "Thinking about *The Mermaid and the Minotaur,*" *Feminist Studies* 4, no. 2 (June 1978): 192–98. Robin Morgan, "The Changeless Need: 'The Great Tribal Forms of Family May Be Vanishing, But New Kinship Systems Flourish All around Us'—A Conversation with Dorothy Dinnerstein," *Ms.* 2, no. 2 (August 1978): 44–46, 90, 92, 94, 97, discusses the thesis of Dinnerstein's book and probes beyond. Not all reviews were favorable, however; see Pauline Bart, "The Mermaid and the Minotaur, a Fishy Story That's Part Bull," *Contemporary Psychology* 22, no. 11 (1977): 834–35; Gottlieb, "Mothering and the Reproduction of Power"; Janice Haaken, "Freudian Theory Revisited: A Critique of Rich, Chodorow, and Dinnerstein," *Women's Studies Quarterly* 2, no. 4 (Winter 1983): 12–15.

30. The term "difference feminism" is used by many, but I recall it most clearly, in print, as used by Katha Pollitt, "Marooned on Gilligan's Island: Are Women Morally Superior to Men?" *Nation,* December 28, 1992: 799–807.

31. The literature here is enormous; major works include Louise Armstrong, *Kiss Daddy Good Night: A Speak-Out on Incest* (New York: Hawthorn Books, 1978); Kathleen Barry, *Female Sexual Slavery* (Englewood Cliffs, N.J.: Prentice-Hall, 1979); Katherine Brady, *Father's Days: A True Story of Incest* (New York: Seaview Books, 1979); Susan Brownmiller, *Against Our Will: Men, Women and Rape* (New York: Simon and Schuster, 1975); Phyllis Chesler, *Women and Madness* (Garden City, N.Y.: Doubleday, 1972); Mary Daly, *Gyn/Ecology: The Metaethics of Radical Feminism* (Boston: Beacon, 1978); Andrea Dworkin, *Woman Hating* (New York: E. P. Dutton, 1974), *Our Blood: Prophecies and Discourses on Sexual Politics* (New York: Harper and Row, 1976), *Pornography: Men Possessing Women* (New York: G. P. Putnam's, 1981); Susan Griffin, *Woman and Nature: The Roaring inside Her* (New York: Harper and Row, 1978), *Rape: The Power of Consciousness* (New York:

Harper and Row, 1979), *Pornography and Silence: Culture's Revenge against Nature* (New York: Harper and Row, 1981); Del Martin, *Battered Wives* (San Francisco: Glide Publications, 1976); Andrea Medea and Kathleen Thompson, *Against Rape* (New York: Farrar, Straus, and Giroux, 1974); Janice Raymond, *The Transsexual Empire: The Making of the She-Male* (Boston: Beacon, 1979); Diana Russell, *The Politics of Rape: The Victim's Perspective* (New York: Stein and Day, 1975).

Within feminist-influenced psychology, a similar shift toward "difference" feminism was taking place; the emphasis was on women's positive psychological traits, born of oppression, perhaps, but ultimately preferable to those exhibited by men. In particular, women were seen as more "relational," more concerned about the feelings of others. The major early work was Jean Baker Miller, *Toward a New Psychology of Women* (Boston: Beacon, 1976). Carol Gilligan, who studied women's moral development, extended this view fully in *In a Different Voice: Psychological Theory and Women's Development* (Cambridge, Mass.: Harvard University Press, 1982). I do not deal with these theorists directly in this work, because although their ideas about women as "nurturers" were widely influential, they did not write about motherhood per se; many other writers of the same school of thought treated motherhood directly.

32. Dinnerstein, *The Mermaid and the Minotaur*, 147.

33. Brown, *Life against Death* and *Love's Body*. My reading of Brown is informed by Roszak, *The Making of a Counter Culture*, 84–123.

34. Dinnerstein, *The Mermaid and the Minotaur*, chap. 7 and passim; Trask, *Eros and Power*, 141–43.

35. Ibid.

36. I am not suggesting that Dorothy Dinnerstein's work was the sole or primary influence on ecofeminist thought. Some ideas that emerged after Dinnerstein's took her work into account, while others simply were influenced by the same trends within feminist thought that influenced her. Ecofeminists did, however, see Dinnerstein as a sympathetic intellect, and she reciprocated; see, e.g., Dinnerstein's leading piece, "What Does Feminism Mean?" in the ecofeminist/feminist peace activist book, Harris and King, eds., *Rocking the Ship of State*, 13–23.

Major ecofeminist works from the late 1970s and early 1980s include Leone Caldecott and Stephanie Leland, *Reclaim the Earth: Women Speak Out for Life on Earth* (London: Women's Press, 1983); Alice Cook and Gwyn Kirk, *Greenham Women Everywhere: Dreams, Ideas and Actions from the Women's Peace Movement* (Boston: South End Press, 1983); Elizabeth Dodson Gray, *Green Paradise Lost* (Wellesley, Mass.: Round Table Press, 1979); Griffin, *Woman and Nature*; Ynestra King, "Toward an Ecological Feminism and a Feminist Ecology," in Joan Rothschild, ed., *Machina Ex Dea: Feminist Perspectives on Technology* (New York: Pergamon Press, 1983): 118–29; Carolyn Merchant, *The Death of Nature: Women, Ecology, and the Scientific Revolution* (San Francisco: Harper and Row, 1981). Irene Diamond and Gloria Feman Orenstein, eds., *Reweaving the World: The Emergence of Ecofeminism* (San Francisco: Sierra Club Books, 1990), serves as an excellent guide to the ideas of this period—the book's bibliography led me to many of the sources listed here; likewise for Judith Plant, *Healing the Wounds: The Promise of Ecofeminism* (Philadelphia: New Society Publishers, 1989).

Let me note, too, that ecofeminism now engages complex, retrospective evaluations of the range of ideas discussed here; see, e.g., Catherine Roach, "Loving Your Mother: On the Woman-Nature Relation," *Hypatia* 6, 1 (Spring 1991): 46–59.

37. Edward P. Morgan, *The 60s Experience: Hard Lessons about Modern America* (Philadelphia: Temple University Press, 1991), 231–50.

38. Morgan, *The 60s Experience*, 231–50; Rachel Carson, *Silent Spring* (New York: Fawcett, 1962); Diamond and Orenstein, *Reweaving the World*, Introduction; Charlene Spretnak, "Ecofeminism: Our Roots and Flowering," in Diamond and Orenstein, *Reweaving the World*, 3–14.

39. My basic chronology of the ecofeminist movement draws from Spretnak, "Ecofeminism"; Merchant, "Ecofeminism and Feminist Theory"; Ynestra King, "Healing the Wounds: Feminism, Ecology, and the Nature/Culture Dualism," and Lee Quinby, "Ecofeminism and the Politics of Resistance," all in Diamond and Orenstein, *Reweaving the World,* 100–105, 106–21, and 122–27, respectively. On the women's peace movement and its convergence with ecofeminism, I have drawn from Harris and King, eds., *Rocking the Ship of State,* most particularly, Ynestra King, "If I Can't Dance in Your Revolution, I'm Not Coming," 281–98; and Irene Diamond, "Ecofeminism: Weaving the Worlds Together (Report on a Conference on 'Ecofeminist Perspectives: Culture, Nature, and Theory,' Held At the University of Southern California, 27–29 March 1987)," *Feminist Studies* 14, no. 2 (Summer 1988): 368–70.

40. Griffin, *Woman and Nature,* 227.

41. King, "If I Can't Dance," 284–85.

42. Ibid., 285.

43. Ibid., 286–89; the quote from the Unity Statement of the Women's Pentagon Action, written by Grace Paley, is in King's piece.

44. Ibid., 289.

45. Linton, "Seneca Women's Peace Camp."

46. On the interconnections among these movements, see Diamond,

"Ecofeminism"; King, "If I Can't Dance," 284; Spretnak, "Ecofeminism," 4–6. Amy Swerdlow, "Pure Milk, Not Poison: Women Strike for Peace and the Test Ban Treaty of 1963," in Harris and King, eds., *Rocking the Ship of State*, 225–37, discusses an earlier use of maternalist rhetoric by "prefeminist" peace activists.

47. Daly, *Beyond God the Father* and *Gyn/Ecology*. Sources on the feminist spirituality movement are voluminous. I have drawn this summary primarily from my reading of Judith Plaskow and Carol P. Christ, eds., *Womanspirit Rising: A Feminist Reader in Religion* (New York: Harper and Row, 1979); Charlene Spretnak, ed., *The Politics of Women's Spirituality* (New York: Anchor Press, 1982). Sidney Oliver, "Feminism, Environmentalism and Appropriate Technology," *Quest* 2, no. 2 (1980): 70–80, actually lists these principles, as they apply to ecofeminism. On goddess religion, see also, especially, Stone, *When God Was a Woman*.

48. Ruddick, "Maternal Thinking." Ruddick developed these ideas further in *Maternal Thinking: Toward a Politics of Peace* (Boston: Beacon, 1989). I do not agree with the critics who see Ruddick's theory as "essentializing" mothers, or as denying the complexity of mothering; Ruddick is quite clear that she is describing a *potential* within the *work* of mothering. Nevertheless, for the purposes of this discussion, it is interesting to note the importance she places on mothering and the terms in which she states that importance.

49. Quoted in King, "If I Can't Dance," 287.

50. Indeed, as discussed in chapter 4, at its inception, cultural feminism aimed to quell controversies over race and sexuality in the movement.

51. For early expressions of feminist opposition to pornography, see Andrea Dworkin, "Why So-Called Radical Men Love and Need Pornography," in Laura Lederer, ed., *Take Back the Night: Women on Pornography* (New York: Morrow, 1980), 148–54; (originally published as "Fathers, Sons, and the Lust for Porn," in *Soho Weekly News*, August 4, 1977); and Nan D. Hunter, "The Pornography Debate in Context: A Chronology of Sexuality, Media and Violence Issues in Feminism," in Ellis et al., eds., *Caught Looking*, 26–29, who includes early feminist actions against pornography in her chronology. See also Morgan, "Goodbye to All That."

52. This recounting of key events is drawn from Lederer, ed., *Take Back the Night*, 1.

53. Griffin, *Pornography and Silence*, passim; on Griffin, see Eisenstein, *Contemporary Feminist Thought*, chap. 12.

54. Dworkin, *Pornography*, passim; on Dworkin, see Eisenstein, *Contemporary Feminist Thought*, chap. 12.

55. Barry, *Female Sexual Slavery*, passim.

56. Lederer, ed., *Take Back the Night*, 6. Diana E. H. Russell, "On Pornography," *Chrysalis*, no. 4 (February 3, 1978): 11–15, expresses similar views.

57. Robin Morgan, "Theory and Practice: Pornography and Rape," in Lederer, ed., *Take Back the Night*, 131.

58. Gloria Steinem, "Erotica and Pornography: A Clear and Present Difference," in Lederer, ed., *Take Back the Night*, 21–25.

59. Barry, *Female Sexual Slavery*, 266.

60. Ibid., 267.

61. This analysis of antipornography rhetoric is developed by many of the writers in *Caught Looking* (Pat Califia, "Among Us, Against Us: The New Puritans"; Kate Ellis, "I'm Black and Blue from the Rolling Stones and I'm Not Sure How I Feel about It"; Snitow, "Retrenchment vs. Transformation"; Paula Webster, "Pornography and Pleasure"), *Powers of Desire* (Echols, "The New Feminism of Yin and Yang"; Ellen Willis, "Feminism, Moralism, and Pornography"), and *Pleasure and Danger* (Echols, "The Taming of the Id"; Gayle Rubin, "Thinking Sex: Notes for a Radical Theory of the Politics of Sexuality").

62. Elshtain, "Feminism, Family and Community"; Griffin, *Pornography and Silence*; Rich, *Of Woman Born*; Ruddick, "Maternal Thinking."

63. Audre Lorde, "Uses of the Erotic: The Erotic As Power," in Lederer, ed., *Take Back the Night*, 298.

64. Barry, *Female Sexual Slavery*, 267.

65. My summary here is informed by works published both during and after the 1976–1983 period. The most comprehensive source for the "pro-sex" critique, and the source I rely on most heavily, is Kate Ellis et al, eds., *Caught Looking*. Some of the articles in this collection appeared earlier in other publications and are important primary sources for the sexuality debates; Pat Califia's "Among Us, Against Us—The New Puritans," for instance, appeared in *Advocate*, April 17, 1980: 14–18, and was highly controversial at the time. Other sources informing my discussion here include Snitow, Stansell, and Thompson, eds., *Powers of Desire;* Vance, ed., *Pleasure and Danger; Heresies 12: The Sex Issue* (1981); Varda Burstyn, ed., *Women against Censorship* (Vancouver: Douglas and McIntyre, 1985); Samois, ed., *What Color Is Your Handkerchief?* and *Coming to Power;* Ann Ferguson et al., "Forum: The Sexuality Debates," *Signs* 10, no. 1 (Autumn 1984): 106–35. Eisenstein's summary of the sexuality debates in *Contemporary Feminist Thought*, 116–24, is especially helpful.

66. This chronology, though reiterated by many sources, is from Hunter, "The Pornography Debate in Context," 27–29.

67. I do not mean to infer here that no feminist women of color

objected to pornography, or that black and Latina feminists used maternalist arguments with less frequency or intensity than white feminists did during this period. To the contrary, see, e.g., Lorde, "Uses of the Erotic"; Alice Walker, "Coming Apart," in Lederer, ed., *Take Back the Night*, 95–104; and most powerfully, reflecting all of the cultural feminist/spiritualist trends discussed in this chapter, Alice Walker, *The Temple of My Familiar* (San Diego: Harcourt Brace Jovanovich, 1989). I am saying, rather, that of the voices of dissent from cultural feminist analysis on these issues, the voices of radical women of color were distinct, arguing a somewhat different point than the white "pro-sex" feminists. Ellen Willis, "Radical Feminism and Feminist Radicalism," 116–17, begins to make these connections between pro-sex feminism and the feminist theory being advanced by women of color.

68. Cherríe Moraga and Gloria Anzaldua, eds., *This Bridge Called My Back: Writings by Radical Women of Color* (New York: Kitchen Table/Women of Color Press, 1981); *Conditions* 5, "The Black Women's Issue" (Autumn 1979); *Heresies* 2, no. 4, Issue 8, "Third World Women: The Politics of Being Other" (1979); hooks, *Ain't I a Woman; Off Our Backs*, "Ain't I a Womon Issue—By and About Wimmin of Color" (June 1979); Vida, ed., *Our Right to Love*.

69. In addition to the sources cited in note 68, see especially Cherríe Moraga and Amber Hollibaugh, "What We're Rolling Around in Bed With: Sexual Silences in Feminism, A Conversation toward Ending Them," *Heresies* 12 (Spring 1981): 58–62; and Cherríe Moraga, *Loving in the War Years: Lo Que Nunca Paso Por Sus Labios* (Boston: South End Press, 1983), passim.

70. Moraga, *Loving in the War Years*, 90.

71. Ibid., 133 and passim; Moraga and Hollibaugh, "What We're Rolling Around in Bed With."

72. Moraga, *Loving In the War Years*, 130.

Notes to the Epilogue

1. See, e.g., Alice Adams, "Maternal Bonds: Recent Literature on Mothering," *Signs* 20, no. 2 (Winter 1995): 414–27; Patrice DiQuinzio, "Exclusion and Essentialism in Feminist Theory: The Problem of Mothering," *Hypatia* 8, no. 3 (Summer 1993): 1–20; Evelyn Nakano Glenn, "Social Constructions of Mothering: A Thematic Overview," in Evelyn Nakano Glenn, Grace Chang, and Linda Rennie Forcey, eds., *Mothering: Ideology, Experience, and Agency* (New York: Routledge, 1994), 1–29; Paul Lauritzen, "A Feminist Ethic and the New Romanticism—Mothering

As a Model of Moral Relations," *Hypatia* 4, no. 2 (Summer 1989): 29–44; Elayne Rapping, "The Future of Motherhood: Some Unfashionably Visionary Thoughts," in Hansen and Philipson, *Women, Class, and the Feminist Imagination,* 537–48; Ellen Ross, "New Thoughts on the 'Oldest Vocation': Mothers and Motherhood in Recent Feminist Scholarship," *Signs* 20, no. 2 (Winter 1995): 397–413; Sheila Rowbotham, "To Be or Not to Be: The Dilemmas of Mothering," *Feminist Review,* no. 31 (Spring 1989): 82–93; Snitow, "Feminism and Motherhood."

2. Echols, *Daring to Be Bad,* 288 and passim; see also the notes for chapter 5 above.

3. I discuss this process of attempted unification and dissent in chapter 5. On the "sex debates" as a response to the totalizing politics of cultural feminism, see Echols, *Daring to Be Bad,* 288–90 and passim; see also the range of writers on the "pro-sex" side of the controversy, but most particularly Snitow, "Retrenchment vs. Transformation."

4. Echols's discussion of dissent from cultural feminism leads her to talk about the development of black feminism in the post-1975 period; see *Daring to Be Bad,* 291–93. While I agree with this analysis and allude to it in chapter 5, I am also referring here to the activism of such groups as Wages for Housework and CARASA (Committee for Abortion Rights and Against Sterilization Abuse).

5. The literature on French feminisms and on newer American feminist psychoanalytic theory is substantial at this point. A good summary of the theories mentioned here can be found in Elaine Marks and Isabelle de Courtivron, eds., *New French Feminisms* (New York: Schocken Books, 1981); Richard Feldstein and Judith Roof, eds., *Feminism and Psychoanalysis* (Ithaca: Cornell University Press, 1989); Rosemarie Tong, *Feminist Thought: A Comprehensive Introduction* (Boulder, Colo.: Westview Press, 1989), chap. 8.

6. The literature on these topics is large and growing; see especially Rita Arditti, Renate Duelli Klein, and Shelley Minden, eds., *Test-Tube Women: What Future for Motherhood?* (London: Pandora, 1984); Gena Corea, *The Mother Machine: Reproductive Technologies from Artificial Insemination to Artificial Wombs* (New York: Harper and Row, 1985); Helen Holmes, Betty Hoskins, and Michael Gross, eds., *The Custom-Made Child? Women-Centered Perspectives* (Clifton, N.J.: Humana Press, 1981); Barbara Katz Rothman, *The Tentative Pregnancy: Prenatal Diagnosis and the Future of Motherhood* (New York: Viking, 1986). As always, Ann Snitow's observations are particularly insightful, in "The Paradox of Birth Technology: Exploring the Good, the Bad, and the Scary," *Ms.* 15, no. 6 (December 1986): 42–46, 76–78.

7. Of course, the antiabortion strategy of endowing the fetus with the full legal rights of a person is not intended, in the end, to create a legal union between woman and fetus; rather, it is intended to give the fetus superior legal staus to that of the woman. But the net effect of the strategy is to tie the rights (and fate) of one to the other. See Mary Ruth Mellown, "An Incomplete Picture: The Debate About Surrogate Motherhood," *Harvard Women's Law Journal* 8 (Spring 1985): 231–47; Faludi summarizes recent writing on the growth of the "fetal rights" movement in *Backlash,* 421–53. On the "sacred bond" interpretation of the Baby M case, see especially Phyllis Chesler's book by that name, *Sacred Bond* (New York: Vintage, 1988). Katha Pollitt's discussion of the case remains one of the best, in "The Strange Case of Baby M," *Nation* May 23, 1987.

8. Judith Arcana, "Abortion Is a Motherhood Choice," *Sojourner* 16, no. 12 (August 1991): 11.

9. On the encroachment of antiabortion iconography and ideology into mainstream and even feminist discourse, see Rosalind Pollack Petchesky, "Fetal Images: The Power of Visual Culture in the Politics of Reproduction," *Feminist Studies* 13, no. 2 (Summer 1987): 263–92. See also Alice Adams, "Out of the Womb: The Future of the Uterine Metaphor," *Feminist Studies* 19, no. 2 (Summer 1993): 269–89.

10. Rothman, *Recreating Motherhood,* 59.

11. On all these trends, the best recent reviews are Ross, "New Thoughts on the 'Oldest Vocation' "; and Adams, "Maternal Bonds: Recent Literature on Mothering."

Selected Bibliography

Books and Articles

Adams, Alice. "Maternal Bonds: Recent Literature on Mothering." *Signs* 20, no. 2 (Winter 1995): 414–27.

———. "Out of the Womb: The Future of the Uterine Metaphor." *Feminist Studies* 19, no. 2 (Summer 1993): 269–89.

Albert, Judith Clavir, and Stewart Albert, eds. *The Sixties Papers: Documents of a Rebellious Decade.* New York: Praeger, 1984.

Alpert, Jane. *Growing Up Underground.* New York: Morrow, 1981.

———. "Mother Right: A New Feminist Theory." *Ms.* 2, no. 2 (August 1973): 52–55, 88–94.

Altbach, Edith Hoshimo. "Notes on a Movement." In Edith Hoshimo Altbach, ed., *From Feminism to Liberation.*

Altbach, Edith Hoshimo, ed. *From Feminism to Liberation.* Cambridge, Mass.: Schenkman, 1971.

Anonymous. "Them and Me." In Shulamith Firestone and Anne Koedt, eds. *Notes from the Second Year.*

Arcana, Judith. "Abortion Is a Motherhood Issue." *Sojourner* 16, no. 12 (August 1991): 11.

———. *Our Mothers' Daughters.* Berkeley: Shameless Hussy Press, 1979.

Arditti, Rita, Renate Duelli Klein, and Shelley Minden, eds. *Test-Tube Women: What Future for Motherhood?* London: Pandora, 1984.

Arms, Suzanne. *Immaculate Deception: A New Look at Women and Childbirth.* New York: Bantam, 1981; orig. 1975.

Armstrong, Louise. *Kiss Daddy Good Night: A Speak-Out on Incest.* New York: Hawthorn Books, 1978.

Atkinson, Ti-Grace. *Amazon Odyssey.* New York: Links Books, 1974.

———. "The Institution of Sexual Intercourse." In Shulamith Firestone and Anne Koedt, eds., *Notes from the Second Year.*

Babcox, Deborah, and Madeline Belkin, eds. *Liberation Now! The Writings of the Women's Liberation Movement.* New York: Dell, 1971.

Bammer, Angelika. *Partial Visions: Feminism and Utopianism in the 1970s.* New York: Routledge, 1991.

Baraka, Imamu Amiri. *Raise Race Rays Raze: Essays since 1965.* New York: Random House, 1971.

Barbour, Floyd B., ed. *The Black Power Revolt: A Collection of Essays.* Boston: Sargent, 1968.

Barrett, Michele. *Women's Oppression Today: Problems in Marxist Feminist Analysis.* London: Verso Editions and NLB, 1980.

Barry, Kathleen. *Female Sexual Slavery.* New Jersey: Prentice-Hall, 1979.

———. "How They Turned the Tables on Us." In Dorothy Tennov and Lolly Hirsch, coordinators, *Proceedings of the First International Childbirth Conference.*

Bart, Pauline. "The Mermaid and the Minotaur, a Fishy Story That's Part Bull." *Contemporary Psychology* 22, no. 11 (1977): 834–35.

———. "Review of Chodorow's *The Reproduction of Mothering.*" In Joyce Trebilcot, ed., *Mothering: Essays in Feminist Theory.*

Baxandall, Rosalyn. "Cooperative Nurseries." In Sookie Stambler, ed., *Women's Liberation.*

Beale, Frances. "Double Jeopardy: To Be Black and Female." In Toni Cade, ed., *The Black Woman: An Anthology.*

Beck, Julian. "Notes toward a Statement on Anarchism and the Theatre." In Judith Clavir Albert and Stewart Albert, eds., *The Sixties Papers.*

Berger, Bennett M. "Hippie Morality—More Old Than New." In Edgar Z. Friedenberg, ed., *The Anti-American Generation.*

Berman, Marshall. "Review of *Haven in a Heartless World.*" *New York Times Book Review,* January 15, 1978: 15.

Bernikow, Louise. "Review of *The Mother Knot.*" *New York Times Book Review,* March 21, 1976: 26.

Bing, Elizabeth, and Marjorie Karmel. *A Practical Training Course for the Psychoprophylactic Method of Painless Childbirth.* New York: American Society for Psychoprophylaxis in Obstetrics, 1961.

"Birth Control Pills and Black Children: The Sisters Reply." In Judith Clavir Albert and Stewart Albert, eds., *The Sixties Papers.*

"Black Caucus Position." *Lesbian Tide* 2, no. 10/11 (June 1973): 19.

Black Unity Party. "Birth Control and Black Children." Reprinted in Patricia Robinson et al., "Poor Black Women." New England Free Press pamphlet in "New England Free Press" file, Schlesinger Library, n.d.

Blumenthal, Samuel. *The Retreat from Motherhood.* New Rochelle, N.Y.: Arlington House, 1975.

Boggs, James. "Black Power—A Scientific Concept Whose Time Has

Come." In LeRoi Jones and Larry Neal, eds., *Black Fire: An Anthology of Afro-American Writing.* New York: Morrow, 1968.

Bond, Jean Carey, and Patricia Peery, "Has the Black Male Been Castrated?" *Liberator* 9, no. 5 (May 1969): 4–8.

Boris, Eileen. "The Power of Motherhood: Black and White Activist Women Redefine the 'Political.' " In Seth Koven and Sonya Michel, eds., *Mothers of a New World: Maternalist Politics and the Origins of Welfare States.*

Boston Women's Health Collective. *Our Bodies, Ourselves.* New York: Simon and Schuster, 1973.

Boston Women's Health Course Collective. *Our Bodies, Ourselves.* Boston: New England Free Press, 1971.

Braden, William. *The Age of Aquarius: Technology and the Cultural Revolution.* Chicago: Quadrangle Books, 1970.

Brady, Katherine. *Father's Days: A True Story of Incest.* New York: Seaview Books, 1979.

Bread and Roses. "Bread and Roses Declaration: The Rights of Women." *Old Mole*, no. 34, March 6–19, 1970: 3.

Breines, Wini. *The Great Refusal: Community and Organization in the New Left, 1962–1968.* New York: Praeger, 1982.

———. *Young, White, and Miserable: Growing Up Female in the Fifties.* Boston: Beacon, 1992.

Breines, Wini, Magaret Cerullo, and Judith Stacey. "Social Biology, Family Studies, and Antifeminist Backlash." *Feminist Studies* 4, no. 1 (February 1978): 43–67.

Brine, Ruth. "The New Feminists: Revolt against 'Sexism.' " *Time*, November 21, 1969: 53–56.

Brooks, Evelyn. "The Feminist Theology of the Black Baptist Church, 1880–1900." In Darlene Clark Hine, *Black Women in American History: From Colonial Times through the Nineteenth Century,* vol. 1.

Brown, Elaine. *A Taste of Power: A Black Woman's Story.* New York: Pantheon, 1992.

Brown, H. Rapp. *Die Nigger Die!* New York: Dial Press, 1969.

Brown, Norman O. *Life against Death: The Psychoanalytic Meaning of History.* Middletown, Conn.: Wesleyan University Press, 1959.

———. *Love's Body.* New York: Random House, 1966.

Brown, Rita Mae. *A Plain Brown Rapper.* Baltimore: Diana Press, 1976.

———. "The Shape of Things to Come." In Nancy Myron and Charlotte Bunch, eds., *Lesbianism and the Women's Movement.*

Brownmiller, Susan. *Against Our Will: Men, Women and Rape.* New York: Simon and Schuster, 1975.

Bryant, Anita. *Bless This House.* New York: Bantam, 1976.

Bunch, Charlotte. *Passionate Politics: Essays, 1968–1986: Feminist Theory in Action.* New York: St. Martin's, 1987.

Burris, Barbara, et al. "The Fourth World Manifesto." In Anne Koedt, Anita Rapone, and Ellen Levine, eds., *Notes from the Third Year.*

Burstyn, Varda, ed. *Women against Censorship.* Vancouver: Douglas and McIntyre, 1985.

Cade, Toni. "The Pill: Genocide or Liberation." In Toni Cade, ed., *The Black Woman.*

Cade, Toni, ed. *The Black Woman: An Anthology.* New York: New American Library, 1970.

Caldecott, Leone, and Stephanie Leland. *Reclaim the Earth: Women Speak Out for Life on Earth.* London: Women's Press, 1983.

Califia, Pat. "Among Us, Against Us—The New Puritans." *The Advocate,* April 17, 1980: 14–18.

———. *Sapphistry: The Book of Lesbian Sexuality.* Tallahassee, Fla.: Naiad Press, 1980.

Caplan, Paula. *Don't Blame Mother: Mending the Mother-Daughter Relationship.* New York: Harper and Row, 1989.

Carden, Maren Lockwood. *The New Feminist Movement.* New York: Russell Sage Foundation, 1974.

Carmichael, Stokely. *Stokely Speaks: Black Power Back to PanAfricanism.* New York: Vintage, 1971.

———. "Toward Black Liberation." In LeRoi Jones and Larry Neal, eds., *Black Fire: An Anthology of Afro-American Writing.* New York: Morrow, 1968.

———. "What We Want." In Judith Clavir Albert and Stewart Albert, eds., *The Sixties Papers.*

Carson, Clayborne. *In Struggle: SNCC and the Black Awakening of the 1960s.* Cambridge, Mass.: Harvard University Press, 1981.

Carson, Rachel. *Silent Spring.* New York: Fawcett, 1962.

Castro, Ginette. *American Feminism: A Contemporary History.* New York: New York University Press, 1990.

Chafe, William H. *The Unfinished Journey: America since World War II.* Second Edition. New York: Oxford University Press, 1991.

Chesler, Phyllis. *Mothers on Trial: The Battle for Children and Custody.* Seattle: Seal Press, 1986.

———. *Sacred Bond.* New York: Vintage, 1988.

Chesler, Phyllis. *With Child: A Diary of Motherhood.* New York: Crowell, 1979.

———. *Women and Madness.* Garden City, N.Y.: Doubleday, 1972.

Chodorow, Nancy. "Consideration of a Biosocial Perspective on Parenting." *Berkeley Journal of Sociology* 22 (1977–1978): 179–97.

———. "Mothering, Male Dominance and Capitalism." In Zillah Eisenstein, ed., *Capitalist Patriarchy and the Case for Socialist Feminism.*

———. *The Reproduction of Mothering: Psychoanalysis and the Sociology of Gender.* Berkeley: University of California Press, 1978.

Chodorow, Nancy, and Susan Contratto. "The Fantasy of the Perfect Mother." In Barrie Thorne and Marilyn Yalom, eds., *Rethinking the Family.*

Christeve, Jackie. "Midwives Busted in Santa Cruz." *Second Wave* 3, no. 3 (Summer 1974): 5–10.

Cisler, Lucinda. "On Abortion and Abortion Law." In Shulamith Firestone and Anne Koedt, eds., *Notes from the Second Year.*

Clarke, Adele, and Alice Wolfson. "Class, Race, and Reproductive Rights." In Karen Hansen and Ilene Philipson, eds., *Women, Class, and the Feminist Imagination.*

Clausen, Jan. "A Flommy Looks at Lesbian Parenting." *Off Our Backs* 16, no. 8 (August–September 1986): 16–17.

Cleaver, Eldridge. *Soul on Ice.* New York: Dell, 1968.

Cleaver, Kathleen. "Black Scholar Interviews Kathleen Cleaver." *Black Scholar* 3, no. 4 (December 1971): 54–59.

Cluster, Dick, ed. *They Should Have Served That Cup of Coffee: Seven Radicals Remember the Sixties.* Boston: South End Press, 1979.

Combahee River Collective. "A Black Feminist Statement." In Zillah Eisenstein, ed., *Capitalist Patriarchy and the Case for Socialist Feminism.*

Conditions 5: "The Black Women's Issue" (Autumn 1979).

Congress to Unite Women. "What Women Want: For Starters." In Shulamith Firestone and Anne Koedt, eds., *Notes from the Second Year.*

Cook, Alice, and Gwyn Kirk. *Greenham Women Everywhere: Dreams, Ideas and Actions from the Women's Peace Movement.* Boston: South End Press, 1983.

Cooke, Joanne, Charlotte Bunch-Weeks, and Robin Morgan, eds. *The New Women: A MOTIVE Anthology on Women's Liberation.* Greenwich, Conn.: Fawcett, 1970.

Corea, Gina. *The Mother Machine: Reproductive Technologies from Arti-*

ficial Insemination to Artificial Wombs. New York: Harper and Row, 1985.

Creamer, Day, and Heather Booth. "Action Committee for Decent Childcare: Organizing for Power." *Women: A Journal of Liberation* 2, no. 4 (June 1972): 7–9.

Daly, Mary. *Beyond God the Father: Toward a Philosophy of Women's Liberation.* Boston: Beacon, 1973.

———. *The Church and the Second Sex.* New York: Harper and Row, 1968.

———. *Gyn/Ecology: The Metaethics of Radical Feminism.* Boston: Beacon, 1978.

Darragh, Janet. "Birth at Home." In Dorothy Tennov and Lolly Hirsch, coordinators, *Proceedings of the First International Childbirth Conference.*

Davidson, Sara. "An 'Oppressed Majority' Demands Its Rights." *Life,* December 12, 1969: 67–78.

Davis, Angela. "The Black Woman's Role in the Community of Slaves." *Black Scholar* 3, no. 4 (December 1971): 2–15.

Davis, Angela, and Bettina Aptheker, eds. *If They Come in the Morning: Voices of Resistance.* New York: Third Press, 1971.

Davis, Ann. "Whose Children Are They? Child Care At the Lesbian Conference." *Lesbian Tide* 2, no. 10/11 (May–June 1973): 11, 18.

Davis, Beverly. "To Seize the Moment: A Retrospective on the National Black Feminist Organization." *Sage* 5, no. 2 (Fall 1988): 43–47.

Davis, Elizabeth Gould. *The First Sex.* New York: Putnam, 1971.

Davis, Flora. *Moving the Mountain: The Women's Movement in America since 1960.* New York: Simon and Schuster, 1991.

Davis, Judy, and Juanita Weaver. "Dimensions of Spirituality." *Quest* 1, no. 4 (Spring 1975): 2–6.

DeBenedetti, Charles. *An American Ordeal: The Antiwar Movement of the Vietnam Era.* Syracuse, N.Y.: Syracuse University Press, 1990.

Deckard, Barbara Sinclair. *The Women's Movement: Political, Socioeconomic, and Psychological Issues.* Second Edition. New York: Harper and Row, 1979.

De Maehl, Sharon, and Linda Thurston. "Caution: Trusting Your Obstetrician May Be Harmful to Your Health." *Second Wave* 2, no. 3 (1973): 21–23.

Densmore, Dana. "Independence from the Sexual Revolution." In Anne Koedt, Anita Rapone, and Ellen Levine, eds., *Notes from the Third Year.*

———. "On Unity." *No More Fun and Games*, no. 5 (July 1971): 53–63.

Diamond, Irene. "Ecofeminism: Weaving the Worlds Together (Report on a Conference on 'Ecofeminist Perspectives: Culture, Nature, and Theory,' Held at the University of Southern California, 27–29 March 1987)." *Feminist Studies* 14, no. 2 (Summer 1988): 368–70.

Diamond, Irene, and Gloria Feman Orenstein, eds. *Reweaving the World: The Emergence of Ecofeminism.* San Francisco: Sierra Club Books, 1990.

Diamond, Stephen. *What the Trees Said: Life on a New Age Farm.* New York: Dell, 1971.

Dick-Read, Grantly. *Childbirth without Fear: The Principles and Practice of Natural Childbirth.* New York: Harper, 1944.

Dickson, Lynda F. "Toward a Broader Angle of Vision in Uncovering Women's History: Black Women's Clubs Revisited." In Darlene Clark Hine, ed., *Black Women's History: Theory and Practice*, vol. 1.

Dill, Bonnie Thornton. "The Dialectics of Black Womanhood." *Signs* 4, no. 3 (Spring 1979): 543–55.

Diner, Helen. *Mothers and Amazons.* Garden City, N.Y.: Anchor, 1973; orig. 1932.

Dinnerstein, Dorothy. *The Mermaid and the Minotaur: Sexual Arrangements and Human Malaise.* New York: Harper and Row, 1976.

———. "What Does Feminism Mean?" In Adrienne Harris and Ynestra King, eds., *Rocking the Ship of State.*

DiQuinzio, Patrice. "Exclusion and Essentialism in Feminist Theory: The Problem of Mothering." *Hypatia* 8, no. 3 (Summer 1993): 1–20.

Dixon, Marlene. "On Women's Liberation." *Radical America* 4, no. 2 (February 1970): 26–34.

———. *The Future of Women.* San Francisco: Synthesis Publications, 1983.

Dobbyn, Dorothy. "A Feminist's Case for Homebirth." *Women: A Journal of Liberation* 4, no. 3 (1976): 20–23.

Donovan, Josephine. *Feminist Theory: The Intellectual Traditions of American Feminism.* New York: Frederick Ungar, 1985.

Downer, Carol. "Covert Sex Discrimination against Women As Medical Patients." Address to the American Psychological Association, September 5, 1972. Reprinted by Know, Inc., Pittsburgh, Pa.

———. "Women Professionals in the Feminist Health Movement." Mimeograph by the Feminist Women's Health Center, Los Angeles, 1974.

Dreifus, Claudia. *Woman's Fate: Raps from a Feminist Consciousness-Raising Group.* New York: Bantam, 1973.

Dudar, Helen, Judith Gingold, and Nancy Dooley. "Women's Lib: The War on Sexism." *Newsweek,* March 23, 1970: 71–78.

Dunbar, Roxanne. "Female Liberation As the Basis for Social Revolution." In Shulamith Firestone and Anne Koedt, eds., *Notes from the Second Year.*

Dworkin, Andrea. *Our Blood: Prophecies and Discourses on Sexual Politics.* New York: Harper and Row, 1976.

———. *Pornography: Men Possessing Women.* New York: G. P. Putnam's, 1981.

———. "Why So-Called Radical Men Love and Need Pornography." In Laura Lederer, ed., *Take Back the Night.*

———. *Woman Hating.* New York: E. P. Dutton, 1974.

Echols, Alice. *Daring to Be Bad: Radical Feminism in America, 1967–1975.* Minneapolis: University of Minnesota Press, 1989.

———. "The New Feminism of Yin and Yang." In Ann Snitow, Christine Stansell, and Sharon Thompson, eds., *Powers of Desire.*

———. "The Taming of the Id: Feminist Sexual Politics, 1968–1983." In Carole Vance, ed., *Pleasure and Danger.*

Edwards, Margot, and Mary Waldorf. *Reclaiming Birth: History and Heroines of American Childbirth Reform.* Trumansburg, N.Y.: Crossing Press, 1984.

Ehrenreich, Barbara. *The Hearts of Men: American Dreams and the Flight from Commitment.* Garden City, N.Y.: Doubleday, 1983.

———. "On Feminism, Family and Community." *Dissent* 30, no. 1 (1983): 103–9.

Ehrenreich, Barbara, and Deirdre English. *Witches, Midwives, and Nurses: A History of Women Healers.* Old Westbury, N.Y.: Feminist Press, 1973.

Eichelberger, Brenda. "Voices on Black Feminism." *Quest* 3, no. 4 (Spring 1977): 16–28.

Eisenstein, Hester. *Contemporary Feminist Thought.* Boston: G. K. Hall, 1983.

Eisenstein, Zillah. "Antifeminism in the Politics and Election of 1980." *Feminist Studies* 7, no. 2 (Summer 1981): 187–205.

———. "Some Notes on the Relations of Capitalist Patriarchy." In Zillah Eisenstein, ed., *Capitalist Patriarchy.*

Eisenstein, Zillah, ed. *Capitalist Patriarchy and the Case for Socialist Feminism.* New York: Monthly Review Press, 1979.

Ellis, Kate. "I'm Black and Blue from the Rolling Stones and I'm Not Sure How I Feel About It." In Kate Ellis et al., eds., *Caught Looking.*

Ellis, Kate, Nan D. Hunter, Beth Jaker, Barbara O'Dair, and Abby Tallmer, eds. *Caught Looking: Feminism, Pornography and Censorship.* New York: Caught Looking, Inc., 1984.

Ellul, Jacques. *The Technological Society.* New York: Knopf, 1964.

Elshtain, Jean Bethke. "Feminism, Family and Community." *Dissent* 29, no. 4 (1982): 442–49.

———. *Public Man, Private Woman: Women in Social and Political Thought.* Princeton: Princeton University Press, 1981.

Erikson, Erik. *Identity, Youth and Crisis.* New York: Norton, 1968.

Estellachild, Vivian. "Hippie Communes." *Women: A Journal of Liberation* 2 (Winter 1971): 40–43.

Evans, Sara. *Personal Politics: The Roots of Women's Liberation in the Civil Rights Movement and the New Left.* New York: Vintage, 1979.

Fairfield, Richard. *Communes USA: A Personal Tour.* Baltimore: Penguin, 1972.

Faludi, Susan. *Backlash: The Undeclared War against American Women.* New York: Crown Publishers, 1991.

Feigelson, Naomi. *The Underground Revolution: Hippies, Yippies and Others.* New York: Funk and Wagnalls, 1970.

Feldstein, Richard, and Judith Roof, eds. *Feminism and Psychoanalysis.* Ithaca: Cornell University Press, 1989.

Female Liberation. "From Us." *Second Wave* 2, no. 3 (1973): 2–4.

Feminist Studies. "Toward a Feminist Theory of Motherhood." 4, no. 2 (June 1978).

The Feminists. "The Feminists: A Political Organization to Annihilate Sex Roles." In Shulamith Firestone and Anne Koedt, eds., *Notes from the Second Year.*

Ferguson, Ann, and Nancy Folbre. "The Unhappy Marriage of Patriarchy and Capitalism." In Lydia Sargent, ed., *Women and Revolution.*

Ferguson, Ann, et al. "Forum: The Sexuality Debates." *Signs* 10, no. 1 (Autumn 1984): 106–35.

Ferree, Myra Marx, and Beth B. Hess. *Controversy and Coalition: The New Feminist Movement.* Boston: Twayne, 1985.

Firestone, Shulamith. *The Dialectic of Sex: The Case for Feminist Revolution.* New York: Bantam, 1970.

Firestone, Shulamith and Anne Koedt, eds. *Notes from the Second Year: Women's Liberation.* New York: Notes from the Second Year: Radical Feminism, 1970.

Fisher, Berenice. "Guilt and Shame in the Women's Movement: The Radical Ideal of Action and Its Meaning for Feminist Intellectuals." *Feminist Studies* 10, no. 2 (Summer 1984): 185–212.

Fisher, Rosalea. "Why Nurse Your Baby?" In Dorothy Tennov and Lolly

Hirsch, coordinators, *Proceedings of the First International Childbirth Conference.*

Fitzgerald, Frances. "The Triumphs of the New Right." *New York Review of Books,* November 19, 1981: 19–26.

Flax, Jane. "The Conflict between Nurturance and Autonomy in Mother-Daughter Relationships and within Feminism." *Feminist Studies* 4, no. 2 (June 1978): 171–89.

———. *Thinking Fragments: Psychoanalysis, Feminism, and Postmodernism in the Contemporary West.* Berkeley: University of California Press, 1990.

Foner, Philip S., ed. *The Black Panthers Speak.* Philadelphia: J. B. Lippincott, 1970.

Foreman, Ann. *Femininity As Alienation: Women and the Family in Marxism and Psychoanalysis.* London: Pluto Press, 1977.

Forfreedom, Ann. "Lesbos Arise!" *Lesbian Tide* 2, no. 10/11 (May—June 1973): 4, 5, 14.

Forman, James. *The Making of Black Revolutionaries: A Personal Account.* New York: Macmillan, 1972.

Fowler, Linda. "Energizing the Feminine Principle Today." *Big Mama Rag* 3, no. 1 (July 1974): 13–14.

Frankfort, Ellen. *Vaginal Politics.* New York: Quadrangle Books, 1972.

Frazier, E. Franklin. *The Negro Family in the United States.* Chicago: University of Chicago Press, 1939.

Fredrickson, George M. *Black Liberation: A Comparative History of Black Ideologies in the United States and South Africa.* New York: Oxford University Press, 1995.

"Free Our Sisters, Free Ourselves." In Leslie B. Tanner, ed., *Voices from Women's Liberation.*

Freud, Sigmund. *Standard Edition of the Complete Psychological Works* London: Hogarth Press, 1966.

Friday, Nancy. *My Mother/My Self: The Daughter's Search for Identity.* New York: Delacorte Press, 1977.

Friedan, Betty. *It Changed My Life: Writings on the Women's Movement.* New York: Random House, 1976.

———. *The Feminine Mystique.* New York: Dell, 1963.

———. *The Second Stage.* New York: Summit Books, 1981.

Friedenberg, Edgar Z., ed. *The Anti-American Generation.* Chicago: Aldine Publishing Company, 1971.

Friedland, Ronnie, and Carol Kort, eds. *The Mothers' Book: Shared Experiences.* Boston: Houghton Mifflin, 1981.

Fritz, Leah. *Dreamers and Dealers: An Intimate Appraisal of the Women's Movement.* Boston: Beacon, 1979.

Fulton, Stacey. "On Racism and Anger." *Lesbian Tide* 3, no. 1 (August 1973): 18.

Gallop, Jane. *The Daughter's Seduction: Feminism and Psychoanalysis.* New York: Cornell University Press, 1982.

Garskof, Michele Hoffnung. "The Psychology of the Maternity Ward: A Study in Dehumanization." In Dorothy Tennov and Lolly Hirsch, coordinators, *Proceedings of the First International Childbirth Conference.*

Gaskin, Ina May. *Spiritual Midwifery.* Summertown, Tenn.: The Book Publishing Company, 1977; orig. 1975.

Gearhart, Sally, and Peggy Cleveland. "On the Prevalence of Stilps." *Quest* 1, no. 4 (Spring 1975): 53–64.

Gibson, Gifford Guy. *By Her Own Admission: A Lesbian Mother's Fight to Keep Her Son.* Garden City, N.Y.: Doubleday, 1977.

Giddings, Paula. *When and Where I Enter: The Impact of Black Women on Race and Sex in America.* New York: Bantam Books, 1985.

Gilligan, Carol. *In a Different Voice: Psychological Theory and Women's Development.* Cambridge: Harvard University Press, 1982.

Gitlin, Todd. *The Sixties: Years of Hope, Days of Rage.* New York: Bantam, 1987.

Glenn, Evelyn Nakano, Grace Chang, and Linda Rennie Forcey, eds. *Mothering: Ideology, Experience, and Agency* New York: Routledge, 1994.

Goldberger, Lisa. "Lesbian Mother Appeal Denied." *The Tide* 3, no. 7 (April 1974): 15.

Goodman, Paul. *Growing Up Absurd; Problems of Youth in the Organized System.* New York: Random House, 1960.

———. *Utopian Essays and Practical Proposals.* New York: Random House, 1962.

Gordon, Linda. *Pitied But Not Entitled: Single Mothers and the History of Welfare, 1890–1935.* New York: Free Press, 1994.

———. "The Struggle for Reproductive Freedom: Three Stages of Feminism." In Zillah Eisenstein, ed., *Capitalist Patriarchy.*

———. *Woman's Body, Woman's Right: A Social History of Birth Control in America.* New York: Grossman Publishers, 1976.

Gordon, Linda, and Allen Hunter. "Sex, Family and the New Right: Antifeminism As a Political Force." *Radical America* 11/12, nos. 6 and 1 (November 1977/February 1978 combined issue): 9–25.

Gorer, Geoffrey. *The American People: A Study in National Character.* New York: Norton, 1949.

Gornick, Vivian. "Review of *The Mermaid and the Minotaur.*" *New York Times Book Review,* November 14, 1976: 5, 70.

Gottlieb, Annie. "Feminists Look at Motherhood." *Mother Jones,* November 1976: 51–53.

Gottlieb, Roger S. "Mothering and the Reproduction of Power: Chodorow, Dinnerstein, and Social Theory." *Socialist Review* 14, no. 77 (Sept.–Oct. 1984): 93–119.

Grant, Joanne, ed. *Black Protest: History, Documents, and Analyses.* New York: Fawcett, 1968.

Gray, Elizabeth Dodson. *Green Paradise Lost.* Wellesley, Mass.: Round Table Press, 1979.

Greenburg, Dan. *How to Be a Jewish Mother: A Very Lovely Training Manual.* Los Angeles: Price Stern Sloan, 1965.

Greer, Germaine. *The Female Eunuch.* London: McGibbon and Kee, 1970.

Griffin, Susan. "On Wanting to Be the Mother I Wanted." *Ms.* 5, no. 7 (January 1977): 98–105.

———. *Pornography and Silence: Culture's Revenge against Nature.* New York: Harper and Row, 1981.

———. *Rape: The Power of Consciousness.* New York: Harper and Row, 1979.

———. *Woman and Nature: The Roaring inside Her.* New York: Harper and Row, 1978.

Gross, Harriet Engel, Jessie Bernard, Alice Dan, Nona Glazer, Judith Lorber, Martha McClintock, Niles Newton, and Alice Rossi, "Considering 'A Biosocial Perspective on Parenting.'" *Signs* 4, no. 4 (Summer 1979): 695–717.

Haaken, Janice. "Freudian Theory Revisited: A Critique of Rich, Chodorow, and Dinnerstein." *Women's Studies Quarterly* 2, no. 4 (Winter 1983): 12–15.

Hacker, Andrew, ed. *U/S: A Statistical Portrait of the American People.* New York: Viking, 1983.

Haden, Patricia, Donna Middleton, and Patricia Robinson. "A Historical and Critical Essay for Black Women." In Edith Altbach, ed., *From Feminism to Liberation.*

Haggerty, Joan. "Childbirth Made Difficult." *Ms.* 1, no. 7 (January 1973): 16–17.

Haire, Doris. "The Cultural Warping of Childbirth." *International Childbirth Education Association News,* Special Issue, 1972.

Hamilton, Charles "Riots, Revolts and Relevant Responses." In Floyd B. Barbour, ed., *The Black Power Revolt.*

Hanisch, Carol. "A Critique of the Miss America Protest." In Shulamith Firestone and Anne Koedt, eds., *Notes from the Second Year.*

————. "The Personal Is Political." In Shulamith Firestone and Anne Koedt, eds., *Notes from the Second Year.*

Hanscombe, Gillian E., and Jackie Forster. *Rocking the Cradle: Lesbian Mothers: A Challenge in Family Living.* Boston: Alyson Publications, 1982.

Hansen, Karen, and Ilene Philipson, eds. *Women, Class, and the Feminist Imagination: A Socialist-Feminist Reader.* Philadelphia: Temple University Press, 1990.

Harding, Susan. "Family Reform Movements: Recent Feminism and Its Opposition." *Feminist Studies* 7, no. 1 (Spring 1981): 57–75.

Harley, Sharon. "Anna J. Cooper: A Voice for Black Women." In Sharon Harley and Rosalyn Terborg-Penn, eds., *The Afro-American Woman: Struggles and Images.*

Harley, Sharon, and Rosalyn Terborg-Penn, eds. *The Afro-American Woman: Struggles and Images.* Port Washington, N.Y.: Kennikat Press, 1978.

Harrington, Pattie. "Nursing a Toddler." In Dorothy Tennov and Lolly Hirsch, coordinators, *Proceedings of the First International Childbirth Conference.*

Harris, Adrienne, and Ynestra King, eds. *Rocking the Ship of State: Toward a Feminist Peace Politics.* Boulder, Colo.: Westview, 1989.

Hartman, Heidi. "The Unhappy Marriage of Marxism and Feminism: Towards a More Progressive Union." In Lydia Sargent, ed., *Women and Revolution.*

Hayden, Casey, and Mary King. "Sex and Caste: A Kind of Memo." In Judith Clavir Albert and Stewart Albert, eds., *The Sixties Papers.*

Hayden, Tom. "The Port Huron Statement." Reprinted in James Miller, *"Democracy Is in the Streets".*

Heath, Louis G., ed. *Off the Pigs! The History and Literature of the Black Panther Party.* Metuchen, N.J.: Scarecrow Press, 1976.

Hermes, Flax. "Mass Women's March in Conn." *Militant* 33, no. 48 (December 5, 1969): 1, 3.

Hewitt, John. *Dilemmas of the American Self.* Philadelphia: Temple University Press, 1989.

Hewlett, Sylvia Ann. *A Lesser Life: The Myth of Women's Liberation in America.* New York: Warner, 1986.

Hine, Darlene Clark, ed. *Black Women in American History: From Colonial Times through the Nineteenth Century,* vols. 1–3. Brooklyn, N.Y.: Carlson Publishing, 1990.

————. *Black Women's History: Theory and Practice,* vols. 1, 11. Brooklyn, N.Y.: Carlson Publishing, 1990.

Hirsch, Jeanne. "Watching a Childbirth at Home." In Dorothy Tennov and Lolly Hirsch, coordinators, *Proceedings of the First International Childbirth Conference.*

Hirsch, Marianne. "Mothers and Daughters." *Signs* 7, no. 1 (Autumn 1981): 200–222.

Hitchens, Donna, and Ann Thomas, eds. *Lesbian Mothers and Their Children: An Annotated Bibliography of Legal and Psychological Materials.* San Francisco: Lesbian Rights Project, 1980.

Hoffman, Abbie. *Revolution for the Hell of It.* New York: Dial, 1968.

———. *Soon to Be a Major Motion Picture.* New York: Perigee, 1980.

Hole, Judith, and Ellen Levine. *Rebirth of Feminism.* New York: Quadrangle, 1971.

Holland, Barbara. *Mother's Day: Or, The View from in Here.* Garden City, N.Y.: Doubleday, 1980.

Holland, Sharon Patricia. " 'Which Me Will Survive?': Audre Lorde and the Development of a Black Feminist Ideology." *Critical Matrix,* Special Issue, no. 1 (1988): 2–30.

Hollinger, David. "Historians and the Discourse of Intellectuals." In John Higham and Paul K. Conklin, eds., *New Directions in American Intellectual History.* Baltimore: Johns Hopkins University Press, 1979.

Holmes, Helen, Betty Hoskins, and Michael Gross, eds. *The Custom-Made Child? Women-Centered Perspectives.* Clifton, N.J.: Humana Press, 1981.

hooks, bell. *Ain't I a Woman: Black Women and Feminism.* Boston: South End Press, 1981.

———. *Feminist Theory: From Margin to Center.* Boston: South End Press, 1984.

———. *Talking Back: Thinking Feminist, Thinking Black.* Boston: South End Press, 1989.

Humm, Maggie. *The Dictionary of Feminist Theory.* Columbus: Ohio State University Press, 1990.

Hunter, Nan D. "The Pornography Debate in Context: A Chronology of Sexuality, Media and Violence Issues in Feminism." In Kate Ellis et al., eds., *Caught Looking.*

Irigaray, Luce. "And the One Doesn't Stir without the Other." *Signs* 7, no. 1 (Autumn 1981): 60–67.

Jackson, George. *Blood in My Eye.* New York: Random House, 1972.

———. *Soledad Brother: The Prison Letters of George Jackson.* New York: Bantam, 1970.

Jaggar, Alison. *Feminist Politics and Human Nature.* Totowa, N.J.: Rowman and Allanheld, 1983.

Jaggar, Alison M., and Paula Rothenberg, eds. *Feminist Frameworks: Alternative Theoretical Accounts of the Relations between Women and Men*. New York: McGraw-Hill, 1978.

Jay, Karla. "Double Trouble for Black Women: An Interview with Margaret Sloan." *The Tide* 3, no. 9 (July 1974): 3, 22–24.

Johnson, John E., Jr. "Super Black Man." In Floyd Barbour, ed., *The Black Power Revolt*.

Johnston, Jill. *Lesbian Nation: The Feminist Solution*. New York: Simon and Schuster, 1973.

Joreen. "Trashing: The Dark Side of Sisterhood." *Ms.* 4, no. 10 (April 1976): 49–51, 92–98.

Karmel, Marjorie. *Thank You, Dr. Lamaze: A Mother's Experience in Painless Childbirth*. Philadelphia: J. B. Lippincott, 1959.

Kanter, Rosabeth Moss. "Communes for All Reasons." *Ms.* 3, no. 2 (August 1974): 62–67.

Kelly, Gail Paradise. "Women's Liberation and the Cultural Revolution." *Radical America* 4, no. 2 (February 1970): 19–25.

Keniston, Kenneth. *The Uncommitted: Alienated Youth in American Society*. New York: Dell, 1965.

———. *Youth and Dissent: The Rise of a New Opposition*. New York: Harcourt Brace Jovanovich, 1971.

Kerouac, Jack. *On the Road*. New York: New American Library, 1957.

Kesey, Ken. *Kesey's Garage Sale*. New York: Viking, 1973.

King, Deborah K. "Multiple Jeopardy, Multiple Consciousness: The Context of a Black Feminist Ideology." In Darlene Clark Hine, ed., *Black Women's History: Theory and Practice*, vol. 1.

King, Mary. *Freedom Song: A Personal Story of the 1960s Civil Rights Movement*. New York: Morrow, 1987.

King, Richard. *The Party of Eros: Radical Social Thought and the Realm of Freedom*. Chapel Hill: University of North Carolina, 1972.

King, Ynestra. "Healing the Wounds: Feminism, Ecology, and the Nature/Culture Dualism." In Irene Diamond and Gloria Feman Orenstein, eds., *Reweaving the World*.

———. "Toward an Ecological Feminism and a Feminist Ecology." In J. Rothschild, ed., *Machina Ex Dea: Feminist Perspectives on Technology*. New York: Pergamon Press, 1983.

Klatch, Rebecca. "Coalition and Conflict among the Women of the New Right." *Signs* 13, no. 4 (Summer 1988): 671–94.

Koedt, Anne. "The Myth of the Vaginal Orgasm." In Shulamith Firestone and Anne Koedt, eds., *Notes from the Second Year*.

Koedt, Anne, Anita Rapone, and Ellen Levine, eds. *Notes from the Third Year*. New York: Notes from the Third Year, 1971.

Koen, Susan, and Nina Swain. *Ain't No Where We Can Run: Handbook for Women on the Nuclear Mentality.* Norwich, Vt.: WAND, 1980.

Kornegger, Peggy. "The Spirituality Ripoff." *Second Wave* 4, no. 3 (Spring 1976): 12–18.

Koven, Seth, and Sonya Michel, eds. *Mothers of a New World: Maternalist Politics and the Origins of Welfare States.* New York: Routledge, 1993.

Kurtzberg, Evelyn. "Recommendations for Change: The Obstetrician and the Pregnant Woman." In Dorothy Tennov and Lolly Hirsch, coordinators, *Proceedings of the First International Childbirth Conference.*

Ladd-Taylor, Molly. *Mother-Work: Women, Child Welfare, and the State, 1890–1930.* Champaign: University of Illinois Press, 1995.

Ladner, Joyce. *Tomorrow's Tomorrow: The Black Woman.* Garden City, N.Y.: Doubleday, 1971.

Laing, R. D. *The Divided Self: An Existential Study in Sanity and Madness.* Harmondsworth, Eng.: Penguin, 1960.

La Leche League International. *The Womanly Art of Breastfeeding.* Third Edition. Franklin Park, Ill.: La Leche League International, 1981; orig. 1958.

Lamb, Myrna. "On the Sanctity of Life." *Second Wave* 2, no. 1 (1972): 9.

Lang, Raven. *Birth Book.* Ben Lomond, Calif.: Genesis Press, 1972.

LaRue, Linda. "The Black Power Movement and Women's Liberation." *Black Scholar* 1 (May 1970): 36–42.

Lasch, Christopher. *Haven in a Heartless World: The Family Besieged.* New York: Basic, 1977.

Lauritzen, Paul. "A Feminist Ethic and the New Romanticism—Mothering As a Model of Moral Relations." *Hypatia* 4, no. 2 (Summer 1989): 29–44.

Law, Sylvia A. "Having It All Is Too Much: Review of Sylvia Ann Hewlett, *A Lesser Life.*" *New York Times Book Review,* March 30, 1986: 10.

Lazarre, Jane. *The Mother Knot.* New York: McGraw-Hill, 1976.

———. "Why Everybody Is Talking about Dorothy Dinnerstein's 'The Mermaid and the Minotaur' " *Ms.* 6, no. 1 (July 1977): 38–43.

Lederer, Laura, ed. *Take Back the Night: Women on Pornography.* New York: Morrow, 1980.

Leghorn, Lisa. "Feminism Undermines." *No More Fun and Games,* no. 4 (April 1970): 60–65.

Lester, Julius. *Look Out, Whitey! Black Power's Gon' Get Your Mama!* New York: Grove, 1969.

Levitt, Cyril. *Children of Privilege: Student Revolts in the Sixties.* Toronto: University of Toronto Press, 1984.

Levy, David M. *Maternal Overprotection*. New York: Columbia University Press, 1943.

Lewis, Diane. "A Response to Inequality: Black Women, Racism and Sexism." *Signs* 3, no. 2 (Winter 1977): 339–61.

Lidz, Theodore, Stephen Fleck, and Alice R. Cornelison. *Schizophrenia and the Family*. New York: International Universities Press, 1965.

Lincoln, Abbey. "Who Will Revere the Black Woman?" In Toni Cade, ed., *The Black Woman*. Reprinted from *Negro Digest*, September 1966.

Lincoln, C. Eric, ed. *Is Anybody Listening to Black America?* New York: Seabury Press, 1968.

Lindsey, Kay. "The Black Woman As Woman." In Toni Cade, ed., *The Black Woman*.

Linton, Rhoda. "Seneca Women's Peace Camp: Shapes of Things to Come." In Adrienne Harris and Ynestra King, eds., *Rocking the Ship of State*.

Litoff, Judy Barrett. *American Midwives: 1860 to the Present*. Westport, Conn.: Greenwood Press, 1978.

Logan, Cory. "From a Black Sister." *Women: A Journal of Liberation* 1, no. 3 (Spring 1970): 46–47.

Lomax, Pearl. "Black Women's Lib?" *Essence*, August 1972: 68.

Lorber, Judith, Rose Coser, and Alice Rossi. "On *The Reproduction of Mothering*: A Methodological Debate." *Signs* 6, no. 3 (Spring 1981): 482–514.

Lorde, Audre. *Sister Outsider: Essays and Speeches*. Trumansberg, N.Y.: Crossing Press, 1984.

———. "Uses of the Erotic: The Erotic As Power." In Laura Lederer, ed., *Take Back the Night*.

Lowman, Kaye. *The LLLove Story*. Franklin Park, Ill.: La Leche League International, 1977.

Lundberg, Ferdinand, and Marynia Farnham. *Modern Woman: The Lost Sex*. New York: Harper, 1947.

Major, Reginald. *A Panther Is a Black Cat*. New York: Morrow, 1971.

Marable, Manning. *Black American Politics: From the Washington Marches to Jesse Jackson*. London: Verso, 1985.

———. *Through the Prism of Race and Class: Modern Black Nationalism in the U.S.* Dayton, Ohio: Black Research Associates, 1980.

Marcuse, Herbert. *Eros and Civilization*. Boston: Beacon Press, 1955.

———. *One Dimensional Man: Studies in the Ideology of Advanced Industrial Society*. Boston: Beacon, 1964.

Marieskind, Helen I., and Barbara Ehrenreich. "Toward Socialist Medicine: The Women's Health Movement." *Social Policy,* September–October 1975: 34–42.

Marks, Elaine, and Isabelle de Courtivron, eds. *New French Feminisms.* New York: Schocken Books, 1981.

Martin, Del. *Battered Wives.* San Francisco: Glide Publications, 1976.

Martin, Del, and Phyllis Lyons. *Lesbian/Woman.* San Francisco: Glide Publications, 1972.

Martin, Emily. *The Woman in the Body: A Cultural Analysis of Reproduction.* Boston: Beacon, 1987.

Martin, Gloria. "Women, Organize Your Own Fighting Forces!" In Redstockings, eds., *Feminist Revolution.*

May, Elaine Tyler. *Homeward Bound: American Families in the Cold War Era.* New York: Basic, 1988.

Mayer, Naomi Lambert. "The Midwife: Liberating Childbirth." In Dorothy Tennov and Lolly Hirsch, coordinators, *Proceedings of the First International Childbirth Conference.*

McAdoo, Bill. *Pre-Civil War Black Nationalism.* New York: D. Walker Press, 1983.

McAllister, Pam, ed. *Reweaving the Web of Life: Feminism and Nonviolence.* Philadelphia: New Society, 1982.

McCabe, Jane. "Review of *Of Woman Born: Motherhood As Experience and Institution.*" *Frontiers* 3, no. 2 (Summer 1978): 77–78.

McKain, Barbara, and Michael McKain. "Building Extended Families." Women: A Journal of Liberation 1, no. 2 (Winter 1970): 24–25.

McNeill, Don. *Moving through Here.* New York: Knopf, 1970.

Medea, Andrea, and Kathleen Thompson. *Against Rape.* New York: Farrar, Straus, and Giroux, 1974.

Mellown, Mary Ruth. "An Incomplete Picture: The Debate about Surrogate Motherhood." *Harvard Women's Law Journal* 8 (Spring 1985): 231–47.

Melville, Keith. *Communes in the Counterculture: Origins, Theories, Styles of Life.* New York: Morrow, 1972.

Merchant, Carolyn. *The Death of Nature: Women, Ecology, and the Scientific Revolution.* San Francisco: Harper and Row, 1981.

———. "Ecofeminism and Feminist Theory." In Irene Diamond and Gloria Feman Orenstein, eds., *Reweaving the World.*

Miller, James. *"Democracy Is in the Streets": From Port Huron to the Siege of Chicago.* New York: Simon and Schuster, 1987.

Miller, Jean Baker. *Toward a New Psychology of Women.* Boston: Beacon, 1976.

Miller, Loren. "Farewell to Liberals." In Joann Grant, ed., *Black Protest.*

Millett, Kate. *Sexual Politics*. Garden City, N.Y.: Doubleday, 1970.

Mitchell, Doris J., and Jewell H. Bell, eds. *The Black Woman: Myths and Realities: Selected Papers from the Radcliffe Symposium*. Cambridge, Mass.: Radcliffe College, 1973.

Mitchell, Juliet. *Woman's Estate*. New York: Pantheon, 1971.

———. "Women: The Longest Revolution." *New Left Review* 40 (November–December 1966): 11–37.

Moraga, Cherríe. *Loving in the War Years: Lo Que Nunca Paso Por Sus Labios*. Boston: South End Press, 1983.

Moraga, Cherríe, and Gloria Anzaldua, eds. *This Bridge Called My Back: Writings by Radical Women of Color*. New York: Kitchen Table/Women of Color Press, 1981.

Moraga, Cherríe, and Amber Hollibaugh. "What We're Rolling Around in Bed With: Sexual Silences in Feminism, A Conversation toward Ending Them." *Heresies* 12 (Spring 1981): 58–62.

Morgan, Edward P. *The 60s Experience: Hard Lessons about Modern America*. Philadelphia: Temple University Press, 1991.

Morgan, Marabel. *The Total Woman*. New York: Pocket Books, 1975.

Morgan, Robin. "The Changeless Need: 'The Great Tribal Forms of Family May Be Vanishing, But New Kinship Systems Flourish All around Us'—A Conversation with Dorothy Dinnerstein," *Ms.* 2, no. 2 (August 1978): 44–46, 90, 92, 94, 97.

———. *Going Too Far: The Personal Chronicle of a Feminist*. New York: Random House, 1978.

———. "Goodbye to All That." *The Rat*, February 9–23 (1970): 6–7.

———. "Lesbianism and Feminism: Synonyms or Contradictions?" *Lesbian Tide* 2, no. 10/11 (May–June 1973): 30–34.

———. "A Maddening Take on Our Movement." *Ms.* 14, no. 9 (March 1986): 74, 76.

———. "Theory and Practice: Pornography and Rape." In Laura Lederer, ed., *Take Back the Night*.

Morgan, Robin, ed. *Sisterhood Is Powerful: An Anthology of Writings from the Women's Liberation Movement*. New York: Vintage, 1970.

Morrison, Joan, and Robert K. Morrison. *From Camelot to Kent State: The Sixties Experience in the Words of Those Who Lived It*. New York: Random House, 1987.

Morrison, Toni, ed. *Race-ing Justice, En-gendering Power: Essays on Anita Hill, Clarence Thomas, and the Construction of Social Reality*. New York: Pantheon, 1992.

Moses, Wilson Jeremiah. *Alexander Crummel: A Study of Civilization and Discontent*. New York: Oxford University Press, 1989.

Moses, Wilson Jeremiah. "Domestic Feminism, Conservatism, Sex Roles, and Black Women's Clubs, 1893–1896." In Darlene Clark Hine, ed., *Black Women in American History,* vol. 3.

Moynihan, Daniel Patrick. *The Negro Family: The Case for National Action.* Washington, D.C.: U.S. Government Printing Office, 1965.

Mungo, Raymond. *Total Loss Farm: A Year in the Life.* New York: E. P. Dutton, 1970.

Murray, Pauli. "The Liberation of Black Women." In Mary Lou Thompson, ed., *Voices of the New Feminism.*

Myron, Nancy, and Charlotte Bunch, eds. *Lesbianism and the Women's Movement.* Baltimore: Diana Press, 1975.

Newton, Esther, and Paula Webster. "Matriarchy and Power." *Quest* 2, no. 1 (Summer 1975): 67–72.

Newton, Huey. *Revolutionary Suicide.* New York: Harcourt Brace Jovanovich, 1973.

———. *To Die for the People: Writings of Huey P. Newton.* New York: Random House, 1972.

New York Radical Feminists. "Politics of the Ego: A Manifesto for N.Y. Radical Feminists." In Shulamith Firestone and Anne Koedt, eds., *Notes from the Second Year.*

Noble, Jeanne. *Beautiful, Also, Are the Souls of My Black Sisters: A History of the Black Woman in America.* Englewood Cliffs, N.J.: Prentice-Hall, 1978.

"No More Miss America: Ten Points of Protest." In Robin Morgan, ed., *Sisterhood Is Powerful.*

Nozal, Bridget. "Some Thoughts on Breastfeeding." In Dorothy Tennov and Lolly Hirsch, coordinators, *Proceedings of the First International Childbirth Conference.*

O'Brien, Geoffrey. *Dream Time: Chapters from the Sixties.* New York: Penguin, 1988.

Off Our Backs. "Ain't I a Womon Issue—By and about Wimmin of Color." June 1979.

Olds, Sally Wendkos. "Breastfeeding Successfully in Spite of Doctors and Hospitals." In Dorothy Tennov and Lolly Hirsch, coordinators, *Proceedings of the First International Childbirth Conference.*

Oliver, Sidney. "Feminism, Environmentalism and Appropriate Technology." *Quest* 5, no. 2 (1980): 70–80.

Olsen, Tillie. *Silences.* New York: Delacorte Press, 1978.

Omolade, Barbara. *The Rising Song of African American Women.* New York: Routledge, 1994.

Ortner, Sherry. "Is Female to Male As Nature Is to Culture?" In Michelle Rosaldo and Louise Lamphere, eds., *Women, Culture and Society.*

Palmer, Phylliss Marynick. "White Women/Black Women: The Dualism of Female Identity and Experience in the United States." *Feminist Studies* 9, no. 1 (Spring 1983): 151–70.

Parker, Andrew, Mary Russo, Doris Sommer, and Patricia Yaeger, eds. *Nationalisms and Sexualities.* New York: Routledge, 1992.

Parsons, Talcott, and Robert F. Bales, et al. *Family, Socialization and Interaction Process.* Glencoe, Ill.: Free Press, 1955.

Patterson, Tiffany R. "Toward a Black Feminist Analysis: Recent Works by Black Women." In Darlene Clark Hine, ed., *Black Women's History: Theory and Practice,* vol. 2.

Patton, Gwen. "Black People and the Victorian Ethos." In Toni Cade, ed., *The Black Woman.*

Pearson, Evette. "White America Today." Reprinted from *The Black Panther,* January 4, 1969, in Philip S. Foner, ed., *The Black Panthers Speak.*

Peck, Ellen, and Judith Senderowitz, eds. *Pronatalism: The Myth of Mom and Apple Pie.* New York: Crowell, 1974.

Peggy and Diane. "Witches Brew." *It Ain't Me, Babe* 1, no. 5 (April 7, 1970): 5, 10.

Peiss, Kathy, and Christina Simmons, eds. *Passion and Power: Sexuality in History.* Philadelphia: Temple University Press, 1989.

Perry, Charles. *The Haight-Ashbury: A History.* New York: Random House, 1984.

Person, Ethel Spector. "Review of Jean Baker Miller, *Toward a New Psychology of Women,* Helen Block Lewis, *Psychic War in Men and Women,* and Dorothy Dinnerstein, *The Mermaid and the Minotaur.*" *Signs* 4, no. 1 (Autumn 1978): 163–67.

Petchesky, Rosalind Pollack. "Antiabortion, Antifeminism, and the Rise of the New Right." *Feminist Studies* 7, no. 2 (Summer 1981): 206–47.

———. "Fetal Images: The Power of Visual Culture in the Politics of Reproduction." *Feminist Studies* 13, no. 2 (Summer 1987): 263–92.

———. "Reproductive Freedom: Beyond 'A Woman's Right to Choose.'" *Signs* 5, no. 4 (Summer 1980): 661–85.

Plant, Judith, ed. *Healing the Wounds: The Promise of Ecofeminism.* Philadelphia: New Society, 1989.

Plaskow, Judith, and Carol P. Christ, eds. *Weaving the Visions: New Patterns in Feminist Spirituality.* San Francisco: Harper and Row, 1989.

———. *Womanspirit Rising: A Feminist Reader in Religion.* New York: Harper and Row, 1979.

Pollack, Sandra, and Jeanne Vaughn, eds. *Politics of the Heart: A Lesbian Parenting Anthology.* Ithaca, N.Y.: Firebrand Books, 1987.

Pollitt, Katha. "Marooned on Gilligan's Island: Are Women Morally Superior to Men?" *The Nation,* 255, December 28, 1992: 799–807.

Potter, David. *People of Plenty: Economic Abundance and the American Character.* Chicago: University of Chicago Press, 1954.

Powell, Linda. "Black Macho and Black Feminism." In Barbara Smith, ed., *Home Girls.*

Price, Colette. "The Self-Help Clinic." Feminist Women's Health Center reprint from *Woman's World* 1, no. 4 (March–May 1972).

Quinby, Lee. "Ecofeminism and the Politics of Resistance." In Irene Diamond and Gloria Feman Orenstein, eds., *Reweaving the World.*

Rabbit, Peter. *Drop City.* New York: Olympia Press, 1971.

Radicalesbians. "The Woman Identified Woman." In Anne Koedt, Anita Rapone, and Ellen Levine, eds., *Notes from the Third Year.*

Rainwater, Lee, and William Yancey. *The Moynihan Report and the Politics of Controversy.* Cambridge, Mass.: M.I.T. Press, 1967.

Rainwater, Lee, ed. *Black Experience: Soul.* New Brunswick, N.J.: Transaction Books, 1973.

Raymond, Janice. *The Transsexual Empire: The Making of the She-Male.* Boston: Beacon, 1979.

Redstockings. "Redstockings Manifesto." In Shulamith Firestone and Anne Koedt, eds., *Notes for the Second Year.*

Redstockings, eds. *Feminist Revolution.* New Paltz, N.Y.: Redstockings, 1975.

Reich, Charles. *The Greening of America.* New York: Random House, 1970.

Reich, Wilhelm. *The Function of the Orgasm: Sex-Economic Problems of Biological Energy.* New York: Farrar, Straus, and Giroux, 1961.

———. *Sex-Pol Essays, 1929–34,* ed. Lee Baxandall. New York: Vintage, 1972.

———. *The Sexual Revolution: Toward a Self-Governing Character Structure.* New York: Orgone Institute Press, 1945.

Reid, Inez Smith. *"Together" Black Women.* New York: Emerson Hall Publishers, 1972.

Rennie, Susan, and Kirsten Grimstad. *The New Woman's Survival Catalogue.* New York: Coward, McCann and Geoghegan, 1973.

———. "Spiritual Explorations Cross-Country." *Quest* 1, no. 4 (Spring 1975): 49–51.

Rheingold, Joseph C. *The Fear of Being a Woman: A Theory of Maternal Destructiveness.* New York: Grune and Stratton, 1964.

Rice, Mary. "Daughters of Demeter: Women and Plants." *Second Wave* 3, no. 2 (Spring 1974): 19–21.

Rich, Adrienne. *Of Woman Born: Motherhood As Experience and Institution.* New York: Norton, 1976.

———. *On Lies, Secrets and Silence.* New York: Norton, 1979.

Riesman, David. *The Lonely Crowd: A Study of the Changing American Character.* New Haven: Yale University Press, 1950.

Riley, Clayton. "Black Nationalists and the Hippies." *Liberator* (December 1967): 4–7.

Ritvo, Lucille B. "Realizing Women's Special Eroticism in Childbirth and Nursing." In Dorothy Tennov and Lolly Hirsch, coordinators, *Proceedings of the First International Childbirth Conference.*

Robinson, Patricia M. "A Historical and Critical Essay for Black Women of the Cities (Excerpts)." In Sookie Stambler, ed., *Women's Liberation: Blueprint for the Future.*

———. "Poor Black Women." In Judith Clavir Albert and Stewart Albert, eds., *The Sixties Papers.*

Robinson, Patricia M., et al. "The Sisters Reply." In Albert and Albert, eds., *The Sixties Papers.*

Rodrique, Jessie M. "The Black Community and the Birth Control Movement." In Kathy Peiss and Christina Simmons, eds., *Passion and Power: Sexuality in History.*

Rogers, Lorna J. "Babies Are Born Not Delivered." *It Ain't Me, Babe*, no. 15 (October 8, 1970): 15.

Rooks, Judith P. "The Women's Movement and Its Effect on Women's Health Care." In Leota Kester McNall, ed., *Contemporary Obstetrical and Gynecological Nursing.* St. Louis: C.V. Mosby, 1980.

Rosaldo, Michelle, and Louise Lamphere, eds. *Woman, Culture and Society.* Palo Alto, Calif.: Stanford University Press, 1974.

Rose, Deborah. "Lookin' Around: How Women Are Regaining Control." *Second Wave* 2, no. 3 (1973): 23–28.

Rosenfelt, Deborah, and Judith Stacey. "Second Thoughts on the Second Wave." *Feminist Studies* 13, no. 2 (Summer 1987): 341–61.

Ross, Ellen. "New Thoughts on 'the Oldest Vocation': Mothers and Motherhood in Recent Feminist Scholarship." *Signs* 20, no. 2 (Winter 1995): 397–413.

Rossi, Alice. "A Biosocial Perspective on Parenting." *Daedalus* 106, no. 2 (Spring 1977): 1–31.

Rossman, Michael. *The Wedding within the War.* Garden City, N.Y.: Doubleday, 1971.

Roszak, Theodore. *The Making of a Counter Culture: Reflections on the*

Technocratic Society and Its Youthful Opposition. Garden City, N.Y.: Doubleday, 1969.

Roth, Philip. *Portnoy's Complaint.* New York: Random House, 1969.

Rothman, Barbara Katz. *Giving Birth: Alternatives in Childbirth.* New York: Penguin, 1982.

———. *Recreating Motherhood: Ideology and Technology in a Patriarchal Society.* New York: Norton, 1989.

———. *The Tentative Pregnancy: Prenatal Diagnosis and the Future of Motherhood.* New York: Viking, 1986.

Rothschild, Mary Aickin. *A Case of Black and White: Northern Volunteers and the Southern Freedom Summers, 1964–1965.* Westport, Conn.: Greenwood Press, 1982.

Rowbotham, Sheila. "To Be or Not to Be: The Dilemmas of Mothering." *Feminist Review,* no. 31 (Spring 1989): 82–93.

Rubin, Gayle. "Thinking Sex: Notes for a Radical Theory of the Politics of Sexuality." In Ann Snitow et al., eds., *Powers of Desire.*

———. "The Traffic in Women: Notes on the Political Economy of Sex." In Rayna R. Reiter, ed., *Toward an Anthropology of Women.* New York: Monthly Review Press, 1975.

Rubin, Jerry. *Do It! Scenarios of the Revolution.* New York: Simon and Schuster, 1970.

———. *We Are Everywhere.* New York: Harper and Row, 1971.

Ruddick, Sara. "Maternal Thinking." *Feminist Studies* 6, no. 2, (Summer 1980): 342–67.

———. *Maternal Thinking: Toward a Politics of Peace.* Boston: Beacon, 1989.

Ruether, Rosemary. *New Woman, New Earth: Sexist Ideologies and Human Liberation.* New York: Seabury Press, 1975.

Russell, Diana E. H. "On Pornography." *Chrysalis* 4 (February 3, 1978): 11–15.

———. *The Politics of Rape: The Victim's Perspective.* New York: Stein and Day, 1975.

Ruzek, Sheryl Burt. *The Women's Health Movement: Feminist Alternatives to Medical Control.* New York: Praeger, 1978.

Sale, Kirkpatrick. *SDS.* New York: Random House, 1973.

Salpin, Beverly. *The Magic Washing Machine: A Diary of Single Motherhood.* Mesquite, Texas: Ide House, 1983.

Samois, ed. *Coming to Power: Writings and Graphics on Lesbian S/M.* San Francisco: Samois, 1981.

Sanders, Fran. "Dear Black Man." In Toni Cade, ed., *The Black Woman.*

Sargent, Lydia, ed. *Women and Revolution: A Discussion of the Un-*

happy Marriage of Marxism and Feminism. Boston: South End Press, 1981.

Sargent, Lyman T. *New Left Thought: An Introduction*. Homewood, Ill.: Dorsey Press, 1972.

Sayres, Sohnya, Anders Stephanson, Stanley Aronowitz, and Fredric Jameson, eds. *The Sixties without Apology*. Minneapolis: University of Minneapolis Press, 1984.

Scheer, Robert, ed. *Eldridge Cleaver: Post-Prison Writings and Speeches*. New York: Random House, 1969.

Schlafly, Phyllis. *The Power of the Positive Woman*. New Rochelle, N.Y.: Arlington House, 1977.

Scott, Joyce Hope. "From Foreground to Margin: Female Configurations and Masculine Self-Representation in Black Nationalist Fiction." In Andrew Parker et al., eds., *Nationalisms and Sexualities*.

Seale, Bobby. *Seize the Time: The Story of the Black Panther Party and Huey P. Newton*. New York: Random House, 1970.

Seaman, Barbara. *The Doctors' Case against the Pill*. New York: P. H. Wyden, 1969.

Select Committee on Children, Youth and Families. *U.S. Children and Their Families: Current Conditions and Recent Trends*. Washington, D.C.: U.S. Government Printing Office, 1983.

Sellers, Cleveland. *The River of No Return: The Autobiography of a Black Militant and the Life and Death of SNCC*. New York: Morrow, 1973.

Shapiro, Jane. "To Tell the Truth: Jane Lazarre's *The Mother Knot*" *Ms.* 4, no. 12 (June 1976): 93–95.

Shelley, Martha. "Notes of a Radical Lesbian." In Robin Morgan, ed., *Sisterhood Is Powerful*.

Shi, David. *The Simple Life: Plain Living and High Thinking in American Culture*. New York: Oxford University Press, 1985.

Silberman, Charles. "Crisis in Black and White." In Joann Grant, ed., *Black Protest*.

Silvermarie, Sue. "The Motherbond." *Women: A Journal of Liberation* 4, no. 1 (Winter 1974): 26–27.

Simons, Margaret A. "Racism and Feminism: A Schism in the Sisterhood." *Feminist Studies* 5, no. 2 (Summer 1979): 384–401.

Slater, Philip. *The Pursuit of Loneliness: American Culture at the Breaking Point*. Boston: Beacon, 1970.

Smith, Barbara, ed. *Home Girls: A Black Feminist Anthology*. New York: Kitchen Table Press, 1983.

SNCC. "Black Women's Liberation." *Women: A Journal of Liberation* 1, no. 2 (Winter 1970): 76.

SNCC. "SNCC Speaks for Itself." In Judith Clavir Albert and Stewart Albert, eds., *The Sixties Papers.*

Snitow, Ann. "Feminism and Motherhood: An American Reading." *Feminist Review,* no. 40 (Spring 1992): 32–51.

———. "Motherhood—Reclaiming the Demon Texts." *Ms.* 1, no. 6 (May/June 1991): 34–37.

———. "The Paradox of Birth Technology: Exploring the Good, the Bad, and the Scary." *Ms.* 15, no. 6 (December 1986): 42–46, 76–78.

———. "Retrenchment vs. Transformation: The Politics of the Antipornography Movement." In Kate Ellis et al., eds., *Caught Looking.*

———. "Thinking about *The Mermaid and the Minotaur.*" *Feminist Studies* 4, no. 2 (June 1978): 192–98.

Snitow, Ann, Christine Stansell, and Sharon Thompson, eds. *Powers of Desire: The Politics of Sexuality.* New York: Monthly Review Press, 1983.

Snyder, Gary. "Buddhism and the Coming Revolution." In Judith Clavir Albert and Stewart Albert, eds., *The Sixties Papers.*

Solomon, Irvin D. *Feminism and Black Activism in Contemporary America.* Westport, Conn.: Greenwood Press, 1989.

Somer, Carol. "How Women Had Control of Their Lives and Lost It." *Second Wave* 2, no. 3 (1973): 5–10, 28.

———. "The Midwife As Witch." In Dorothy Tannov and Lolly Hirsch, coordinators, *Proceedings of the First International Childbirth Conference.*

Spelman, Elizabeth V. *Inessential Woman: Problems of Exclusion in Feminist Thought.* Boston: Beacon, 1988.

Spiegel, David. "Mothering, Fathering, and Mental Illness." In Barrie Thorne and Marilyn Yalom, eds., *Rethinking the Family.*

Spretnak, Charlene. "Ecofeminism: Our Roots and Flowering." In Irene Diamond and Gloria Feman Orenstein, eds., *Reweaving the World.*

Spretnak, Charlene, ed. *The Politics of Women's Spirituality.* New York: Anchor, 1982.

Stacey, Judith. "The New Conservative Feminism." *Feminist Studies* 9, no. 3 (Fall 1983): 559–83.

Stambler, Sookie, ed. *Women's Liberation: Blueprint for the Future.* New York: Ace, 1970.

Staples, Robert. *The Black Woman in America.* Chicago: Nelson-Hall, 1973.

Starr. "Unspoken Culture." *It Ain't Me, Babe* 1, no. 5 (April 7, 1970): 14.

Starrett, Barbara. "I Dream in Female: The Metaphors of Evolution." *Amazon Quarterly* 3, no. 1 (1974): 13–27.

Steinem, Gloria. "Erotica and Pornography: A Clear and Present Difference." In Laura Lederer, ed., *Take Back the Night.*

St. Joan, Jackie. "Who Was Rembrandt's Mother?" *Quest* 2, no. 4 (Spring 1976): 67–79.

Stone, Chuck. "The National Conference on Black Power." In Floyd B. Barbour, ed., *The Black Power Revolt.*

Stone. Merlin. *When God Was a Woman.* New York: Dial Press, 1976.

Streshinsky, Shirley. "Are You Safer with a Midwife?" *Ms.* 2, no. 4 (October 1973): 24–27.

Sullivan, Deborah A., and Rose Weitz. *Labor Pains: Modern Midwives and Homebirth.* New Haven: Yale University Press, 1988.

Swerdlow, Amy. "Pure Milk, Not Poison: Women Strike for Peace and the Test Ban Treaty of 1963." In Adrienne Harris and Ynestra King, eds., *Rocking the Ship of State.*

Swigart, Jane. *The Myth of the Bad Mother: Parenting without Guilt.* New York: Avon, 1991.

Tanner, Leslie B., ed. *Voices from Women's Liberation.* New York: New American Library, 1970.

Tennov, Dorothy, and Lolly Hirsch, coordinators. *Proceedings of the First International Childbirth Conference.* Stamford, Conn.: Moon Publications, 1973.

Teodori, Massimo, ed. *The New Left: A Documentary History.* Indianapolis: Bobbs-Merrill, 1969.

Thompson, Mary Lou, ed. *Voices of the New Feminism.* Boston: Beacon, 1970.

Thorne, Barrie. "Feminist Rethinking of the Family: An Overview." In Barrie Thorne and Marilyn Yalom, eds., *Rethinking the Family.*

Thorne, Barrie, and Marilyn Yalom, eds. *Rethinking the Family: Some Feminist Questions.* New York: Longman, 1982.

Tong, Rosemarie. *Feminist Thought: A Comprehensive Introduction.* Boulder, Colo.: Westview Press, 1989.

Trask, Haunani-Kay. *Eros and Power: The Promise of Feminist Theory.* Philadelphia: University of Pennsylvania Press, 1986.

Trebilcot, Joyce, ed. *Mothering: Essays in Feminist Theory.* Totowa, N.J.: Rowman and Allanheld, 1983.

U.S. Bureau of the Census. *Historical Statistics of the United States, Colonial Times to 1970.* Part 1. Washington, D.C.: U.S. Government Printing Office, 1975.

Vance, Carole, ed. *Pleasure and Danger: Exploring Female Sexuality.* Boston: Routledge and Kegan Paul, 1984.

Van DeBurg, William L. *New Day in Babylon: The Black Power Move-*

ment and American Culture. Chicago: University of Chicago Press, 1992.

Vida, Virginia, ed. *Our Right to Love: A Lesbian Resource Book.* Englewood Cliffs, N.J.: Prentice-Hall, 1978.

Viorst, Milton. *Fire in the Streets: America in the 1960s.* New York: Simon and Schuster, 1979.

Vitale, Sylvia Witts. "Black Sisterhood." *National Black Feminist Organization Newsletter* 1, no. 3 (September 1975): 3.

Vogel, Lise. "Marxism and Feminism: Unhappy Marriage, Trial Separation, or Something Else?" In Lydia Sargent, ed., *Women and Revolution.*

Von Hoffman, Nicholas. *We Are the People Our Parents Warned Us Against.* Chicago: Ivan R. Dee, 1989; orig. 1968.

Walker, Alice. *In Search of Our Mothers' Gardens: Womanist Prose.* New York: Harcourt Brace Jovanovich, 1984.

———. *The Temple of My Familiar.* San Diego: Harcourt Brace Jovanovich, 1989.

Wallace, Michele. *Black Macho and the Myth of the Superwoman.* New York: Verso, 1990; orig. 1979.

Walsh, Joan. "The Mother Mystique." *Vogue* 183, no. 8 (August 1993): 96.

Ware, Cellestine. *Woman Power: The Movement for Women's Liberation.* New York: Tower Publications, 1970.

Warrior, Betsy. "Females and Welfare." In Leslie B. Tanner, ed., *Voices from Women's Liberation.*

Watkins, Mel, and Jay David. *To Be a Black Woman: Portraits in Fact and Fiction.* New York: Morrow, 1970.

Wattenberg, Ben J. *The Birth Dearth.* New York: Pharos Books, 1987.

Webb, Marilyn. "We Are Victims." *Voice of the Women's Liberation Movement* 1, no. 6 (February 1969): 1, 4–5, 12.

Webster, Paula. "Pornography and Pleasure." In Kate Ellis et al., eds., *Caught Looking.*

Weinbaum, Batya. *The Curious Courtship of Women's Liberation and Socialism.* Boston: South End Press, 1978.

Weiner, Lynn Y. "Reconstructing Motherhood: The La Leche League in Postwar America." *Journal of American History* 80, no. 4 (March 1994): 1357–81.

Weisskopf, Susan (Contratto). "Maternal Sexuality and Asexual Motherhood." *Signs* 5, no. 4 (Summer 1980): 766–82.

Weisstein, Naomi. "Woman As Nigger." In Leslie B. Tanner, ed., *Voices from Women's Liberation.*

Weisstein, Naomi, and Heather Booth. "Will the Women's Movement Survive?" *Sister* 4, no. 12 (1975): 1–6.

Wellish, Pam, and Susan Root. *Hearts Open Wide: Midwives and Births.* Berkeley: Wingbow Press, 1987.

Westkott, Marcia. "Mothers and Daughters in the World of the Father." *Frontiers* 3, no. 2 (Summer 1978): 16–20.

White, E. Frances. "Listening to the Voices of Black Feminism." *Radical America* 18, no. 2–3 (1984): 6–25.

Williams, Brooke. "The Retreat to Cultural Feminism." In Redstockings, eds., *Feminist Revolution.*

Williamson, Nancy. "The Mean Mothers." *Lesbian Tide* 3, no. 5 (December 1973): 10.

Willis, Ellen. "Declaration of Independence." *Voice of the Women's Liberation Movement* 1, no. 6 (February 1969): 1, 4–5, 14.

———. "Feminism, Moralism, and Pornography." In Ann Snitow et al., eds., *Powers of Desire.*

———. "Radical Feminism and Feminist Radicalism." In Sohnya Sayres et al., eds., *The Sixties without Apology.*

———. "Sisters under the Skin? Confronting Race and Sex." *Village Voice Literary Supplement,* no. 8 (June 1982): 1, 10–12.

———. "Toward a Feminist Sexual Revolution." *Social Text* 6 (Fall 1982): 3–21.

WITCH. "Pass the Word, Sister." In Leslie B. Tanner, ed., *Voices from Women's Liberation.*

Wolfe, Tom. *The Electric Kool-Aid Acid Test.* New York: Bantam, 1968.

"Women Support Panther Sisters." In Leslie B. Tanner, ed., *Voices from Women's Liberation.*

"Women's Workshop on Sexual Self-Determination." *It Ain't Me, Babe,* December 1, 1970: 5.

Wright, Nathan. *Black Power and Urban Unrest: Creative Possibilities.* New York: Hawthorn Books, 1967.

Wyland, Francie. *Motherhood, Lesbianism and Child Custody.* Toronto: Wages Due Lesbians, 1977.

Wylie, Philip. *Generation of Vipers.* New York: Rinehart, 1942.

Yablonsky, Lewis. *The Hippie Trip.* New York: Pegasus, 1968.

Yates, Gayle Graham. *What Women Want: The Ideas of the Movement.* Cambridge, Mass.: Harvard University Press, 1975.

Yette, Samuel F. *The Choice: The Issue of Black Survival in America.* New York: Putnam, 1971.

Zaretsky, Eli. "The Place of the Family in the Origins of the Welfare State." In Barrie Thorne, ed., *Rethinking the Family.*

Journals

Amazon Quarterly
Berkeley Women's Health Collective Newsletter
Big Mama Rag
The Black Scholar
Childbirth Alternatives Quarterly
Chrysalis
Conditions
Female Liberation Newsletter
Feminist Forum
Feminist Issues
Feminist Studies
Frontiers
Helicon Nine
Heresies
Hypatia
It Ain't Me, Babe
The Mole
Momma
Mom's Apple Pie
Monthly Extract
Ms.
National Black Feminist Organization Newsletter
No More Fun and Games
Off Our Backs
Quest
Sacred River: A Women's Peace Journal
Sage
The Second Wave
Signs
Sinister Wisdom
Sister Courage
The Tide
Voice of the Women's Liberation Movement
Womanspirit
Women: A Journal of Liberation
Women's Studies
Women's Studies International Quarterly
Women's Studies Quarterly

Files at Schlesinger Library, Harvard University

Alliance Against Women's Oppression
Another Mother for Peace
Berkeley/Oakland Women's Union
Birth Project
Bread and Roses
Cambridge Women's Center
Cell 16
Chicago Women's Liberation Union
Coalition for Abortion Rights and Against Sterilization Abuse (CARASA)
Female Liberation
Feminist Antinuclear Task Force
The Feminists
Foundation for Matriarchy
Gay Revolution Party
Happiness of Womanhood
Martha Movement
National Black Feminist Organization
National Organization for Women
National Women's Conference to Prevent Nuclear War
National Women's Political Caucus
New England Free Press
New England Women's Coalition
New York Radical Feminists
New York Women's Liberation
Peace Links
Radical Feminist Organizing Committee
Radical Women Publications
Redstockings
Third World Women's Alliance
Wages for Housework
Wellesley College Center for Research on Women
WITCH
Women against Violence against Women
Women and Life on Earth: An Ecofeminist Conference
Women's Action for Nuclear Disarmament
Women's Campaign for Social Justice
Women's Encampment for a Future of Peace and Justice
Women's Equity Action League.

Index